Jane Goldberg

MY
MOTHER
MY
DAUGHTER
MY
SELF

D1453592

FA^B

FREE ASSOCIATION BOOKS

First published in 2016 by
Free Publishing Limited

A CIP Catalogue of this book is available from
the British Library

ISBN: 978-1-9113830-5-5

Cover design and typeset by
www.chandlerbookdesign.co.uk

Printed in Great Britain by
4 Edge Limited

Parenting is the number one health issue on our planet: to grow up with not love but indifference, rejection and abuse leads to self destructive behavior, revenge and violence. Read Jane's words of wisdom and learn how to be a loving parent.

Bernie Siegel, MD
author of best-selling books:
Love, Medicine and Miracles
The Art of Healing
365 Prescriptions For The Soul

What do we know about the relationship between mothers and daughters? In this incredibly moving and lyrically written "memoir," psychoanalyst Jane Goldberg has answers that resonate and make you think twice about your own family connections. It is a hugely ambitious—and altogether successful—endeavor at co-mingling theory with beautifully drawn stories—both clinical from her practice, and personal from her family, blending the two in an eloquent and compelling voice. Deserves attention of all those who are mothers and all those who have or had mothers.

Elizabeth Loftus, Ph.D.
Author of:
The Myth of Repressed Memory: False Memories and
Allegations of Sexual Abuse
Witness for the Defense: The Accused, the Eyewitness and the
Expert Who Puts Memory on Trial
Eyewitness Testimony

Referred to as "the woman who changed the world"
in *The New Yorker*, May 19, 2014 issue: "Partial Recall: Can neuroscience help us rewrite our most traumatic memories?"
by Michael Specter

Distinguished Professor University of California, Irvine
Past President - Association for Psychological Science
Ranked 58th in the *Review of General Psychology*'s list of the 100 most influential psychological researchers of the 20th century, and was the highest ranked woman on the list.

Goldberg's remarkable capacity to recount her life from both subjective and objective points of view animates her journey toward self-discovery in such a way that it touches our hearts as well as our minds. Her insights are brilliant; her language is elegant, accessible and well-crafted; her openness and revelations (about both herself and her patients) are moving and uplifting. For all these reasons and more, her ability to draw in the reader is remarkable and convincing.

This book should be required reading for all students and practitioners of psychotherapy and psychoanalysis, all mothers, and all adult sons and daughters. Alan Watts wrote a book in the 60's called *The Book*. His intention was to create THE book that would be so inclusive, so profound that if there were only one book in the world, this would be it. Similarly, if there were one book to read about being a mother, being a daughter or a son, being a person with an interest in the kind of self-discovery that is gleaned from the process of psychotherapy and psychoanalysis, *My Mother, My Daughter, My Self* would be that book. More than any book I have read, it captures the art, the beauty and the magic that is created when the internal work is done that leads to self-understanding and the consequent self-transformation. When this book is published, it will become required reading for all psychoanalytic candidates and faculty members of each of the institutes that I founded. Reading it is like eating a scrumptious, nutritional, utterly satisfying meal. So satisfying, you will feel like you will never have to eat again.

Respectfully Submitted:

Phyllis Meadow, Ph.D.
author of:
Treatment of the Narcissistic Neuroses
The New Psychoanalysis
Ethics for Psychoanalysis: In the Interest of the Patient
Founder of three psychoanalytic institutes
Center for Modern Psychoanalytic Studies, New York, NY;
Boston Graduate School of Psychoanalysis, Boston, MA;
The Cyril Z. Meadow Institute, Dummerston, Vermont.

Once again, Jane Goldberg has created a tour de force, a stunningly smart body of work that should be required reading for all mothers and all daughters. With sensitivity, compassion and humility, she traces the inevitable steps of the separation process between mothers and daughters. The stories themselves—sometimes about herself and her own mother, sometimes about herself and her daughter, and, too, about her patients—are riveting and illuminating. All is surrounded by sound and documented research and theory. Hats off to Jane Goldberg for her accomplishment in this magnificent book.

Mimi G. Crowell, Ph.D.,
President, Center for Modern Psychoanalytic Studies.

This wonderful book by Dr. Goldberg is warm, moving and so very true about the relationships of mothers ourselves and our daughters. Who would think a psychoanalyst could write so beautifully and yet clinically about the relationships of mothers and daughters?

Vicki Semel, Ph.D.
Director of Academy of Clinical and Applied Psychoanalysis, New Jersey

---

This is the story of one woman's journey into and through the experience of motherhood. It is a deeply personal and emotional story, often gripping and forceful, and has all the elements of a novel and, in many ways, reads like one.

At the same time, it is replete with insights and facts that would be invaluable to any mother and would-be mother, saving them from much of the inevitable confusion, mistakes and misunderstandings that happen as a result of bringing human beings into the World.

This book should be required reading for all mothers and would-be-mothers on the planet. Perhaps for men too, so they can get a better idea of how to be more attuned to the realities of motherhood and be better, more effective in their role as mate and father.

Arthur Jaffe
NY State licensed and certified in
Biosync Neuromuscular Therapy
Yogic Neuromuscular Therapy
Detoxification Acupuncture
Shiatsu
Reiki
Amma (Ancient Chinese Bodywork)
Alternative Pain Control and Management

CONTENTS

Introduction   1

PART I **MY MOTHER**

1. The Smallest Fraction into which Time can be Divided   5

2. Being Irredeemably Separate and Unrelentingly Close   9

3. Dress Rehearsals for Death   21

4. The Shallow Years   26

5. In Love with Love   39

6. Growing Down   53

PART II **MY DAUGHTER**

7. Imaginative Leaps of Delusional Anxiety About a   69
Misbegotten Fantasy

8. An Unbroken Continuum   76

9. The Senses of Symbiosis   86

10. Fear and Trembling (and trauma too)   100

11. The Journey of the Soul Between Life and Death   109

12. The Pas de Deux of Anxiety   132

13. An Affliction of Muteness   139

14. Recognising the Squeezed Tightening in Another   147

15. The Loss of the Omnipotent Mother   156

16. Dreams of Flight (and other desires of the soul)   170

17. The World of Words   185

PART III **MY SELF**

18. Who I was Meant to Be 199

19. In Search of History 211

20. Sex as an Act of Betrayal 226

21. When Men Matter 236

22. Murder as Metaphor 253

23. A Grotesque Frankensteinian-Combo 275

24. A Zombie without a Mother 293

25. The Year my Sexuality went Public 307

26. An Unmentionable Skeleton in the Closet 316

27. Wandering around in Psychic Space 322

28. Giving in to Complete Abandon 331

29. The End of Longing 346

Bibliography 367

Introduction

This is what I know most emphatically: I know from having been my mother's daughter, I know from being my daughter's mother, I know from being a psychoanalyst to others, and I know from my night dreams and from having lived through my own frightening demons—there is no fear worse than the primal fear of abandonment—the fear of aloneness that comes from separation.

Separation is the very first challenge we meet at entering life when we go from our symbiotic biological unity with mother to our separation from her that is called birth. Our urge to become our own person—really an instinct more than an urge, like an imprint seen in animals—is primary as we confront its various later iterations in our life's journey. With each step of our separation travel, we can either welcome it, or fight against it. And each step we take toward successful separation moves us in the direction of the development of a secure, confident and wholly integrated sense of self.

I have come to believe that the process of separation between mother and child is one of the most difficult challenges that we, both as parents and as children, face. Throughout my life as the daughter I was to my mother, I had a near constant interest in positioning myself in relation to her, at times honouring our mutual attachment, and at other times denouncing it and bolting from it. And, as a new mother, I found myself struggling with my feelings of concern and anxiety, hovering over my newborn, wrapping her in a cocoon of safety while simultaneously strenuously seeking the perfect balance of distance, both for me—to retain some semblance of the forty-seven-year-old life I had before she came, and the life I still wanted to live away from her—and for her, too, so that she would continue her growth into a self that has its own distinctive definition.

In my work with my patients, too, I have found other mothers and daughters battling with the same issues that I confronted in my relationship with my mother, and that Molly and I encountered in the early time of our being together, coming to know each other as biologically separate, yet emotionally bonded individuals. In my practice, I find mothers and children who strive to form a coherent story of their complex, contradictory relationships with each other, struggling with the same preoccupation of being able to contextualise themselves in relation to one another that I did with my own mother, that I now do with my daughter, and that my daughter will surely do with me as she gets older and grows more and more into her separate self.

All of us are capable of being terrified of our essential aloneness, a feeling that arises from all the difficult separations we have encountered in our lives. Perhaps we all remain children in this way.

I have written this book to help me to think about women searching for oneness with each other, sometimes stumbling, but always, in the end, triumphing. I have written about the struggle of women to honour our commonality of femaleness, the closeness that we, as mothers and daughters to each other, and as women with each other, are able to achieve. The book is about, as well, the conflicting and simultaneous search for individuality and separation. Every mother and child's ultimate challenge is to exalt in the harmony of their initial symbiotic togetherness, and then, to welcome joyously the creation of their separate selves. The book is about maintaining intimacy with both closeness and separateness: we want both; we need both.

PART I
MY MOTHER

1

The Smallest Fraction into which Time can be Divided

I was with my mother the moment she died. After what seemed like an eternally long anguished sigh, my mother's struggle for breath and life ended, and the withering stillness turned absolute. Death had been lurking around for hours, so close to her that it would have heard her whistle to it.

For the last few days of my mother's life, as she reached laboriously for breath, her struggle to stay alive had been almost too much for me to witness. Finally, that last day, her imminent death seemed to call out to me, pulling me out of my own bedroom where I had been in hiding, taking a reprieve from having to listen helplessly to her sparse breaths. I believe that she needed me to be with her those last few minutes of her life and that she, somehow, in (and despite) her comatose state, communicated to me to come and be with her to share together our final, irrevocable separation.

Blique and I were flanking her. Blique—my nanny who was there for my birth, and who was still there all these years later for my mother's dying-time—was standing on the far side of the bed, closest to the door; I remained on the side next to her closet. We watched my mother's distorted/contorted body lying supine on the bed that had been her prison for that last year of her life, observing her struggle, reaching out with her mouth and stretching her lungs to gasp in a morsel of air. And then, there was silence. I whispered: *"Blique, she stopped breathing."* I said it as though it were a most unexpected turn of events, that it couldn't be true. I guess the surprise in my tone convinced Blique that I was wrong, and she responded by saying, *"No, she's still breathing."* We were looking at her chest, waiting for a sign of movement, examining my beloved mother as though she were an inert specimen, imagining that she was/must be still breathing (as she always had) shallowly, imperceptibly. I suppose that I had not quite been able to grasp that this towering figure of a woman who had been my mainstay for thirty-seven years could be gone. And I think that I had not given up hope for eking out one more precious moment of life with her.

That's all death takes: a moment in time, an instant, the smallest fraction into which time can be divided. She was breathing, and then she was not. I had been wanting for that moment to come, wanting her to end the suffering that the last days of her life had brought. But then when it came, I wanted time to be reversed. I wanted her back; the stillness of her death was too final, too absolute.

In that instant of her death, everything that had defined her as the human being that she had been—as my mother; as my mother who had showered me with adoration and the feeling that I was her completion; as my mother who held on to me fiercely and protectively, even obsessively at times; also, as a mother to two other children; as a wife; as an ambitious, intelligent woman who lived ahead of her time and took a profession when other upper middle-class southern women were content to be housewives; as a woman of warmth, courage and compassion, humour and cunning, as well as coldness and dispassion—all of her life left her when she inhaled and exhaled her last, not too regretful, breath.

At that moment, I reached out for her, both afraid to touch her, and needing to touch her, wanting to extend longer the last moments I would ever be able to see her face. I looked at her, at the bed that I had spent so many mornings, decades ago, snuggled up against her welcoming warm body.

I let the streams of tears run down my face as I backed out of the room, moving indecisively toward her closet. I stretched my head back, as the wall began to block my view to her. I could still see the sliding glass-door drapes, the footboard of her bed, and then, when I had finally made my full exit out of the room, I could see nothing at all that had to do with her. I retreated into her closet, the space where I had spent so much time from childhood on, breathing in, feeling, absorbing all her clothes, shoes, jewellery. I wanted to run back into the bedroom, and be with her, stay with her, stay with her until I was all grown up, and asked myself when that would be. I suppose I thought that being ready for her death would indicate I was, finally, a complete adult; but, feeling alone and scared at that moment, I wondered if that day could ever come.

There had always been a feeling of safety when I was with her, and amongst her belongings. I understood, even as a child, and then later, all through her struggles to stay alive in her long cancer years, that I was part of the anchor that breathed life into her, filled her with joy and delight. She had had such a desultory flirtation with death all through those years: the cancer threatening her, disappearing, then coming back. And, despite these agonising last moments—the suffering she had endured in the last few months, from her bones breaking when she merely turned over in the bed, and all else of her body disintegrating as we watched—I still wanted her back.

Selfishly, I wanted her to be breathing—even if it was only breath that she was capable of.

I went back in the bedroom to be with her again. I searched the room for her; I looked in the air around her. I was looking for *her*, not the lifeless body that was next to me, but the *her* I had known. I wondered if space itself might still hold some remnant of her living energy, her spirit.

I think I must have grabbed out at my mother's spirit, grasping onto whatever was left before it had gone stratospherically too far. And then, maybe I was able to pull this *her*—this spirit, or energy, or soul—tightly into myself. And she became eternally inside me, part of me, as I had been part of her, inside her, thirty-seven years earlier.

Regardless of all my previous protests about the differences between us, in spite of our sometimes conflicting desires and needs over the years of our being mother and daughter to each other, despite our past disagreements about my behaviours and decisions, her dislike of some of my men, and our ambiguous understandings of who was who: who was she, and who was I—from that moment on, all conflicts about our separateness vanished. In that final, irreversible act of separation that death invariably signifies, my mother and I were able to recapture a moment of the union of togetherness that we had begun our lives with. My mother remains alive inside me, surely as much a part of me now in her death as I had insisted, at times, that she was not a part of me during her life.

I sat with my mother as she lay in her bed, a place that was stiller than any place on earth. The rest of my family— my brother, sister, and aunt—all were waiting in the front of the house. Stephen, the funeral parlour representative was waiting. The day persisted; the darkness of the day's ending sifted down from the sky as I continued to wait, though I knew not for what.

2

Being Irredeemably Separate and Unrelentingly Close

was there, too, when my mother informed my father that she had been diagnosed with terminal cancer. I think my mother experienced telling my father that she was dying as, for her, a little like what people feel when they are telling a bad joke: you know the joke is bad; you know the only thing the joke has going for it is the punch-line, so you draw out all the material before the punch-line, you make it endless so that by the time you get to the punch-line, everyone is so grateful just to get to the end of the joke. So when my mother told my father that she had something to tell him, she started to tell a story—the story of her imminent death—in true southern form, which means going around in a lot of circles first in order to stretch out the suspense. He, a southerner of a different breed, a man who never minced words, the kind of man that basically grunted a lot, grumbled out before she got to the punch line, "All right. Do you have to go to Shreveport and back to get to the point?" (No New Orleanian wants to go to Shreveport because it's just too damned far, and there's nothing there once you get there. I think that's what my father was afraid of all his life: that there would be nothing there once he got to wherever he was going. I think that's why he beat my mother to the punch in terms of dying first. He couldn't have borne all that nothingness. (At least her chatter, as long as she was alive, distracted him.)

The moment after she told us, for a long time, we clung to each other in a desperate hug—more like a hanging on to each other for dear life—reassuring ourselves that we were still there. I became aware in those moments—frighteningly aware—of a sense in which I was encircling my mother. I had suddenly become larger than she. In my arms, her body felt small and alarmingly vulnerable.

While my mother was not a large woman, she had always appeared large to me. The fact is that after I was full-grown, I was probably the same height as she. Yet I would never say that this was so, and I did not believe it to be so.

When asked her height, she would always say five feet, one and three-quarter inches. She would then explain that in college she had just missed the five-foot, two-inch mark that would have enabled her to get on the basketball team.

When I was a teenager and people would ask me my height, I would say that I was five feet, one and a half inches. I was, indeed, over five feet, but I was not, I was sure, as tall as my mother. That day, the day I became taller than my mother, I became, as well, my mother's mother.

An odd droll fantasy

In the process of letting go of my mother in her last bed-ridden year, her "dying time" as I think of it now, I made frequent trips between my childhood home in New Orleans, and my adopted home in New York. My trips to be with her were made for so many disparate, even contradictory, reasons. They were made out of a need to snatch every last minute still left to us; out of guilt, and love; from a sense of responsibility as well as generosity. They were made to replace the sense of aloneness that had taken hold in my mother's life since my father's death. They were made in order to cling to the closeness between us, and they were made out of the fear of aloneness that I envisioned as my future without her.

On this particular night during my mother's dying time, I found myself sitting in the backyard of our house, next to the pool. It was a typical lovely but sultry evening in June, yet not even the breeze carrying the familiar sweet scent of night-blooming jasmine could shake me out of my deepest fear—that of falling into a dark and solitary abyss from which there would be no return. The fear was, on its most primitive level, the fear of losing "me"—because in so many ways, it felt as if losing my mother was going to be tantamount to not having a self of my own. Losing my mother was going to mean entering an undescribed unknowable world, losing the foundation from which all that I now call "me" has sprung.

During this time, the big ranch-style house that had once been home to a family of five had become home to only one. Except for my mother, the whole family had moved out: Lee, the oldest of we three children, had stayed close to home, having moved next door with her husband and two children; my big brother, David, also stayed close, moving a mile away with his partner; I had moved north for graduate school; and my father had died a year earlier, moving I suppose, in some sense, to a place further away from my mother than all of the rest of us. (This, in spite of a rather odd, droll fantasy, an illusionary idea of immortality my mother held on to, reflecting her hopeless, desperate attempt to imbue life into my father for just a little longer than the timeframe of his physical life had allowed. She seemed to be only half joking when she told me right after his death of her idea of having him "stuffed," like a huge teddy bear, positioning him on the living room couch, and waving hello and good-bye to him as she wandered through her day. Without this man, who was the only man she had ever loved, the only man she had ever had sex with, the man she defined as her one-and-only, life was unimaginable. For the two years after his death that my mother remained alive, living still in our family home, the image of my stuffed-father stayed with me, unbidden. I suppose I took my mother's idea a little seriously, and her fantasy came to have a realness of its own for me. Every time I, too, passed the living room couch, I gave a silent nod to my ephemeral father.)

Like a thief

During my trips to see her and care for her that last year, and through the ethereal stillness that had become her, I scampered around the house, moving from room to room, surveying all that still was, anticipating all that would no longer be. I became like a squirrel readying for winter—obsessed with holding on to my mother's belongings, attempting to close that looming gap of eternal separateness that was threatening to come between us. On each trip back home, I found something else of hers that I wanted with me up in New York: an inexpensive knick-knack (a white ceramic snail); an antique bowl (eighteenth-century Chinese); a dress. This was when I took her white winter wool, still with the price tag hanging on it. I would never have taken any of her lavish gowns. But, the white wool was a bit more practical, a dress I could wear on an evening out in New York. Still, it was a dress so excessive (all white in the winter?), I never would have allowed myself to actually purchase it. It fit me perfectly, as did all of her clothes.

I justified my raids on the home and her closet: the knick-knacks were too cheap for her to care about; the Chinese bowl would stand attractively on my elaborately wood-carved curio cabinet that she had given me some years earlier; I would wear the white winter wool and she wouldn't/couldn't. She wouldn't miss the clothes; in her bedridden state, couldn't even see whether they were there still in her closet or not. Yet, even after the white winter wool was brought to New York, possession claimed by its new owner, it remained hanging in my closet as desolate and unused as it had been in hers. I could not bring myself to wear it. There was a sanctity about her dress/about all her possessions. I wanted them to be mine; I took them to be mine, but they were hers; they would always be hers.

On one visit, I reclaimed the pretty jar with the jewelled top that I had given her for Mother's Day when I was thirteen. It was a precious little thing, a rounded amber-tinted glass bottom gave it an antique feeling, and the top encrusted with coloured pieces of glass that glistened and glowed. It was the first present I had ever bought for her, the first time I eschewed drawing a picture for her or making a Popsicle-stick box. She kept all my childish creations; she displayed them and I know she treasured them. But the jar was special to her because I gave it to her when I was old enough to have developed a taste for beautiful things; it was special to me because I had really wanted it for myself, but I lovingly made that sacrifice. It was a gift that I had independently given her, chosen without her help, paid for out of my own allowance. Through all the rest of my teenage years, and into my twenties, I would walk into her bathroom, spy it sitting in the prized place of honour she had accorded it—atop the veined black marble countertop—and I would covet it. I would wonder whether I selfishly should have kept it for myself. That conflict was so much what we two were about: genuinely wanting to share, but also giving to each other even when we didn't want to, even, on occasion, to the detriment of our own well-being.

That dying year, as I roamed the house, I felt like a thief furtively planning my next steal. Piece by piece I was trying to move my mother's home into mine. I was trying to ward off her death by acquiring her, by becoming her.

Intent on defining the differences

And yet, even in this dying time of convergence between my mother and myself, I had never been quite so intent on defining the differences between us. My sense of my parents' bedroom was that it had a softened, hushed hue. The intense southern afternoon sun—setting every evening behind the now famed 17th Street Canal (the canal that was breached during Hurricane Katrina, causing all manner of difficulty for my house, my neighbourhood, and for the city itself)—was filtered out by the green shading of the sliding glass doors. But during the time of my mother's illness, that softness seemed to turn dark and morbid. During those dying days, I craved sunlight, as though it represented life itself—the antidote to her dying, the anti-death. I would flee from that darkness into my own sun-filled bedroom.

In the face of the hopelessness of her condition, I refused to acquiesce in my own body to the immobility that she embodied. I focused on our differences, our separateness, in making sure that I kept moving—as if to convince myself that it was not both of us who were dying, and if only because, unlike her, I *could* keep moving. I trained for a mini-triathlon, running six miles a day, followed by a one-mile swim and, finally, the obligatory bike ride. The more my mother's body waned, through no fault of hers, the more mine waxed, through effort and determination. As she lay immobile, I rejoiced in the strength of mine. And the buckets of exercise-sweat that poured from me—those were my tears.

I defined our differences, too, in how we each dealt with

her mother, who, though elderly, was still living and healthy. Dutifully, my grandmother trudged out to our suburban/country home from uptown New Orleans to make her visits. It was during this final year that my mother was able to inflict upon her own mother a final revenge for the bad mothering she felt she had experienced. My mother made my grandmother sit in the front part of the house, the living room, trip after trip, never permitting her into the back bedroom for a proper in-person visit, not even for a final goodbye. I think my mother was recreating for her mother the feeling that she believed she had had when she was a baby: *"Hello, is there anyone out there to care for me? Hello, I hear someone, but where is she? Why is she not here with me?"* This was the story of my mother's childhood that I had grown up hearing—a mother not there, a mother who couldn't/wouldn't love, and a child with no subsequent secure sense of self, no confidence; a child filled with self-loathing.

I sat with my aging grandmother—well into her eighties at this point—during these times of her banishment, sharing her shame and humiliation, both of us wanting my mother to be able to rise above her hatred, above her anger, and above the awful disappointment in her mother that had defined so much of her life. I sat with my grandmother as she endured her daughter's rejection in mute silence, hiding her pain as she had learned to do as a proper southern woman. I sat with my grandmother as we tried to make small talk when there was no small talk to be made—only big talk about life and death, and pain and rejection, and togetherness and loss, and love and unlove.

A towering presence

I was used to spending time in my mother's closet. So much of her life had been represented by her closet. It was her most private, and most valued, space in the house.

When I was young, we moved from uptown New Orleans to what was then the "country" (and is now a large suburb) in order to build my parents' dream house. They gave themselves the grand extravagance of each having their own closet—and splendid closets they were. All the closets felt like rooms to me, special, secret and mysterious rooms with places to situate myself, under and over things. I was not yet tall enough to reach the highest pole from which my mother's best dresses hung. But it didn't matter. I remember standing amongst her dresses, gently moving her clothes hanging over my head, swaying with them as though they and I were dancing together. I would keep the door to the closet open, and I could see the milky light from the back yard filtered through the green sliding glass doors and the eyelet drapes in front. The play of shadows from the old live oak trees out back painted a soft carpet of stippled light on the floor beside me, soothing me in its familiarity. I would open and shut the closet door, playing with the light sources: the living sunlight, but, as well, the overhead light that went on and off mysteriously as I opened and shut the door. It was a modern convenience that we didn't have in the older uptown house, and I never ceased to be amazed by the wondrous power of sudden-light, and then light-no-more, and I couldn't quite figure out the magical mechanism. And when I sat on the floor, I was surrounded by a treasure trove of her shoes on the shoe rack that I could touch and smell and dimly see in the cavernous safety of her inner sanctum.

Hiding in her closet gave me an assurance about our relationship. It wasn't strictly a hide-and-seek game we played because we never gave name to the game. It was more freewheeling, without rules. But there was pleasure in my disappearance from her, not because I would get "lost," but because I would get "found." I knew that when she would find me there (even when she wasn't aware that I had gotten "lost"), as she often did, she would smile and say lovingly, acceptingly, "So there you are." At this young age, and still without the claustrophobia that came with her worry and anxiety about me that developed later, I understood that she would always want to know where I was. And she accepted, still without fear, that, as much as I wanted to be just like her, there were times, too, when I wanted to hide from her, to be altogether separate and away from her. Sitting on the floor next to her shoes, I pulled a high-heeled shoe over my foot. It was heavy and unwieldy. I marvelled at how much room was left—how much more I needed to grow to fit into her shoes. Yet, as much as I yearned to be like her, I felt a chick-like contentment that I was still her little girl, an adjunct to her towering presence.

Within my mother's closet, beside her clothes, shoes and jewellery, was her vast collection of umbrellas. She had, it seemed, one for every occasion and for every outfit: dressy, elegant umbrellas with sleek, fitted covers and beautifully carved wood handles. These hung together in her closet in an ordered row, too excellent to be used. And there were the everyday umbrellas that folded into small carry-size packets, also with matching covers: still elegant, but casual in their foldable sizes. These little folded umbrellas, however, were the perfect size to get lost. When the famous New Orleans torrential rains came, my mother would get frantic in her search for one of them. I was always the one who mounted a search for them. My brother was too busy with his cars and motorcycles. My sister, at that point in her teenage life, was simply uninterested in pleasing my mother the way I was. My father was either at work or sitting in his easy-chair, not to be disturbed from reading his newspapers. Only I would bother to look, and only I would find the lost umbrellas.

Cars were an important feature of our family life. My father earned his living through cars: he owned an auto parts store. My parents met because of cars: in the waning days of the Great Depression, my mother was one of the first young women in New Orleans to independently acquire a car. So the story of their meeting goes: she needed a licence plate for her new automobile, and someone told her that a young man, who had just arrived in New Orleans, would be able to get her one. Throughout my growing up years, my mother always had her own car—I remember a Studebaker, a Chevy Impala—but the family car was my father's, always a large one—sometimes a Lincoln, sometimes a Cadillac—with bucket seats in the front. My sister and brother always sat in the back, but I, as the "baby" of the family, got the throne— the armrest dividing the front seats—the "horsey," as I called it. I would ride the horsey, and I would stretch out my arms, aspiring to touch my mother on my right and my father on my left, as though the act of touching them simultaneously was what held them—and all of us—together.

I never revealed the secret of my search for the lost umbrellas that led to my success in finding them—that they were always in the same place, invisible to everyone's eyes except for mine. The horsey was the key to my being an under-aged genius detective. The umbrellas were almost always trapped below my horsey throne, wedged against the floor, forgotten victims of my mother's last use of them. I would hand the lost umbrellas to her with a celebratory smile, and she would praise me for my cleverness. I would swell with pride, drinking in her love and admiration.

Filled with trepidation

The last time I saw my mother's collection of umbrellas was when she was just a month away from her death. I had flown to New Orleans into yet another rainstorm. Like most of the local rainstorms, the rainfall was rapid and created deep pockets of flooding throughout the city. When I arrived at the house, Blique had completed her day's work. (This is a euphemism—Blique had no real work, as she was aged and didn't walk well; yet my mother continued to pay her, and she continued to come faithfully to work, and would, at best, pick up my father's newspapers to place them in a pile.) She was ready to go home. I was happy to drive her. I was used to driving Blique home to the Desire Street Projects. I had done it often with my mother when she was still healthy and mobile. Together, we had ventured into the projects— the same projects where in the late sixties, there had been a shoot-out between the police and the Black Panthers. Yet, my mother and I hazarded into this place fearlessly because we were with Blique. Blique, who raised my sister, brother and myself as surely as my mother did, a black woman of the all-black projects: seemingly surrounding us white folks with a halo of safety.

But, for this trip, I needed a sturdy umbrella, not one of the cheap foldable ones. The rain had transitioned into torrential. I was filled with trepidation at the thought of having to use one of my mother's precious, dressy umbrellas, so savagely protected all those years from wear and tear.

I snuck stealthily into my mother's closet. I made my selection—a pretty, frilly fire engine red umbrella, one of the umbrellas reserved for only dressy-use—though in spite of its femininity, it looked sturdy enough. I walked into her bedroom to tell her that I was leaving to take Blique home. Furtively, I held that umbrella against the side of my body away from her vision so that she couldn't see it. With my mother's body almost useless, with her having become mostly deaf, her partially paralysed mouth making her speech slurred, this frail, terminally ill woman still held such immense power over me that I snuck and hid rather than openly defying the order she had fought so valiantly to create. Or, had my furtiveness nothing to do with the hierarchy of power in our relationship? Was it simply my way of loving her not to disturb the small bit of order that she was able to wield in those last days of her incapacity? Perhaps it is difficult to know which it was because, at times, I have been unable to distinguish between the two: fear or love.

3

Dress Rehearsals for Death

Having been with my mother at the moment of her death, I suppose I can say that something—my mother's soul perhaps—did happily take flight from that decrepit body at that last exhalation of hers. But, too, some piece of my own soul drifted out with her, away from myself, when she died. As life left her, there was a sense in which I gave chase to her vaporous spirit as it floated away from her body. Part of me kept right on going with her airborne/space-borne, perhaps even heaven-borne journey, and I think I lost a little of myself in the travel that day of death. Her death marked for me the final, from-which-there-is-no-return end of our symbiosis, end of hope for union and togetherness. I felt more alone than I ever had felt, and my sense of self began a process from solidarity to dissolution, much like the Wicked Witch's body melting down into a pool of water. It felt as if there would never in my life be a love for me as strong, as unconditionally accepting, as unambivalent as was my mother's. For me, her death was an emotional event like no other. It was an event from which my psyche and my soul, now many years later, are still recovering. It is a mourning for which there is no end.

A pause in my memory-moments

I find myself reaching out for my memories of her, grabbing onto those that come spontaneously to me, searching for those that have begun to elude me. I want to keep her real and alive for me, even if only in the interior of my mind. Yet, my memories come intermittently; they are, unlike a film, neither streaming nor continuous. They are more like snapshots placed on a gigantic-sized album page with large spaces between the pictures—static memories frozen in time—of sensations, feelings, events, places and people—my mother featuring most prominently, staring out at me, even beckoning me to walk through the page and be with her again.

My strongest memory of the early years with my mother is of the endless hugging between us. This went on all through my childhood, big bear hugs, ending with her asking me, "Will you ever grow too old for 'lovin'?" (as she called it). So sure was I in my absolute and eternal devotion to her that. without hesitation, I declared that I would never, ever grow too old for lovin' and that she was the "best, most beautiful mom in all the world."

And then, in the midst of these sweet-filled memory-moments, there is a pause—as though the album pages are getting glued together, stuck to each other as though they are wet leaves, one having fallen on top of the other, married and unwilling to be separated, and I am unable to turn the page to the next picture series. Then I have a startling and disquieting realisation: in the midst of thinking about the whole line of ancestry on my mother's side—my grandmother, who we called *Momie*; my great-grandmother, who we called *Mère* (French for "mother"); my great-aunt, who we called *Tante* (French for "aunt")—in the midst of all these vivid memories of names of all the women in my family who preceded me, I can't remember what I used to call my mother. I have forgotten my name for her. I know I didn't call her *Mommy*; it's too close to what we called her own mother, and anyway, it feels too childish as a term that I, eager always to grow up fast and furious, would have chosen. It could have been *Mama*; but this, too, doesn't seem right—too old-fashioned—what I imagine my father might have called his mother from the old country, still, as I knew her (as *Muna*), with her thick Polish accent and heavy bosom. I'm inclined to think it was *Mother*, but if it were, I would gloomily wonder about myself. I know she and I did better than my calling her *Mother* would indicate—with that hint of stoic reserve that *Mother* suggests. I am compelled to wonder about myself: could I really have separated myself and my memory this much from the woman who raised me, this woman who adored me, and whom I adored in return.

Or was it the other way around? Did I adore her first? Beginning with our original oneness, there was never a moment, throughout our life together, that I was not certain of my mother's love and devotion to me. She gave me the feeling that there was always a "yes" emanating from her, stretching over to me. I think I must have cooed lovingly into her face when I slid out from her womb, and she immediately became enchanted with me and with my pleasure in her. As I grew up, she and I enjoyed talking with each other, having dialogues about the "important" as well as "unimportant" things in life. But most of all, there was a physicality between us. My mother liked snuggling with me, expanding her individual body boundary to incorporate me. Throughout my childhood, I was utterly responsive to her affection.

Maybe I can't remember what I called my mother because I am still insisting, even after her death, on declaring our distance from each other, just as I did for long stretches of time when she was alive. Maybe I can't allow myself to know that she and I are irredeemably, irrevocably separate. And perhaps the only way to wipe out the fact of our separateness is to attempt to obliterate memory, to forget our life together. Maybe all the separations that I had insisted on while she was alive—my acts of rebellion, my deceits, my leaving home, even fleeing from her, moving 1000 miles away—were all preparations for her death. They were dress rehearsals— attempts to prove that she and I were not the same, behaviours to show that I could have life independent of her, insisting in these acts that we were not fused, as it seemed she often thought of us as being.

Un-separateness in the face of separateness

And now that my childhood has passed, with it, too, has gone the pleasure and excitement I used to enjoy hiding in closets. Yet, I am in my mother's closet again. Albeit, with faint pleasure now. We have sold the house, and we need to take everything from it, remove all vestiges of the life my mother had, the family that we once were. Lee, three inches shorter than my mother was, has no need, no wish for any of her adornments—not for her clothes, nor her shoes or handbags. My brother doesn't have a wife. I, alone, am looking at what is in my mother's closet, trying to decide what I want to keep for myself, what I want to give to Goodwill. The finely crafted shoes of course—the soft Italian leathers, blue, tan, and red. And the brown and gray scaly crocodile and alligator skins—those shoes that even now are still slightly too big for my own feet. Never mind. I take them. I take all the glitzy sequined gowns—the rich brocades, the pastel chiffons and the deep-hued velvets, all the plush dresses she wore to weddings and bar mitzvahs. She wore them well. She looked elegantly luminous in them. (When dressed for these occasions, she bore an uncanny resemblance to Nancy Reagan, and looked ready to assume a role as the President's wife, greeting distinguished foreign leaders with beauty, aplomb and elegance.) I take them all, even knowing that my sneakers/no lipstick/down-home style will never accommodate her gowns. Yet I cannot bear to part with them. And, of course, I take the umbrellas. All of them. Too many to use in a lifetime.

In the face of such utter, unending separation, I am trying desperately to make my way toward un-separateness. As I have gotten older, I think about how my mother looked, and I know that I am increasingly looking more and more like her. I will allow myself to wear her jewellery (her jade earrings that she bought when we went to China together, trying against all odds for both of us to escape the searing pain of my father's/her husband's recent death). I will put to good use a few of her clothes (her winter coat is still in good shape). I will live with her furniture (the headboard of her first marital bed will be mounted handsomely above the door of my own bedroom; the antique armoire will stand in my psychoanalytic office). I startle myself sometimes when I clear my throat, and the sound is so intimately familiar to me; it's as though she is in the room with me, alive again, readying her voice to talk to me. Or, even closer. She is within me; it is in some non-physical, not-real way, *her* throat that is being cleared. It is as though, in some sense, I have become, am still becoming, her. No matter what effort I have tried to make in the past to get away from our togetherness, there is no flight from that which is within.

4

The Shallow Years

I am indiscriminate in what I box up and bring to New York to live with me: the furniture my parents lived with, bedding they slept on, a full set of Encyclopedia Britannica, my father's books of stamps, and multiple boxes. Large and small boxes, filled with things I know I will never use, but can't bear to throw away. And, amongst all this conglomerate of old belongings, there is the box of papers containing my parents' wills and passports, old family photographs, my old drawings from when I was in sixth and seventh grades. There is also the letter that my father brought with him when he rode his Harley-Davidson from southern Georgia to New Orleans, a young man in search of a life beyond the insular farm on which he grew up. The letter is dated May 17th, 1930 (my father is twenty years old at this time), written on a fading letterhead piece of stationery from:

FARMERS & MERCHANTS BANK
CAPITAL $25,000.00
SURPLUS AND PROFITS $45,000.00
MONTICELLO, FLORIDA

and signed by an undecipherable name, a gentleman who is apparently a banker at said bank. The letter says:

> *TO WHOM IT MAY CONCERN:*
> *The bearers hereof Messrs Meyer Goldberg and Frank J. Settler, Jr. are both young men of high standing in this city and are Children of highly respected families who have resided here for some years. They are both young men of good moral character and entitled to any confidence that may be bestowed upon them. They are making a sight seeing tour of the Country, and I am cheerfully giving them this letter in order that any one with whom they may come in contact with may be assured of their good character. They are both deserving young men and any favors shown to them will be appreciated, and we will gladly respond to any inquiry that may be made regarding them or their movements.*

I see that F. J. Settler is listed as the Vice President of the bank, presumably Frank Jr.'s father. My father was travelling in good company as he rode his Harley around the country, first to New York City (where, so the story goes that he relished in telling, he went to college by "walking in the front door of NYU and out the back"). I was told that his Harley broke down only twenty miles from his home on the return trip; he got it repaired, and then proceeded on to New Orleans where he decided to stay for a spell (forty-eight years, until his death). I set aside this precious document of familial history.

The intrusiveness I decide to commit

And then, I spy my mother's diary.

I decide that it is time to take my mother's diary out from this dusty storage bin where it has, apparently, been hidden away for decades. I want to read it, to come to know my mother in a way different from the ways I knew her when she was alive. I want to know her as she herself experienced herself and her life—not through my eyes, but through her own. I want to come to know my mother, not just as the mother she was to me, not just as I knew her, but as the woman she was, independent of me. Madeleine Malvina Levy Goldberg was, too, a daughter, a wife, a friend. She taught school. She collected antiques. She was southern and she was Jewish. It was these attributes, and more, that made her into the complex personality that she was.

I forgive myself for the intrusiveness I am about to commit. Even this invasion into her private world—our willingness to cross over into each other's boundaries—describes our relationship when she was still alive; and now, after her death, it seems like a mere extension of what we already had, already did, with each other (mostly without resentment).

This is a diary whose existence I have known about for a long time. I was a teenager when I accidentally discovered it in her desk in her bedroom (the desk that now sits in my New York office). It was a day when I was rummaging around in my mother's belongings—papers, photos, jewellery, the things people keep in desks—thinking that in seeing and touching and holding her belongings to my cheek, something essential of her would somehow rub off on me. I stopped reading the diary as soon as I opened it when I found myself on a page where my mother was asking herself whether or not she was a lesbian.

I closed the book back then because I was an uninvited intruder into this private space—away from her husband, away from her children—that my mother had carved out for herself. I was peeking into areas that my mother had not meant for me to see. Yet, for all these years since I opened that diary, I have remembered that my mother asked herself that question.

My mother's diary is one of those five-year calendars—about an inch deep into the page for each year. The inventor of this diary obviously didn't expect its writer to have anything of any consequence to say because there is no room to say it. My mother proved herself to be compliant with the inventor's intent. She says nothing of any consequence: "I slept late." "I should have studied, but didn't." "Drove to Baton Rouge for the day." She says all this in microscopic script, which is the only way this diary permits its writer to write.

I find her writing reassuring to me in its familiarity. This is the same script that she used in the hundreds of letters she wrote to me over the years—letters to me at sleep-away camp, at college, letters waiting for me at each new post (France, Germany, Austria, Italy, Greece) during my summer trip to Europe after my sophomore year in college. This is the same script that was then barely readable for its size, but here even more exaggerated in its smallness because the page is itself so small. So perfect is the clarity of her handwriting that this diary could be in a museum for miniatures. I realise, then, that the microscopic size of her writing is a metaphor for her personality and for her conflicts. It's not just that she didn't want to take up space because of low self-esteem, or a defective sense of self, interpretations that any psychoanalyst/psychologist might be tempted to make. More significantly, it's the adaptation that she has made to the constraints of the diary. She didn't fight that sadistic inventor who made a mockery of any burgeoning ability to write thoughtfully or lengthily (or largely). She stayed within his intended limits, squeezing her words, crimping her hand. Such, I think, defined her life. Such, I think, defined her pain: a reluctance to separate herself out from what was expected of her, from the demands of her environment, from the wishes of those who surrounded her.

1937–1938–1939: these are the years that my mother

chose to write about. She had another two years that the diary afforded her. But by 1939 she had accomplished what she must have felt was her main life's work: she had met her husband-to-be. And her writing stopped.

I call these years her "shallow years." On the world stage, Hitler had become a world terror. Germany was supporting the fascist overthrow of the government in Mexico, just a stone's throw away from New Orleans. The Nazi Bund was demonstrating in the streets of Manhattan. The world was on the brink of war. Yet, my mother makes no mention of these events. In terms of the larger world around her, it seems as though she is in a dark corner, facing a wall.

My mother writes as though she has no concerns other than her fitting into the society around her. She writes without conflict about who she is or what she does. She drones on, as though life were nothing more than worrying about her grades, getting a job when she graduates, hanging out with friends. She has no idea yet that she is a repressed tornado, waiting to be released, unleashed. She doesn't know yet that beneath her concern with her quotidian life is a continent of pain that relates to her relationship with her mother. She doesn't know yet that her destiny, determined by the particular brand of relationship she had with her mother in her growing-up years, would result in her never feeling entirely comfortable within herself, within the society around her.

My mother's compressed handwriting about essentially nothingness goes on for the whole year of 1937. "Saw Elsie." "Can't get the car for parade. Damn it." "Freshman hygiene lecture very interesting." "Late for basketball practice." Basketball and swimming are featured well in my mother's diary. She's planning to be a physical education teacher. It is clear that an important part of her identity is in the athletic use of her body, and I remember with pride that she had been

Southern Champion in both breast and butterfly strokes when she was a teenager. She had stayed close to her adolescent swimming coach, Roy Brenner, even as an adult. I remember many times visiting Roy's modest uptown house. When we built our swimming pool, it was Roy who donated the ornate tile dragon that decorated the bottom of the pool.

"Tommy called." Here things get a little more interesting because after a point Tommy is mentioned in practically every entry. Tommy, sometimes alternately and inexplicably referred to as Hank, is an important person in my mother's life in these years. It sounds like she is in love with Tommy/Hank. She gets excited when he calls, and sad when he fails to call. I feel betrayed for my father. I was always sure that my father was my mother's one and only, forevermore, there-will-never-be-another-even-in-heaven. I have to consider the possibility that my father was not my mother's first and only true love, but her second. And then, there is a telling pronoun and I am startled to realise that Tommy/Hank is a woman.

I realise that I am at the point in my mother's life when she is first beginning to experience a passion for relationships. It is an extraordinary moment for me. It's like seeing, for the first time, a home-movie of your mother before you were born. But this is much more personal—she's both protagonist and author (unlike in most films where the players are not also the directors). My mother is telling me, through her free associative writing as the author describing her own character, that her first passion is for a woman. I realise that I am not surprised, for, as far back as my memory goes, there were always my mother's women. These women were like satellites that my mother had launched into a trajectory orbit. She kept them circling around her home with her husband and her children, but she never let them get too close to us. Her women were her private life.

It was always obvious to me that her relationships with

her women never sated her. And this search, of course, had its origin in those early years of feeling unloved and unwanted by her mother. She was always searching, always reaching for these women. They were always older, women whom she adored and admired, women whom she aspired to be like. They were women who she perceived as being the diametric opposite to her mother and for whom her feelings were, too, polar opposite to her feelings for her mother.

For these women she sacrificed much personal time to be with, to do errands for, to buy things from. They were almost always working women. They were busy women, women not readily available for the intense loving that my mother sought to give and receive. I remember (only faintly now) frequent phone calls, attempts to make plans—overhearing my mother's requests for time, and listening to her willingness to meet these women on their terms, any time/any place. My mother never grasped the significance of this small point: they were women who, like my mother's own mother, first by necessity and then later by desire, reached beyond the expectations of women of their day and became highly successful in business.

It was my grandmother, through her business acumen and determination, who enabled her family to survive the days of the Depression. She took the last hundred dollars she and her husband had, hopped on a train—a woman alone travelling from New Orleans to New York—and came back home having learned to teach bridge. She became the first bridge teacher in the state. And later, when my grandmother decided to work for Mutual of Omaha, she sold so much life insurance that she became a lifetime member of the Million Dollar Club. When she decided to dance, she became Arthur Murray's prize student, travelled from contest to contest, filling her whole house with trophies that trumpeted her triumphs. I remember my dismay (and teenage embarrassment) when my grandmother (old lady that I saw her as being then at the age of sixty or so) appeared on local TV, dancing my generation's dance, the jitterbug, resplendent in her jewelled and sequined dance gown. The point is: whatever my grandmother aspired to do, she did well. She excelled. She did what she did without apology and with a kind of gaudy, shimmering drama.

And perhaps this, too, was part of the reason for my mother's rage. Perhaps she knew that my grandmother had it in her to be a better mother, could have been the loving mother that she needed, because my grandmother really could have done anything she set her mind to. But instead of making the choice of being a loving mother, she took the path, unusual for her time (but of economic necessity), of success as a woman in the world. My mother, though she was her mother's firstborn, was not her mother's first passion in life, and my mother was well aware of this circumscription of their relationship.

My mother never felt that she had a mother at all—only a woman who gave her the gift of life and then alternately hated or ignored her. My mother used to tell me that she felt her mother wanted her dead. I understand—and I think that my mother understood—that my grandmother did not "really" want her dead. It was a feeling that reflected the "spirit of the law" (the felt-reality) rather than the "letter of the law" (the actual reality).

(I stand in good company in understanding there is not as big a difference between felt and actual realities as we might think. One of Freud's great contributions was his understanding that the "spirit of the law" counts almost as much as the "letter of the law." He made his argument around the pivotal issue of childhood incest and molestation. Streams of patients were coming into his Vienna office, complaining about having been sexually abused by relatives. At first, Freud believed them—the "letter of the law." But eventually he came to understand that these so-called "memories" were constructions of the mind—"phantasies," as he called them. His understanding led him to see that the mind is active and imaginative in its attempt to organise its experience. Memories of childhood abuse may or may not be "real" memories. The difference between an actual memory and a fantasised memory is a crucial distinction for issues of morality, for acquiring a true clinical picture, and for treatment. But for assessing the importance of Freud's idea that memory is created as much as it is remembered, that distinction is irrelevant.)

I can't say for sure whether or not my grandmother was a rotten mother to my mother. She had two other children, and neither of them hated her as much as my mother did. (In fact, just the other day, my aunt made reference to being blessed with such a "wonderful mother.") All I can know is that in terms of my mother's emotional experience—real or imagined—she felt hated, and returned to her mother the same feeling in spades. I never saw my mother demonstrate a single kind emotion or sweet word to her mother. Her mother would call on the phone, and my mother's voice would become disembodied, cold, and distant. She would become transformed from the loving mother I knew, into a hateful, vengeful daughter. This Jekyll/Hyde transformation was so much a part of my growing-up that it ceased to surprise me when I would witness it.

I believe that my mother must have gotten a strong message from her mother that she wasn't good enough the way she was, that she should be different. I believe that my mother did all those athletic activities that she mentions in her diary (and that she continued through the raising of her children, fulfilling her college ambition of becoming a physical education teacher—though she had a double major in chemistry and a minor in German as well) in order to keep moving away from her feelings, to keep her emotions at bay—to move away from the pain of the unloving relationship she felt she had with her mother.

My mother never seemed to grasp the significance of her choice of the women who populated her adult life. She never understood her repetition of the experience of, first, an unloving mother, and later, re-creating that same experience with a cadre of women who were sufficiently busy with their professional lives that they were unable (and, I think, too, unwilling) to return my mother's passion. My mother seemed compelled to keep repeating her early experience with her mother, re-finding over and over again the feeling of frustration and incompleteness with a woman/mother/mother-figure.

The irony, then, in my mother's choice of women—Tommy/Hank first, and then all the others who followed—was that they were, like my grandmother, motivated by success. They, like my grandmother, were untypical New Orleans Jewish women in that they worked, either out of pleasure or necessity. One was an early widow, looking for a productive way to occupy her time; another was a divorcee, in need of an income. With them, as with my grandmother, the relationship with my mother came only after business. But with these women, unlike with my grandmother, my mother forgave them their unavailability and stretched herself out to reach them on their turf and on their terms. Whatever particular trade they happened to be in was where my mother directed her energy for the time of that involvement.

Ultimately, in each of the relationships, my mother's frustration became the more powerful force—stronger even than her attraction to any particular woman. She was never able to really sit down and rest in any of these relationships.

My mother's searching out the women she found—going

to their places of work, joining with them in their interests, volunteering to do all manner of errands for them—was as much a part of my growing-up experience as was anything else. I shared my mother inordinately. The whole time I was growing up, there were other Tommy/Hanks, a long list of them, whom she pursued, really chased down almost, with the fervour of a lover. I remember these women, each of them. I remember my mother's attempts to see herself in the light of their reflections. Because they were all working women, they were women whom my mother had to fight for her time with, women who squeezed my mother in between their other activities.

One was a fine dress saleswoman. During those years of her involvement with Madelyn, my mother bought all the evening gowns that I found in her closet after her death, now stored in a chest in my apartment: pristine, still elegant, waiting to be used perhaps as dress-up costumes. My mother bought more gowns than any woman could wear in a lifetime, gowns that would rival any in a Givenchy fashion show. It was also during this time that my mother changed the spelling of her own name, Madeleine (which she had always proudly pronounced with an impeccable French accent, thus showing off her regal Alsatian heritage) to match her friend's more Americanised version.

After Madelyn came Emery, who owned an antique furniture store on Magazine Street. It was during her friendship with Emery that my mother re-decorated the house. This was when she acquired the antique armoire, and the English library table, and the demilune chest—all pieces of rarity, precious antiques that make my apartment in New York practically a showroom for cultivated taste.

The lavishness of her collections—of the gowns, the antiques, her jewellery—paralleled her consuming desire to please these women (as well as giving her an excuse to be with them), or even to become like them, even to become them, as witnessed by her name change.

Tommy/Hank seems, then, to be the first in my mother's list of women who fascinated her and whom she desperately wanted to be close to and emulate. Soon enough, however, it becomes clear from my reading the diary that this is a relationship that never exceeded the bounds of convention and conversation, and Tommy/Hank probably remained unaware of my mother's ardent interest in her.

I move on to my mother's March cold that lasted too long, and all the football games between Tulane and LSU. In 1938, Tulane, apparently, had a better team than LSU (amazingly, because in my high school years, LSU was king); she reports cheerfully that Tulane won: 14–0; and she goes on reciting the scores of the games between Tulane and Mississippi, and Tulane and Alabama. She mentions going to the games with her Daddy, and it takes me a minute to remember that her Daddy is not my Daddy, but is my grandfather, my Papa.

Paying attention to what is not said

I am now more than halfway through this diary, and there has been a reasonably large cast of characters. Yet, there is one person who is noticeably absent from any mention. In psychoanalysis, the analyst pays as much attention to what is not said as to what is said. My mother, in over seven hundred entries, every day, never missing a day for more than two years, has not mentioned her own mother once. This is my mother already putting distance between them, not yet even knowing that this is what she is doing. This omission of mention is my mother killing off her mother whom she herself felt killed off by.

I know, though, that at this point in my mother's life when she was writing her diary, just at the end of her teens, she herself would not have made much of her omission. She might have dismissed her avoidance of her mother as a topic as unimportant, explaining that, after all, her mother was a businesswoman, and her father—who worked from the back of their home selling mosquito bar netting—simply had more time to spend with her. I know, too, that already—before my mother had become consciously aware that she hated her mother and felt hated by her mother—that she is attempting separation from her. I know that her omission of her mother in her diary is the telltale sign that she has taken her distance, that she is unwittingly attempting to relegate her mother to stick-figure status in her life.

My mother's diary, so far, has confirmed for me what I already know about her mother and her mother substitutes, her search for closeness with the latter and her insistence on distance from the former. I begin to get a little impatient for some unexpected revelation. I want to see if there are any hints of what is to come in this woman, any suggestion that she will transform from the somnolent unconscious girl/woman whose efforts are to live the same way all her friends do, into the woman I knew her as being: a woman of daring, uncommon sensitivity, and crystal clear (and astonishing for her time) consciousness. I jump ahead, scouring the pages for some material that will catch my eye.

5

In Love with Love

There's an old saying in New Orleans; actually it's a word—*lagniappe*. Lagniappe is a French/Cajun/Creole/only-in-New Orleans word that means *a little something extra*. It's that maraschino cherry on top of the Gambino's Bakery Charlotte Russe ladyfingers that my grandmother used to always have for us. It's a good description of how you make gumbo: you make the roux, then throw in some okra, celery and bell pepper, then a ham hock, and you think you're almost done, and then suddenly you see hiding behind something in the refrigerator, a big ripe Creole tomato. You had forgotten you had it, you hadn't planned on cooking with it, but there it has appeared suddenly, and you know that it is that little something extra that's going to make your gumbo even better than you had planned. Or, it's hanging out in the French Quarter on a perfect sunny day, enjoying all the street scenes, walking around sipping your mint julep as you can do only in New Orleans, and then unexpectedly, around the corner comes a jazz band with their big black umbrellas and their soulful moans of trumpets and trombones. The day has gone from perfect to sublime. It's gilding the lily. It's lagniappe.

The thing about lagniappe is that you can't look for it. It just appears unexpectedly. New Orleans is founded on the principle of lagniappe. New Orleans is a town that's always pushing to the edge of the envelope. With the driving age at 15 when I was growing up, and the drinking age at 18, it's never been satisfied with being ordinary. It wants to be a little bit more than any other town. It works at creating lagniappe—unexpected little extra treats—by creating a frenzy. For instance, the holidays start, like everyone else's, with Thanksgiving. Then we get into Christmas when people actually move out of their homes because the Christmas lights and decorations are so exaggerated that the homes are rendered uninhabitable. The rest of the country settles down then with post-Christmas blues. But not New Orleans. It's just gearing up for Mardi Gras, which is not a week-long of revelry, as most outsiders think. Rather, it's months of balls and parades, only culminating on the day of Fat Tuesday known to the rest of the world as Mardi Gras. And, if that's not enough, then the town gets into its Jazz and Heritage Festival weekends, expanded to two weekends because the original one weekend just didn't satisfy the New Orleans spirit for more, and more, and then even yet more.

A lesson in contradictions

New Orleans, as a town, is nothing if not a lesson in contradictions. First, there's the question of never quite being able to decide on its identity. Maybe it's French, maybe it's Spanish. You think it's French, its reputation is French and its food is a (some feel improved) perversion of French. Then you get there and realise that a lot of its old architecture is Spanish. And, with its location at the mouth of the biggest river in the land, it should have become one of the biggest cities around. It, in fact, once was—the sixth largest city in the country before the Civil War. But then it shrank. It's actually a small city, nestled in the crescent of the river, and closed up for expansion by a huge lake, Pontchartrain, on its other side. It has an air of sophistication and worldliness. You come to expect a kind of cosmopolitan attitude. Then you look at the newspaper, the one newspaper in town, and you see that local news is about all that anyone cares about. A lot of the news is about what's happening with the zoo, and the ponds and the social scene. The townspeople threaten yearly to not support its symphony orchestra; and the art museum, until the 1980s, was so nondescript that it could hardly justify its existence. Next to the French Quarter's den of iniquity on Bourbon Street, where hawkers on the street try to suck you in, one block away—literally a single block over—is a stretch of road named Royal Street that carries antiques as exquisite and precious as those found anywhere else in the world.

And, of course there's the race issue: the subliminal issue that I grew up with that was never talked about. Some of the uptown neighbourhoods are integrated in a way that doesn't exist in any other city in America. You can have one block that is completely gentrified, homes gracious and lovely with some delicate colour of pastel, and the next block is the same kind of house, a shot-gun cottage (named so because its linear architecture allows one to stand at the front door of the house, shoot a shotgun, and a nanosecond or so later the bullet will exit the back door), not renovated, still looking just as it did 100 years ago, and occupied by blacks. The neighbours, black and white, all say hello to each other; they're friendly; their hellos are genuinely warm. For many of the young professionals who have gentrified the neighbourhoods, black nannies raised them as surely as did their mothers, so living with, amongst, or close to black people seems entirely normal. Yet, this is the town that when integration was legally mandated in the 1960s, decided to close Audubon Park Pool rather than share it with black people (the pool my mother taught swimming in). The town decided they'd rather have seals than blacks in its pool (and, indeed, the seals got a new, nice home). Later, in 1993, thirty years after enforced integration, the town's judicial system, with a decade long history of black mayors, ordered its Mardi Gras parades to integrate. The premier parades, the ones that represented the cream of New Orleans high society, decided they'd rather not parade than have blacks join them. Comus, Momus and Proteus, parades that had been part of the town's history for over 100 years, then no longer travelled the streets of New Orleans.

Too, New Orleans is a town of differences. It has more diversity than anywhere except perhaps New York. For the most part, its subcultures co-exist rather peacefully. It has Catholics who live in the 9th Ward Irish Channel and sound like they have just got off a fast train from the deepest heart of Brooklyn. The town has so many Catholics, and they permeate the culture so vividly that you begin to think Catholicism defines New Orleans. Then, of course, you remember the blacks and jazz, and you realise that New Orleans ain't New Orleans, and never has been, without them. Next, you find out about the Protestants and Episcopalians who make the Garden District one of the prettiest residential sights in America. There're the I-talians who own neighbourhood restaurants that serve better food than the four-star eateries in New York. There's the New Orleans Mafia, headed by my old down-the-street neighbour Carlos Marcello, who owned the favourite restaurant of native New Orleanians (and known only to New Orleanians), Mosca's, and, as well, according to some theorists, the architects who coordinated the JFK assassination. New Orleans has the Cajuns who no one else has—who no one even comes close to simulating—who still retain their own language, their own food and their own music and live as though 200 years ago were still here.

And finally, New Orleans has its Jews.

Southern Jews had been a rarity since the first expeditions from eastern and western Europe, as well as from Russia. New Orleans, like most of the rest of the world, wanted to hate the Jews and drive them out. Their history together begins in the mid-1700s. In 1724, France passed a *Code Noir*, effectively banning all Jews from living in the French colony of Louisiana. Nevertheless, six brave Jews defied the edict (but who's counting?), and settled in New Orleans. In 1759 the *Commissaire Ordonnateur* of New Orleans announced that

> … *Jews, who according to the edicts and ordinances must not remain in a colony more than three months, under penalty of imprisonment and confiscation of their property, are forming establishments here by the progress and the danger of which have been observed by the whole country. There are, at present, six of them here …*

Yet, for most of the town's history, Jews, though they were being counted, were ignored, and left to prosper, which they did. Within a short period of time, they had established themselves as the some of the city's leading retailers and richest citizens.

My own ancestors came over on different boats in different influxes. The western European Jews, among them my mother's great grandparents, were fleeing the violence and chaos of Alsace-Lorraine in the 1850s as it passed from French to German hands. This violence, though, had nothing to do with the usual European embrace of anti-Semitism. The Jews weren't hated for their religion, and they weren't afraid of being killed. They left because there was another home beckoning to them where they would find a cultural commonality, in a place where they already spoke the language.

The eastern European Jews, on the other hand, were being persecuted in Russia and Poland in the late 1880s precisely because of their religion. When they left their homeland, they were running for their lives. If they were lucky, as were my father's parents, they got rides from Poland/Russia/Latvia/Lithuania to Hamburg, hidden in hay wagons, pulled by oxen or mules; the unlucky ones walked. When they had saved enough money to come to the New World, they brought over few precious heirlooms, and little commonality of culture to their new home.

The western European Jews wanted to look indistinguishable from the New Orleans community in which they were rapidly becoming acculturated. They embraced Reform Judaism: they threw off their yarmulkes and tallis; they sat through religious services conducted in English; organ music filled the rafters in the glorious synagogue built in the best and most expensive Moorish tradition (as was Touro Synagogue, the temple I went to until I was confirmed in tenth grade). And they did the unthinkable—they broke with strict tradition by having men and women sit together. Except for the small amount of Hebrew prayers, these services could have been in any Christian church in the land. Such was the aspiration of the western European Jews: to look Christian; to stay Jewish, but look Christian.

The eastern European Jews, on the other hand, kept their old-world religion, and remained observant. This is a religion of prayer. These were Jews who took life seriously because they had had, for so long, worried about which direction the next death threat was going to come from. Assimilation was the farthest thing from their minds. They stayed Orthodox; they didn't wear fox-fur coats to Yom Kippur services because praying was serious business, not show-time. They didn't join the Jewish country club because Saturday (Shabbos) was for God.

The seeds of the rest of their life together

In continuing to read my mother's diary, and all of her references to the local scene, her talking about the unique place that New Orleans has always been, finally, I spy my father's name. I become alert at the name *Meyer Goldberg* because where their story begins is where my story begins. It is, of course, a Jewish name. In those days, my mother being interested in, or dating, a Gentile, would have been inconceivable. By the time of my mother's up-bringing, the small Jewish sub-culture in New Orleans (still smaller, at one per cent, than any other major city in the country) had become firmly entrenched and a distinctive part of the larger culture surrounding it—not precisely an integrated part of it, but standing next to it at least.

From reading my mother's diary, it seems to me that not much has changed in New Orleans between her growing up years and my own. She went to the same school as I did, *Isidore Newman School*, originally founded in 1909 to educate children living at the Jewish Orphans' Home. The first house we lived in was a mere six blocks away from the house she grew up in. She moved this short distance from the Levy home on Jefferson Avenue to the Goldberg home on Nashville Avenue.

My mother's verbal meanderings in her diary describe the culture of her day in much the same way I would describe my own: Jewish New Orleans, for both her and me, was a circumscribed society. The Jewish women stayed mostly with other Jewish women. Most of them didn't work; many volunteered for the *New Orleans Museum of Art*, and for the Jewish organisations associated with the temples. Husbands were faithful, and the families gathered for dinner every night. Life was fairly routine, predictable and safe. This was the culture she was raised in, and this was the family life that I was exposed to, as well.

I've always thought there is a difference between those who grow up in one place and live the rest of their lives there, and those who have the urge—an itch that has to be scratched—to move away, to experience more than the little world that they have thus far known. As with many native New Orleanians, it did not occur to my mother to ever leave the town she had been born in and become accustomed to. Unlike myself, who fled to the North as soon as I could, no future other than staying in New Orleans came to my mother's mind. And this is one reason why her diary, at first glance, seems so uninteresting, so filled with everyday trivialities. She has not yet been released. She still strove then, as a young woman, to succeed within the defined, ordinary limits that were familiar to her.

It is November 1938, and after one date my mother is in love. I see what she saw in him from an old photograph I have of him: a handsome man who has newly dusted off his pants, blown into town from a farm in southern Georgia, striking in his leather jacket as he sits smartly upon his Harley Davidson.

> November 25, 1938
> *My first date with Meyer, and on the way home he kissed me, first my forehead, then my cheek, and finally my lips. But such sweet kisses. I do like Meyer more than I've ever liked any boy—excluding none.*

And two days later:

November 27, 1938

A wonderful day. Out riding with Kaplans in back.
Victor, Meyer, and I in front. Meyer squeezed my hand
quite often on the way back while Victor drove. Then
supper alone. Meyer came back. To the show we went—
then for a whirl around while he told me I was sweet and
kissed me. I know I'm in love for the first time in my life.

And this, too, was the story I heard when I was old
enough to hear about love—that my mother fell exquisitely,
wonderfully in love with my father and stayed in love,
presumably, until the day she died. And I know that from
my mother's perspective, from the point of view of her
understanding of love, her story of instant romantic love that
never died felt true enough to her.

One theory I have developed over the years is that upon
first meeting someone who will contribute to shaping your
future, someone who will gain importance to us, that we all
know everything that is psychically important, everything
that is going to be pertinent to the specific nature of the
ensuing relationship, within the first few meetings. We never
pay attention to the cues, and we live out the relationship
with all that precious information staying deeply hidden in
the unconscious so that the absolutely inevitable, only-way-
it-could-have-turned-out end comes as a surprise. Union was
our first experience with love, and it is union to which we
all want to return. I think we all want to love and to fuse, to
reunite, so badly—to be back in the symbiotic bliss with our
mothers—that we make ourselves not look at all at that which
might render us apart. We ignore irreconcilable differences;
we refuse to see signals of imminent disaster; we deny the
obvious—all in order to preserve love and all in the name of
love. All for the sake of union. All because separation is too

painful to contemplate. We are more in love with love than with a person. And it is for this reason that my mother could never let go of her version of her marriage, even after the evidence contradicted it.

Already, by my mother's third date with my father, I see the seeds of the rest of their life together (and ultimately, the legacy about men that she left with me, the seeds of my own life). She waits for him to call; he doesn't and she tries to be a mythical princess, waiting patiently, undemandingly, femininely. She can't pull it off. She goes to his work, drops off a note for him, and then obsesses that she has destroyed the relationship:

> December 3, 1938
> *He told me I was so silly and shouldn't write such silly notes like that. He didn't hold my hand until the show was almost over, so I thought he probably wouldn't kiss me, but he did. Gee, I know I've spoiled everything. Yet he asked me for another date.*

She: the archetypal female principle since the world began, the repository of feeling, emotionality, and love; he: the archetypal male principle since the world began, the iron hand of rationality and common sense, alternately attracted to and revolted by too much feeling. These differences between female and male, between my mother and father, accounted both for my mother's initial attraction to Meyer Goldberg and her later difficulty in being his wife; and, too, for his initial attraction to her, and his difficulty (seemingly from the beginning) in having her as his wife.

Some months later my mother begins to get more confident in her role:

February 23, 1939
Meyer didn't want to see me, but I made him. He wanted to bring me home at 10, and I wouldn't let him. Tears came to my eyes at A&G [the local grocery store] and he told me not to be foolish. I was so happy in school all day about last night.

This is not about female domination, nor is it about control or manipulation. It is about feeling and pain. It is about longing for union, and it is about the fear of separation. Such was the dance my mother and father did until the day they died. She felt; he didn't. She sought closeness; he sought distance. No woman "makes" her beloved see her when he doesn't want to, and no woman doesn't "*let* him bring (her) home" when he wants to if she is feeling truly, really loved. This behaviour is a defence against not feeling loved, a hiding from the fact that your hunger for him is stronger than his is for you. This is being so in love with blissful togetherness that the reality that you are not altogether together is denied. This object of my mother's affection is a man, but it is her mother-conflict that she is re-enacting all over again. She dreams of his love and affection, as she originally wished for her mother's, and she becomes terrified at the thought that, like her mother, he might not reciprocate.

Familiar distance

I believe that my mother could not have fallen in love with another kind of man. Her love would not have been so passionate if she had chosen a man who returned her ardour with equal fervour. My father's silent distance gave her all the room she needed to project onto their relationship her romanticised vision of their love, her belief that their union reflected something akin to cosmic harmony. His distance must have felt awfully familiar to her too—a repeat of what she had experienced with her own mother.

This repetition—choosing the familiar as opposed to the best, or healthiest, or even most pleasurable—held sway here with my mother's choice of her husband (as it does in many marriage choices). In choosing my father, my mother, in fact, chose her mother. She chose a man who, like her mother, was overwhelmed by her emotions and who would have preferred that she keep trying to squash herself into a box in which she couldn't fit.

My father did not embrace symbiotic bliss, my mother's romanticised version of their relationship, the way she came to convince herself he had. He may have loved her in a fashion, in his own restrained way; but compared to what she felt for him, he might as well have been an iceberg. There were times, I remember some of them, when he was downright crotchety or mean. I remember that it was always she who reached for his hand, never he hungering for the physical contact. And, I remember her calmness in the face of his irritability.

Yet, even in the face of overwhelming evidence, my mother persisted in mythologising their relationship, insisted on believing that he felt as close to her as she did to him. My mother never admitted that her husband did not love her the way she desired, the way she insisted was so. Separation, emotional distance, needing to take space—the qualities my father excelled at in his relationship with my mother—these were not concepts of which my mother allowed herself to be even dimly aware with her husband.

Had my mother's "silly" feelings been merely her being in love and the concomitant feelings of pain and fear and insecurity that falling in love often brings, the two of them probably would have gone along merrily without any hitches. She would have grown out of the being-in-love anguishes she refers to in her diary, and they would have fit into the template of New Orleans Jewish couples without seeming particularly odd.

Such was not to be their fate. My father must have made the mistake that all lovers in trouble make. He must have thought that marrying her, settling her into domestic life, being a true and dutiful husband—giving her what she said she wanted, what she thought she wanted—would take away her "silly" feelings—her feelings that, in truth, unbeknownst to either of them, came from her incomplete separation from her mother. Like all lovers, my father must have thought that love is stronger than character and that it supersedes history. When we are in love, we think that bestowing upon our beloved the right feelings, the right circumstance, the right amount of money, will take away the person's feelings of insecurity, unhappiness, fear, or sense of being unloved. I think my father assumed that his wife would become a traditional southern lady, find her place with the other women, be content with life and thus release him from her overpowering needs. Real feelings, "silly" feelings, feelings of needing an intimacy that matched the symbiotic closeness of mother and child—these he was not used to dealing with and not comfortable with. They would not have been a part of the equation he was expecting. But, having been denied these feelings from her mother, these were, indeed, the feelings that my mother had most fervently.

Misguided lovers who think that their gifts (even their gifts of emotion) will transcend character and will obliterate the legacy of history are invariably wrong, and my father was wrong. Character and history always win. Insecurity, doubt, feelings of inadequacy—when they are your legacy from childhood—usually return no matter the ecstasy that the reprieve of being in love may have given momentarily.

Water seeks its lowest level, and so does character once the freshness of initial sweet blooming love wears off. We are each capable of regressing back to our most needy, most infantile, and most unappealing selves, the dependent self that needs closeness as much as the body needs air and water. My father never succeeded in making my mother's "silly" feelings vanish because they were too deeply entrenched, and, ultimately, had nothing at all to do with him.

6

Growing Down

I realise, after having finished reading my mother's diary, that there is another diary—a missing one. I have scoured every page of my mother's diary and there is nowhere in sight the question I remember reading when I was thirteen—the one about whether or not she was a lesbian. This is one of those memories that you are certain happened, but as with all those things that happened about which you have no vivid memory— you have seen it maybe in a picture that you can no longer find, or your mother has told you about it a dozen times and it is completely etched in your memory bank—you have no real proof that it happened. You just remember it—irrationally even. I know I saw that question in a diary years ago, and if it's not in this diary, it must be in another one. A later diary. A diary that would have been written after my mother became a person capable of deeper, self-reflective thought. After my mother had begun, or finished, being analysed.

The official explanation

Perhaps it was my mother's needing an answer to the question of her sexuality that impelled her, some eleven years after writing this first diary, into undergoing a psychoanalysis. Or perhaps it was the riding stable event with my sister. This was her official explanation to me as to why she entered analysis the one time I asked.

My sister and I loved horses. We pleaded with our father to buy us one until we wore him down. We kept Crackers in a barn in our backyard, and from the time I was in seventh grade all the way through to high school graduation, my sister and I spent every day after school riding her. But it was my sister who first developed the passion for horses. It was she who first asked for riding lessons when she was eleven, a seasoned summer camper, a veteran horse-rider (at seven, I was not yet a camper, not yet enthralled). My mother—always the devoted mother, the mother who, more than any other mother, became involved in her children's lives (she was den mother for my brother's Cub Scout group, Girl Scout leader for both my sister and me, swim teacher to all of us and many of the children of New Orleans)—never hesitated in saying yes. But my mother's ambitions as a mother sometimes stretched beyond her actual level of comfort and adequacy. (The truth is I remember her being a fairly mediocre scout leader.)

They sat parked in the car, my mother and my sister, their first visit to the riding stable. They sat, waiting. My sister finally asked if they were going to go in. My mother told her that she should go on in alone. My sister said she was afraid to go in alone. Confronted with a motherly necessity, my mother realised that she was as afraid as her eleven-year-old—afraid to meet a new person, feeling incompetent to deal with the vagaries of setting up lessons—in short, inadequate to deal with life outside the family home—and she knew that this was no kind of mother to be. My mother's self-stated reason for deciding to be analysed was out of her need to be a better mother to her children than her own mother had been to her.

It was after this episode that my mother began her analytic journey—her exploration into the origin of her anxieties and feelings of inadequacy, the exploration that led her, as it does for everyone who undertakes it, back to her own mother.

One doesn't get analysed without being in pain. It's not like going to the doctor, a one-shot deal for a check-up—what would be the equivalent of an emotional tune-up to see if the state of your psyche is alright. With the body, there are things that you don't really know a lot about, things that can go wrong that the doctor can discern before you know about them. That's not true about the psyche. If there is something wrong, you know. You know because you feel it, or worse, you know because you don't feel it. You may not feel at all. It is true you can go along for a long time not feeling, and never know that you're effectively asleep, but sooner or later something happens. At some critical juncture, we are jolted into awareness that we have been living in a coma. Maybe a husband leaves for a younger woman. Maybe a mother dies and we fall, inexplicably to ourselves, into a deep depression. Maybe everything seems hunky-dory, but we feel this acute sense of dissatisfaction that we can't shake because the real, unadorned truth is that everything is not hunky-dory at all.

Seeing an analyst is also not like going to a doctor to get medication to take away your symptoms for some disease like diabetes or for high cholesterol. You can try that route for a diseased psyche. Many do. They see a psychiatrist and get medication for depression or anxiety, or for too many fantasies about sex (one of my patients came in at the age of fifty, still a virgin, a good-girl Catholic who had grown up thinking she would be a nun, now plagued, actually tormented, by unending sexual fantasies), or for feeling unloved by their spouse. If this plan worked routinely, or even frequently, psychoanalysts and psychotherapists would be out of business. Psychoanalysis is a long haul, the slow, low road. It isn't a Band-Aid and, lots of times, it ain't fun. You don't do it unless you have to.

Not only did my mother's "silly" feelings never go away, but in fact they began to plague her. As she settled into her marriage, as her relationship with my father became routine and predictable, her "silly" feelings found recipients other than my father—her women. I'm not sure whether it was a sudden epiphany or a slow dawning, but at some point my father became aware that he was married to a woman with complex, contradictory needs, and that many of these needs were unrelated to him. He was a farm man, of simple ideas and straightforward solutions. At some point, my father, rather than choosing the route of seeking understanding, chose, instead, the route of simply withdrawing.

The more my father withdrew, the more his soft blue eyes went vacant when he looked in her direction, the more my mother went back to her original passion, her fascination, her longing for the care of a woman. It was this longing, I believe, that ultimately led her to her analyst. She would have only chosen a woman; a woman hired, presumably, to give her the care and attention that she never got from her mother. A new mother, so to speak.

It wasn't really psychoanalysis, then, that I believe appealed initially to my mother. It was in this woman's being interested in her—the first woman who showed sufficient interest to be able to contain the intensity of my mother's need for love—that my mother came to feel loved. I think for my mother, and perhaps for most of those who enter analysis, the process is a bit like having a visitation from God. The patient lies on the couch, and the analyst remains out of sight (like God, even like the god of the underground, Hades—invisible). The voice of the analyst drifts over to the patient, seemingly disembodied, hovering over the patient, enveloping the patient like a blanket.

Or, perhaps the analogy is closer to the mother of infancy: a shimmering but indistinct presence; an omnipresence.

By her analyst, my mother finally came to feel loved: by her analyst, to whom she confided everything, every secret confession, including, undoubtedly, her sense that she didn't deserve to be loved (an almost unavoidable legacy from a mothering experience where you don't feel loved); by her analyst, who knew the worst of her, who knew her deepest, darkest undeservedness, my mother felt. And in coming to feel loved, she came to feel more whole, more deserving. Her analysis freed her to know her desires—her wish to be loved by a woman, a female mother replacement who would ease the pain of her having felt unloved by her real mother. And, in feeling this, it gave her the confidence to pursue the satisfaction of her desires—even when those desires must have felt awfully frightening to her.

Feeling like she was going crazy

I believe that when my mother began her analysis, she had no idea what she would find. What surfaced were ideas, thoughts, and feelings. They were all rumbling around, long ago submerged to the subterranean, and grumbling only a deep moan that she had effectively ignored, been able to ignore, up until then.

I have the feeling that at some point after my mother married my father, she felt like she was going crazy, or that she was crazy and she could no longer ignore those uncomfortable feelings. I think this, then, is what propelled her to question whether or not she was a lesbian. In the years of the early 1950s, in the still provincial town of New Orleans, to have strong feelings about other women would have been seen as quite crazy. At this point she would have known that she was unlike her friends who felt themselves to be, and who would have seemed to my mother to be, quite normal. It took her analysis to help my mother to understand that her desire for other women, given her history, was itself quite normal and that, in fact, her feelings for women were not sexual feelings at all. They represented, rather, an infantile need to redo symbiosis, to get better mothering than she had gotten the first time around.

My mother told me that psychoanalysis had saved her life. I do not doubt the veracity of this statement. Psychoanalysis is intended to save lives, the emotional lives of its patients. I think that until her analysis, my mother felt only half alive. Too much of her spirit had been squashed.

My mother felt that her mother wanted her to be less filled with all those prickly feelings of doubt and insecurity that demanded attention from those she was involved with. And for that message of "I wish you were different," my mother hated her mother back. Until the day my mother died, she and her mother never ceased engaging in their little acts of dismissal and anger toward one another. My mother's omission of any reference to her mother in her diary shows to me that she is trying to forget even that she has a mother. She is attempting to bury whatever feelings—whatever rage—she has about this mother who she felt wanted to kill her. But after she met my father and had her children, after she began her analysis, she just couldn't run fast enough to elude her feelings. Feelings, submerged for so long, kept surfacing and resurfacing. She couldn't have known what to do with them.

If you are filled with feelings you don't understand—anger, disappointments, insecurities, fears that seemingly have little to do with your present life—if you think you're crazy, and if the lesson you learn is that those feelings have good reason to be there because your emotional history has created them, the only thing that remains still puzzling is how and why these feelings got there inside you in the first place. But if you learn that even that question has a good, compelling, logical explanation, then I would say that the lesson that you've learned about yourself, the lesson that psychoanalysts give to their patients, is worth its weight in gold. You would be inclined to say, as my mother did, that this process of learning that you're not crazy has saved your life.

The process of being grown down

I think of the process of exploring one's inner self—the domain of psychoanalysis and psychotherapy—as a *growing down*. In order to be free from the past, you have to grow down into that past, return to it, defenceless and open. You must return to that psychic place where the pain began, and allow yourself to re-experience it. This is the only way to find out who you really are, who you were and who you should have been, who you would have been, if you had been left to your own devices and grown up normally and naturally, unimpeded by whatever forces threw you a curveball and knocked you off track.

Being psychoanalysed is the process of being grown down on purpose and with intent. The people who avail themselves of it are those who have had trouble with the normal growing-up process. The job of the analyst is to return the patient to that period of time before there was a walling off of feeling, before defences were erected that created unconsciousness, before there was a tightness in the chest instead of a raging anger, before there was numbness instead of unbearable hurt. This was the time when feelings were still raw, unfiltered, conflicting, and irrational. All this stuff is the natural state of the child, but becomes the unconscious of the adult.

When analysis is done properly, this growing down happens quite artfully. It is a guided tour. This excursion into one's internal landscape is quite a different matter from when one stays grown down because one simply can't grow up. The former has maturity as its goal, and is organised and freeing; the latter is chaotic and constricting. The analytic process is done with great deliberation and control. It is the analyst's job to make sure that this delicate, even dangerous, growing down heals rather than harms.

But the thing about being analysed is that it is definitely a mixed blessing. Who wants to feel all that pain? If you can keep it safely tucked away, unfelt, unseen, unheard, why not? But for the patients who seek psychoanalysis, the method of hiding doesn't work for them, just as it had stopped working for my mother after she became a mother herself. Entering psychoanalysis isn't really a choice, because you have come to feel, as my mother had, as though your life—your emotional life—depends on it.

My mother learned from her analysis that it was the unlovingness that existed between her and her mother that made her feel crazy. This unlovingness did not exist between my mother's sister and my grandmother, nor between my mother's brother and my grandmother. It was particular to the two of them. Something about those two people and those two personalities that didn't work too well together left my mother with a profound sense of having a ground beneath her which had no stability, no mother-earth solidarity.

Anyone can be a stand-in for the mother

Without a sense of stability, time becomes warped. Our mental and emotional life confuses us because of this issue of psychic time. We live with awareness of a past, present, and future. But modern physics has concluded that these demarcations are illusory, and that time actually follows more approximately the rules of the unconscious. In the unconscious, there is no time. Everything is now. As we are hurtled toward our destiny, moving toward our desires, we return to our past. The past keeps surprising us, creeping up on us by manifesting itself in the present.

Freud discovered this phenomenon in his sessions with his patients. He found that his patients often mistook the present for the past, leading their lives in the present as though it were the past. For instance, we fall in love. We think we are in love with the man we see in front of us, but in our psyches, he is not the man he really is. We have turned him into our mother. Anyone can be a stand-in for the mother. Anyone in our present life can assume the psychic position of the mother from our past, and we remain utterly unaware that we have made this misidentification.

The answer my mother found about her sexuality, through her analysis, was that she was looking for another mother, a better mother, a mother who wanted her to soar with her feelings. But in order to come to know this, she had to go back to all those feelings unfelt for so long, all those pains in relation to her mother and her feeling of rejection by her mother. She had to *grow down* into those pains in order to grow up.

Tommy/Hank was only a forerunner—the first stand-in for the role of a new and better mother. Finally, my mother found her analyst. In being analysed my mother came to be able to experience herself, undefensively, as a woman—as a woman in search of the company and love of other women. In finding a model of womanness that she could latch onto, she was able to give herself licence to let her feelings for women define her. This was an emotional life that was altogether separate from her life with men—her father and husband—as well as from her children.

It has taken me the reading of my mother's diary to understand the link between her relationship to her mother and how this mother relationship fashioned the whole of the rest of her life. I understand, for instance, that her disinterest in her mother, so strikingly demonstrated in her first diary, was precisely the key to her "silly" feelings that were deposited on my father's lap, and then, throughout the rest of her life, on the laps of her chorus of women. I understand that her romanticised version of her marriage and her endless search for happiness in another relationship, a love that would seize the heart of another woman, were both related to her own mother. I understand that these working women who were squeezing her in between their other activities, including even her analyst with whom she had to share other patients, were mere replications of her mother.

It was my mother's feeling of needing to be squeezed in, of having felt crushed by her mother that compelled her to make sure, above all else, that this compression was never a feeling that I would get from her. The release she experienced from her analysis is what freed her into understanding the kind of mother that she herself needed and wanted and thus allowed her to become the kind of mother to me that she herself needed and wanted. I became for her, I think, the kind of person she would have been had she had that kind of mother, the kind of person she never ceased struggling to be after her analysis. I became for her, I think, a personification of her best true self.

As a result, we developed an uncommonly close bond. I was, most of all, more than her other children, more than her husband, more than her female friends, her most-favoured/ most-valued beloved. By the time she had me, her last child, she was more comfortable, more freewheeling as a mother. She was more in touch with her loving nature, and all this created a child who was, in response, more tied to her and more in love with her than her other two children were. She and I had an easier time than she ultimately did with my father because his attitude toward her feelings changed from a permissive, accepting *"Don't be silly"* to a critical, intolerant *"Don't be silly."* And finally, I was more steady than her women friends who changed with the seasons—all the latter-day Tommy/ Hanks whom I knew as I was growing up—because either her desires for them were too enveloping for their tastes, or she tired of their inaccessibility and moved on to the next one, seeking an easier conquest.

About me, there was no ambivalence, no conflict. We were as though we were living from one soul shared, not two. This search, this attempt to capture the feeling of oneness between herself and another person—this is what my mother was seeking. The elusiveness of this feeling of oneness was what defined her life as much as anything else. It defined her pain. Try as she might, she was unable to create for herself this feeling of oneness with either man or woman. Having been denied this with her own mother, she had trouble finding it later. I was the sole exception; I became for my mother, like her analyst, a replacement for the love she never felt from her own mother. I believe that in the same way that she felt her life depended on her analyst, she came to feel, too, that her life depended on me and on the closeness between us. I was her willing and appreciative recipient of all the love that was newly freed up by her analysis, releasing her from her unconscious hate both from and toward her own mother.

As my mother, she made sure that I would never suffer this same pain of longing for oneness in our relationship. Her pain of feeling separate from her own mother became transmuted into my joy of feeling together with her, my wonderful, exquisite mother who gave me the feeling that my birth and my life were the most blessed events that had ever happened to her.

Even the potential pain of having to share my mother was diluted. I think it must be a terrible insult to any child when a mother brings home a newborn. She is saying, in effect, to the child: "I want yet another child, to fill me just as you have." Most children feel the insult. They become aggressive and competitive with the newborn. We call it sibling rivalry. We forget that it is the mother's lack of complacency with the existing child, the need to create yet another, that is the cause.

I, as the youngest—without being subjected to the tragedy of a younger sibling's birth inflicted upon me—grew up without real awareness that my brother and sister were, too, my mother's children, that they had my mother as a mother, too. I think I lived for many years with an eerie and, of course, utterly false, sense of being the only real child to my mother. I knew in my mind that my sister and brother were both there, part of the family, as was my father. But I felt that they were more like addendums, afterthoughts to my mother and me—not really part of her as I felt I was, not merged with her as I was. It somehow escaped my attention that my mother might have done with my older sister and brother before me the same things that she did with me. I know that my mother felt joined to me in a way that uniquely defined our relationship. If I saw my sister and brother as addendums, she and I were more like appendages of each other, doing a close dance of togetherness, unseparate.

Still ashamed

I don't know where my mother may have stashed away her missing diary. It's possible that she threw it away, still ashamed of her impulses toward women even after her analysis provided her with an intellectual understanding of what drove her. Perhaps her emotional acceptance didn't fully track with her intellect.

If this were the case, it would explain her disdain for my multiple serial relationships with men—her *"Oh Jane"*'s that referred to my propensity to fall in love so easily. In seeing me flit from man to man, she was seeing herself, and she felt the same non-acceptance with my pattern that she had experienced with her own.

My equivalent to my mother's diaries is my dream notebook. I have been writing down my dreams since I was a teenager. Like a diary, my dream notebooks are personal fragments, anecdotes from deep within the night when all the world around me is asleep (my family, my pets, the street life outside), and they are from the place in my psyche where night lives. I have written down my dreams as I am only faintly awake, still living in the twilight of my unconscious, before this state evaporates into the glaringness of daylight and the day world. My dreams have taken me from the distressingly morbid to the astonishingly creative; from the savagely melancholic to the inspired imaginative. Taken as a whole, they, as my mother's diaries did, trace my unique psychic development.

I plan to destroy these books before I die. I want no one to see me as I am in my dreams, as I am in my search for the meaning of my inner self. (Even the analyst waits to be invited into the inner sanctum of the psyche of the patient. We typically ask our patients to tell us what they would like us to know. The patient's desire to keep psychic doors closed is always respected.) I do not think that my missing mother's diary was one of the victims of her inherent disorganisation, like the wandering umbrellas that kept getting lost in the car "horsey." I believe that this diary was deliberately removed from a place where anyone would ever find it.

PART II

MY DAUGHTER

7

Imaginative Leaps of Delusional Anxiety About a Misbegotten Fantasy

nd now, a decade after my mother's death, life, brimming life, is defining my time as much as death did in those earlier years. I am standing at the gate of the airport. I am with Gregg, the man with whom I live, anticipating the arrival of the plane we have come to meet.

We are unreasonably (ridiculously) early—long before the ETA of the plane. Plenty of time for my mind to take me to the farthest reaches of imaginative wanderings. I develop the fanciful idea that the plane will develop engine trouble somewhere along its route from Louisiana to New Jersey, sputtering along until it has to turn back, returning from whence it came, never to return again.

That last moment of irrevocable despair

The gate attendant tells us that the plane is late. She informs us that it is right above us, circling around, waiting for permission to land. I gaze upward, seeing only the vaulted ceiling of the terminal, yet expecting to see magically through walls and roofs, as though affixing my eyes upon the plane can will it into an existence that I have yet to believe in.

Having allowed myself this single flight of fantasy of a plane that never arrives, I apparently now give my brain permission to really run amok. At this point, it is fair to call my mental wanderings unadulterated delusional anxieties. I am thinking that the plane, rather than turning back to whence it came, will just keep right on flying speedily along on its predetermined path, and then go beyond its rightful destination, whizzing past all of New Jersey, leaving huge New York State in its air-rippled wake—on to Canada, or maybe even farther, to some far-flung, unheralded land, perhaps the Arctic tundra. Or, that the plane is never going to land at all, not back in Louisiana, nor in Canada, and not at the Arctic, but that it is going to go into some infinity twilight zone of a netherworld, sucked into a Bermuda Triangle kind of place, and my still-unclaimed, un-delivered baby in flight on the plane will disappear forever more with it.

Despite my firm commitment to disbelief, the plane lands. The passengers begin their disembarkation, one by one, all of them in a steady procession. Then the flight attendants disembark; the co-pilot; then the pilot, seemingly (and appropriately) the last person to leave the plane, makes his walk down the landing tunnel. I catch his attention, and ask: "Is there another passenger still on board?" He thinks not. I get more specific: "A passenger perhaps with a baby?" "A baby?" he asks dubiously, as though the word "baby" is a foreign language that he does not speak. I am poised to be crestfallen, an inch away from the certain knowledge that I was never meant to be a mother, that this is all some misbegotten fantasy.

And then, at just that last moment of an approximation of irrevocable despair, one lone passenger holding a baby begins her slow and deliberate exit from the plane to the gate. She comes toward me, spearing her eyes into my own, and wordlessly, she stretches out her arms to give me the infant she is holding. Yet my arms remain paralysed at my side. I can generate no movement anywhere in my body. While my body remains frozen, my mind keeps going into its own erratic whereabouts. It is a jumble: *I am not this baby's mother; I don't know this baby; the woman holding this infant is more her mother than I am, more mother than I ever will be; I don't know what to do with a baby; I'm not even sure I have ever before held a baby.* And then I force myself to do the right thing, to do the thing that everyone here—I have the concentrated attention now of the flight attendants, the pilot, even the clean-up men—is expecting me to do. I raise my arms to take the child. If someone had asked me at that moment what I was feeling, I would have answered, "Nothing. Nothing at all." I am an empty vessel—no coherent thoughts, only a maze of inarticulateness, and an absence of emotions. And that is why it is so strange that tears have started flowing uncontrollably down my face, forming a mist that falls on the small body of this, my new baby, my daughter.

Born into existence and differentiation

After several years of stops and starts, unsuccessful fertility treatments, looking into babies from Romania to Russia, Ecuador to Cambodia, it is, finally, the picture of this specific mother-to-be that has captured me irretrievably. One glance at her face and I know that she is the one I needed to bear the baby I have been waiting for. Staring out at me is an all-too familiar-looking face. She has the same thin, very adult-like nose, the same dark hair, the same refined chin that meets the world at a challenging angle. She is a contemporary version of my mother, whom I had never known at the same age as the woman in the picture—about eighteen—but whose pictures at that age I had seen in various old albums. This young woman is an emblematic reincarnation of my mother, and it is her baby girl who is to become mine.

My daughter has been delivered to us by the woman who has served as her foster mother for the first week of her life while the adoption was being finalised. During this first tantalising week of my daughter's earthly existence, while she is still living with her foster mother, my aunt calls. She is my mother's sister, and implores me to give my impending daughter the name of my mother. She explains that she has compiled a family tree, and that she now sees that it has been a tradition for many generations back to give this long-held family name, my mother's name, to a girl child. The practice, she explains, has adhered for every other generation. My mother is named after her grandmother, and her grandmother named after her grandmother, and so on down the line. In choosing the names for my sister and myself more than forty years ago, my mother continued the hallowed tradition of skipping a generation for the family name. My sister, however, broke the line of tradition, giving both her daughters entirely different, nonfamily names; and so, it now falls on me to give the last remaining granddaughter the continuation of the naming lineage of the richly textured French Alsatian Oberdorfer-Levy line of ancestry. Or not.

My daughter's name could have come to me instantly, like a sudden, dazzling romance; or it may have appeared like writing in the sky made by an aeroplane, visible between suspended clouds; or from a mysterious sand name that has materialised miraculously as we walk along a beach. But none of those magical things have happened. And so, Gregg and I are left to work assiduously at finding my daughter's true name. We buy a naming book; we ask our friends; we look at the family tree that my aunt has sent us. We do not take this task lightly, as the name we give our daughter will define her, identify her, make her detectable and recognisable for the whole of her life, both to others and to herself. And, too, it is her name that will give her immortality. Her body will die; even memories of her will eventually cease to exist, as those who have known her and loved her will carry with them into the ground their memories of her when they themselves die. But her name will live on forever: in town records, on her gravestone, on the backs of old photographs scratched in pen by me, her loving mother, years, even decades, earlier. Her name, identifying her being, will remain available to be found for anyone interested in the search, one hundred or perhaps even a thousand years hence. Given the weight of the meaning of her name, through her life and beyond, I want her name to be charming and charismatic, playful and profound. I want it to both be imbued with as well as to impart a sense of "wowness" as a launching pad for the rest of her life, and onward into eternity.

Bestowal of a soul

Among preliterate peoples, the act of naming is a bestowal of a soul on the one who receives the name. In some pre-modern cultures, the verb meaning *to name* is the same word as the verb *to be*. Naming brings into existence. But naming doesn't just create; it separates, too; naming gives differentiation and distinction. It defines this newly born being as no longer an entirely attached add-on to its mother.

Different cultures have different procedures and ceremonies for finding the name of a newborn. Cultures with a keen sense of ancestry give children their names from the totems or family trees of their parents (as my own family has done). The Chinese, both ancient and modern, conceptualise the universe as comprised of five elements; when they envision that a newborn fails to embody all five elements, they choose a name that ostensibly makes up for the deficiencies of the inherent character of the child. In some cultures, names are taken from events that happen during the pregnancy of the mother, or shortly after the birth of the child. In others, names are divined through magic and incantation.

I like best the process of finding the right name for infants performed by the Khasi people who migrated from Africa to Northeastern India, and took their tradition of naming their infants with them. They begin their search for the right name of their offspring by pouring rice meal into small dishes, and then filling a gourd with rice liquor. After an invocation, the liquor is poured into the rice meal while various names are recited. The name the child will inherit is the one that is said during the pouring of the drop of liquor that takes the longest to leave the bottle.

In the end, the method Gregg and I choose to name our daughter is not so different from the Khasi's. It is the name that we keep coming back to, that seems to have the longest staying power for us—the name that takes the longest "to leave the bottle." Indeed, on the third day after we have received her, my mother's namesake, my daughter, is born into her name, signifying both her newly acquired existence, and, as well, her differentiation into a separate being. And now, having acquired a name, my daughter has entered into a symbolic contract between herself and the society around her. She will henceforth be considered to be a part of the history of her generation and her culture. Her deeds will exist separate from the deeds of all others. She has become legally identical to her name, and thus a person with distinct and unique definition.

And, as I discovered my daughter's true name by waiting to see which drop of liquor took the longest amount of time to leave the bottle, I now begin the process of eagerly awaiting the time when my daughter will engage in the same process. In the not too distant future, she will begin the arduous but thrilling endeavor of attaching sound to meaning, and within that feat of unique human mastery of language, she will search for and find her true name for me. I don't think it will be *Mother* (again, too stoic, too detached from the natural warmth of our relationship). I think it will be *Mommy*, or *Mom*. But the name she finds for me will be her own decision, as she brings me into existence within her world, creating differentiation and distinction between me, her mother, and all other beings and objects in the universe. And when that time comes that she first calls me by name, I will know that she has taken yet another step in the ongoing, inevitable process of relinquishing our exquisite time of symbiotic togetherness, and that she will be moving further into the experience of being the unique and magnificent being known forever more as *Molly Malvina Goldberg*.

8

An Unbroken Continuum

I was born shortly after the death of my maternal grandfather's mother. My grandfather was convinced that his mother had left him too soon, and in order to stay still close to him, had given herself new life by implanting her existence within my body. As long as he was alive, my grandfather found evidence of how like his mother I was: the way I looked, the turn of my little toe, specific mannerisms, even (actually, most of all) the preponderance of moles on my body from birth.

And now, with my daughter, I see, as my grandfather saw with his mother, a symbolic rebirth of my own mother whose name continues on once more. As Gregg and I settle into our home with our child, as the new threesome we are, I find myself thinking about my daughter, not just as my daughter, but also as my mother's granddaughter, and the line of mothering and daughtering, an unbroken continuum, that we three females have created. There are times in these early days of our being together when I wake up and look at my daughter, and it seems as though she has grown overnight. I am, as I was that first day when I met her, still vulnerable to thinking that I am not her mother, not her "real" mother, that

I am merely borrowing her for a while. For just an instant that is quicker than any measurement of time, I look in her bed, and I envision that there is a changeling there, that I do not know her; and then the realisation rolls over me as mist from the sea that she and I are bound together indivisibly and eternally. We are as one, together, as my mother and I, too, were once one.

A kind of ghostly guide

My memories of my mother seep into the empty space that now exists between my mother and me; they bring us back together. Though my conscious memory may fail me, at times, I feel that my mother is solidly in me. Perhaps the conscious memories aren't so important, as the after-effects of the intertwining of our lives remain deep within me, below awareness even. I understand the enormity of her impact on me. I know that each of the strengths that I have—my energy, enthusiasm, and essential satisfaction in life—each has its origin in the contentment that I felt with my mother in my early years. My relationship with her has not been segmented off from the rest of my life. It has influenced most aspects of who I am, strong and weak, good and bad: my decision to become a psychoanalyst; my relationships and anxieties with men; my passion for athletics and for swimming; my love of music and reading; the particular brand of my spirituality; and, of course, now that I am a mother myself, the ways in which I will mother my own child.

It feels particularly important to me, now, to keep my mother alive in me as a kind of ghostly guide to the raising of my newborn daughter, to escort me to the place of good mothering that she herself informed me with. I think about these two females in my life who have meant the most to me and moved my life in the direction it has gone. In mothering

Molly, I see the vestiges, still alive in me, of my own mother. I recognise that it is I who serves as the connection between my mother and my daughter; it is I who serves as the link between these two people who have been the most important to me. I am the fulcrum, the living link, between them.

And so, as my daughter and I develop a whole new framework of experiences that will eventually become memories for us both, I commit to continuing the process of capturing the remembrances of the woman who birthed me, raised me, loved me, and then, in her death, left me. Memories created; memories discarded; memories recaptured.

The nowness of a present-day Buddha

The state of nothingness that I had fallen into upon first receiving my Molly—the tears streaming down my face with no connection to conscious thought or feeling—this state is only the purview of adults. From observing baby Molly, and from getting to know her in the first few weeks of our togetherness, I see that she is incapable of this kind of disconnect.

While Molly was still inside her bio-mom's womb, she existed as a unified being. And after birth, she was, like most babies, born into a state of complete integration with soul and body. I think of this state of harmony as being the "baby-soul time."

Although most spiritual believers embrace the concept of an eternal soul, they differ as to when the soul enters the body. Some maintain it is at conception, as most Christians and creationists believe; the ancient Vedas and the Shastras say it is 120 days after conception; rabbinic literature suggests it is at birth. Despite the differing opinions, I think that it must be correct that by the time of birth, some vital, invigorating energy, or spirit, or force has implanted itself within the newborn that makes the infant a whole and complete being that is in a state of potentiality, like the small seed that grows into a towering oak.

Molly's experience of her baby-being gives her a direct connection to her soul—her "actual Me" as Walt Whitman has called it. This early time for Molly, her first experience of the world around her, as for all infants, represents a realm of sensations and impulses, pre-feelings, unthought thoughts, and the reaching out for the immediate satisfaction of needs. At this stage of development, there is no sense of before or after because there is no notion of temporal order, no understanding of causality. There is no sense of an Other because Baby can't yet differentiate between itself and Mother. There is only actual, raw experience, and it is, largely, this inner tone of experience that forms Baby's sense impressions.

Molly is a living example of these concepts of the wholly integrated world of infants. Only the present counts for her because it fills the entirety of her consciousness, minute to minute. A minute ago was the past and is no longer relevant to this moment. Molly's feelings fly out of her, released into the air to rise away from her, soaring freely as a butterfly in flight. Molly, living from her soul, is like a present-day Buddha, truly experiencing only a "nowness"—no thoughts of before or since.

A crier, a singer, a laugher, a howling screamer

Molly's first cry, the cry at birth that all doctors and mothers anxiously await, served as an essential sign of independent life. This birth wail is the first visible sign of an autonomous act on the part of the infant. Now that she has found her first voice, cleared out her respiratory tract of mucus from her first breath (the biological function of that first cry), I watch/listen in awe as Molly continues her exploration in the various expressive potentials of her voice. She exercises it with abandon: sweet, endearing sounds, but just as often, by loud, communicative (and maddening to the listener) wails.

All babies have four acoustically distinct cries that arise from their various states of pain, frustration, hunger, or anger. I hear them all in Molly's vocalisations. I marvel at their sheer intensity and emphatic-ness. Molly's cries are so different from those of an adult, which are ejected out merely from the throat. She exploits her full vocal range, from deep to high, like a gifted opera singer who is soprano, tenor, and bass all at once. Molly's cries fill her whole self, her body serving as a container for screams that find their route all the way to the outer perimeter of her body/self/being. Only her skin, serving as a barrier between who she is and that which surrounds her, prevents all of what is inside her from exploding outward into the air. This is how infants live, and this is how we should all aspire to live—from our centre outward to the farthest boundaries of our bodies, filling our selves with ourselves.

Molly, like most infants who are born healthy and are well cared for, lives entirely from her soul in these first few exquisite months of her life. This oneness within herself reflects a complete synchrony—a coincidence—between what she feels and what she expels in her vocalisations. Although without words, and despite the limited number of ways she can express herself, she is able to use both her voice and her body in an entirely unified way. As well as being a crier, she is a singer. Molly has what I call her "sleep-song"—a little baby hum that actually goes up and down the scale a few notes. She puts herself to sleep every night with her sleep-song, and then she wakes up the next morning with a hardy, full-bodied laugh, as though no time has intervened between the two. I see her laughing, and then I laugh, too, filled with the joy of her existence on earth. The laughters between us become contagious.

And as well as being a crier, a singer, and a laugher, Molly is also a screamer. Or, perhaps she is closer to being a howler. It is in her howling shrieks that I see her as remaining most emphatically connected to her essential self, the self that receives the fullest most explosive expression. I understand that the Japanese have baby screaming competitions for the loudest infant screamers, and they have confidence that the winner will be bestowed with good and long-lasting health for the vigorous use of its voice. (As the Japanese proverb says: "Crying babies grow fast.") Molly's screams, qualitatively different from her cries, are from the sheer joy of having a voice that wants to be used—a voice that doesn't yet form words but that, nevertheless, imparts subtle yet distinctive meaning.

It is through all these numerous uses of her voice—her crying, singing, laughing, and screaming—that Molly is able to express her soul-being. Indeed, it is the sounds of Molly's and my togetherness that are our greatest pleasure—our first "conversation." It is in Molly's screams that she manifests her own self most insistently, but it is, as well, in the screams we do together that we have the richest choreography of our twosome.

Our screams have no purpose other than our mutual engagement. There is no topic of discussion, no subject matter, no past to explain, no intention for the future: there is just pure togetherness. In this togetherness, we scream in high screeches and in low schrooches; we scream together in unison and then our voices follow each other's in a sequence; we scream imitatively and responsively, one as chorus to the other's melody. We, together, try every kind of scream known to mankind. We find exquisite pleasure together in our screams.

Now that Molly and I have found each other, the closeness we are able to create—from her laughter, her cries and screams, and her little sleep-songs—is unrelenting. There is no greater joy for me than holding her, loving her, listening to her, looking at her. I know she needs this attention, and wants it. As my daughter Molly Malvina Goldberg gasps in through every lively breath as much energy as her small body can serve as a container for, she invigorates me, inspires me.

Soul-meeting

French psychoanalyst Jacques Lacan refers to the symbiotic fusion of mother and child as the *Realm of the Real*, the only occasion of perfect unity and completeness. There is no distinction between self and other, between child and mother. Words are unnecessary. The world is experienced as all fullness, with no absence, no sense of loss, because there is no sense of separateness. I think Lacan was right (though perhaps betraying a perverse sense of humor) when he suggested in his name for this developmental stage that this psychic place of unity is more "real" than all that follows, irretrievably lost when one enters into the capacity for language.

Infants and mothers meet on the deepest level possible. They are everything to each other, and they are all this from the depths of their being. Their various encounters of absolute authenticity reflect a kind of soul-meeting. Baby needs to do nothing to create this meeting; it is simply in the nature of Baby to live from this place that represents the centre of Baby's being. And mothers, too, in their interactions with their newborns, are stimulated by their infants to connect to and express this same depth of feeling and authenticity of self. Freud referred to the experience of symbiosis between mother and child as "oceanic," meaning vast, deep, and total. I think his descriptive adjective is right, and I suspect that the bond between mother and infant is the strongest possible bond between human beings. When I have asked women the difference between their love for their children and their love for their husbands, a frequent answer is that they would, without forethought and without hesitation, give their lives for their children. They do not offer themselves as sacrificial lambs with the same lack of reservation, nor the same frequency, for their husbands, parents, or other loved ones. It is, I believe, the all-encompassing symbiosis that confers on mothers this willingness to give value to their infant's life above even their own.

I believe that infants' souls are intimately tied to the souls of their mothers. This soul-meeting is, I think, the real meaning of "symbiosis." This, then, is at the root of the unshakeability of the bond between mother and child. And this place of unbreakable bonded-ness is where Molly and I meet in these early months.

In our early time together, I give Molly the closeness she needs because her whole future depends on it. I give it to her because in agreeing to be her mother, I have assumed the responsibility of tending to her needs. But I give it to her, also, because I myself need it. I need this closeness with her as intensely as she needs it with me. She fills me psychologically in my need to be a mother, a need I didn't even know I had until she came. She is my completion (as I know I was my mother's so many decades ago). With my Molly, I feel full.

I know that it is only through this initial symbiosis between Molly and myself, through our shared togetherness, that she will come to develop a separate self. This early social interaction between us lays the foundation for her later ability to interact and read others' behaviours, and should she become adept at this, the skill will likely stay with her the whole of her life. My job as her mother is to mirror (auditorially, visually, and tactilely) who she is. We know from research that this mirroring takes place in the brain itself—"mirror neurons" according to researchers Valeria Gazzola and Christian Keysers. Mother and child have "shared circuits." They are in constant action of observing and listening to another; and then the same actions are performed, the same emotions are expressed, the same sensations are experienced. These copycat processes exist within the substrate of the brain. On the level of electrical and chemical activity in the brain, then, mothers and infants serve as mirrors to each other, copying each other. This mirroring (both conscious and deliberate, as well as unconscious and chemical) aids the baby in the long procession of psychological/physiological/neurological events that culminate in the formation of a stable self-identity.

I know, then, that my job as Molly's mother is to mirror for her a self that is connected to who she is and who she wants to become. I need to give her an experience of mothering that will help her to stay close to her soul and to find herself in the reflection of my soul, an emotional involvement that will enable her to be able to access her soul as the inevitable process of separation from me continues its progression toward her separate self. I know that in this time I need to sing, to laugh and to yelp and squeal and howl with her, as she does with me. During this time together, Molly mostly hears my voice as a singsong. I laugh and hum and croon with her when I am feeding her, when I am bathing her, and when we play our games together.

Respective visits into eternity

The ancient Chinese philosopher Zhang Zai has said that every birth is a condensation; every death, a dispersal. The Mesoamerican mythology has a similar concept of duality. They believed in two suns: the young Day sun; but countering the energy of newly-created light was the ancient Black sun, the female origin of all. Both womb and tomb were embodied in the opposing qualities of the suns, forever linking birth and death.

From being with my mother ten years before Molly's birth, sharing with her the last moments of her life on this earth, I understand (and perhaps even felt at the time) her "being" as having scattered from her body, dispersed out into the universe as pure eternal energy for which time no longer existed. And, now, from being with Baby Molly, I understand (and absolutely feel) this idea of energy being intensely concentrated and coalesced in infancy. What I see when I am with Molly is that for her, as for all infants, her world is the immediate present, the now, and now is eternity because it is all there is. She's like the big bang at the beginning of the universe, dense energy expanding ever outward. My mother and my daughter are linked through their respective visits into eternity.

Being with Baby Molly is so like the experience I had of being with my mother as she was fighting against her encroaching death. For vibrantly alive Molly, and for my quivering dying mother, the world is/was ever-present; there is/was an immediacy to every precious moment for each of them, and for me, too, in being with them. But while their sense of non-time is what unites them, it is also what separates them. For Baby Molly, the future stretches out into an almost infinite number of possibilities; for my now long-dead mother, the future has already come and gone.

9

The Senses of Symbiosis

M olly and I spend a lot of our initial time together gazing into each other's eyes, searching for and finding our place of emotional contact, using our eyes as the conduit through which our feelings pass from one to the other. British psychoanalyst D. W. Winnicott described the process of the mother gazing at the baby in her arms, and the baby gazing back at the mother's face and "finding (her)self therein."

I <u>feel</u> the depth of our eyes meeting (as well as experiencing this emotional meeting/contact visually). It is the same eye contact that I experienced with my dying mother. There were then, and similarly are now, no defences, no holding back; there was/is just pure meeting, seeing each other and looking into the deepest selves of one another. The closer my mother came to death, the more profound the contact between us became. Similarly, Molly's closeness to her birth gives her the same innocent, trusting openness.

Seeing and symbiosis

When I realised that I would not be having my own biological child, and decided on adoption as the route to my becoming a mother, there was no question that I wanted a girl. Girls are different from boys. I knew nothing about boys—nothing other than that they grew up and then broke my heart. When I told the adoption agency that I wanted a girl, they informed me that the girl waiting list was longer. I could get a boy baby sooner. There was not a moment's hesitation: I decided to wait.

I knew intuitively what science has proved: girls are easier to emotionally connect with than boys. Research shows that gender differences between males and females is evident from the first day of life from how they use their eyes. A one-day-old girl baby will look at her mother's face. A one-day-old boy baby, however, prefers to find a mobile in his field of vision. Within the next three months, mutual face gazing between mother and daughter will increase by over 400 percent. A daughter will use her mother's face as a visual mirror. Boys, however, in the same three months, will still prefer staring at the mobile. This difference is simply a hard-wired fact. Girls look for and want emotional communication. They want it at the age of one day old, and they want it throughout the rest of their lives.

It has been said that the eyes are the window to the soul. I think it is more accurate to say that the eyes are the window to the emotional brain. The brain chemical oxytocin—often called the "love hormone"—is crucial to bonding, essential to the first experience of attachment that mothers feel for their newborns, and that the newborns experience for their mothers. Oxytocin is produced in all intimate emotional communication. (Parenthetically, it is also produced in dogs when there is eye-to-eye contact between the dog and a human. When a dog gazes into your eyes, it is giving you the dog-equivalent of a hormone-hug.)

It is this eye-to-eye contact that facilitates the bonding process. I have heard from other mothers, both biological and adoptive, about the feeling of deep connection through eye contact. The depth of the experience of eye contact between mother and infant is one reason why adoption agencies prefer that birth mothers do not see their child. They know that when the child gazes up into Mother's eyes, the mother will recognise their bond, and it will be more difficult for her to let go of her child. During the time of my search for Molly, I met a woman who had travelled to Romania to find "her" child. She had seen him on a *60 Minutes* television segment about the plight of orphaned children in Romania. She felt this one specific child calling out to her. It took her nine months of living in a foreign land, travelling all over the country from orphanage to orphanage, learning the language, to find this one child whom she had seen for only an instant on her television set. I asked her what it was about him that had inspired her to undertake such a monumental task. She said, without a moment's hesitation, "It was his eyes."

For Molly and me, and for all mothers and infants, the immediacy of this visual meeting through eye contact has been prepared for by her, worked toward during the many months of pre-birth. As the biological mother's body primes itself assiduously for nine months, readying itself for its final alteration, so too is the baby-to-be busy, organising, consolidating and unifying itself for its eventual birth.

Sounds and symbiosis

Pre-Molly began the development, the construction of the person who I now call Molly, long before she came to me. Even in *utero*, Molly's auditory system was sufficiently developed for her to hear a cauldron of muffled sounds. She would have heard a constant pounding that was her bio-mom's heartbeat, gurglings that were digestive sounds, swooshing that was the circulatory system of her bio-mom. These sounds of the biology of the mother, all fetuses share.

But more than the sounds of the biology of her bio-mom, it was her first mother's voice that came to have special meaning to her. It is likely that her bio-mom's soothing voice had the ability to calm Pre-Molly's heart rate, and that her excited voice would have activated Molly. Because her bio-mom's voice travelled (like all expectant moms) from her throat, down her spine, through her pelvic arch and into the amniotic fluid, Molly was able to experience this auditory simulation as both sound and as tactile vibration. The vibrations on Molly's eardrums and skin were felt as well as heard. For all mothers and babies-to-be, when mothers speak, they are giving their future baby not just localised auditory stimulation, but a whole body-to-body experience of togetherness.

It was, too, her bio-mom who gave Molly her first experience of separation through sounds—long before the natural biological separation of birth, and long before the unnatural separation of bio-mom and child that occurred in Molly's first mother giving up her daughter for adoption. In utero, Molly experienced her bio-mom's voice as ebbing and flowing; loud and soft; it was present, and then it was absent, and these sounds and non-sounds would have been experienced by pre-Molly as unpredictable and random. It is here, then, in the very stopping and starting of the intrauterine sounds of each biological mother's voice, that painful and frightening separation begins for the fetus.

Just as seeing the eyes serves as a visual mirror for infants, "seeing (them)selves within," similarly hearing the mother's voice, serves as an acoustic mirror in which infants first hear themselves. After birth, newborns—as young as two hours old—prefer the human voice above all other sounds. They can distinguish and favour their own mother's voice over any other female voice, and this recognition holds true even if they have spent most of their time in a hospital nursery and have been barely exposed to their mother's voice *ex utero*. A four-day-old infant can distinguish one language from another: French babies will suck more vigorously when they hear French spoken; similarly, Russian babies are more activated by Russian than by French. The mother's voice is probably the strongest aspect of continuity between prenatal and post-natal life, a "sonic version of amniotic fluid," as author Anne Karpf has referred to it. Unlike her visual presence, which is detected through directional looking and can be blocked out either by will or by accident, the mother's voice is more like surround sound from acoustical equipment, a 360-degree sound bath for the infant. And so, long before Molly came to me, even before her birth, through the sounds of her first mother's voice serving as an acoustic mirror, the formation of an early sense of self was begun for Molly.

The newborn first hears its own independent voice upon the initial birth wail. Beyond this, an infant's cry will be mostly exclamations of desperate discharge, signalling discomfort. Newborns haven't yet learned that crying is their most effective tool, their best instrument (and sometimes weapon) for communication. But after six to eight weeks, the infant will become interested in exploring the use of crying as interactive. This is what I observe in newborn Molly, and this is what all mothers observe: at two months, Molly goes silent after a bout of crying. It is as though she is waiting to see if there is going to be a response. She will look as though she is staying vigilant on high alert, listening for my voice, anticipating my appearance. I call out to her from another room that I am coming, and the sound of me—my voice coming to her, seemingly floating in the air—reassures her of my presence and my imminent arrival. And this "heard but not seen" communication is perhaps, for Molly, the most miraculous of all communications from me to her (and perhaps why hide-and-seek is such a favourite game for children, a reawakening of this early experience of mother's simultaneous visible presence and invisible disappearance).

Even without the comprehension of language, my voice serves to help Molly to feel secure, to establish strong emotional ties, to develop empathy as well as a host of other social skills. After I leave Molly for a while, and then reappear, my voice has, to her, the magical ability to repair the stress induced from our separation.

I see the same thing with Oscar (poodle dog Oscar). After we have been apart, the sound of my voice immediately soothes him. We know through animal studies that the effect of separation between mother and offspring is not just psychological, but affects the brain as well. In one study, rodents separated from their parents were shown to have changes in the limbic (emotional) system of their brains. Yet, for both animal and human babies, maternal vocalisations have the power to repair these brain changes.

And, a few weeks later, I notice that Molly is interested not only in my vocalisations, but in creating a symphony of her own sounds. It is in her creating her language of sounds (not yet words) that my Molly continues the journey of her awareness of her separate self. Hearing her own sounds enables her to distinguish between "self" and "not-self." Her voice sounds become the externalisation of her inner self, calling out to be heard, begging to be responded to, bridging inner and outer, spanning the distance between herself and me.

The audio-vocal communication between a mother and her infant cannot be over-estimated—not only in terms of the particular relationship that is forged between specific mother and child, but also in terms of its evolutionary significance. Brain researcher and theoretician Paul MacLean has postulated that the separation cry of the infant has served as the driving force in the evolution of the neo-cortex, the newest part of the brain that is distinctly human, the place from which language derives. We are the smartest species on the planet, in part because babies don't like to be separated from their mothers, and they cry to tell us it is so.

Touch and symbiosis

Once I have had my first experience of holding my Molly, you couldn't have ripped her from my arms. She goes everywhere with me, fastened to my back, my front, my side. Mothers want/need to touch their babies; babies want/need to be touched by their mothers.

Molly, like all infants, was born already used to being touched. It is another one of the aspects of continuity from pre- to post-natal life. Not only does the fetus hear the sounds of its mother's body working, the fetus's skin is constantly caressed and stroked by these sonic reverberations. And, too, the fetus touches itself, rather prolifically in fact. An eight-week-old fetus will touch a hand to the face, grab one hand to the other hand, clasp its feet, bring its hand to its umbilical cord, and perhaps most miraculously, turning and walking up and down the amniotic sac wall. And finally, at the time of childbirth, the intense labour contractions, signifying an active uterus ready to release its living package, give tactile stimulation to the baby's internal organs, preparing the baby for ex-utero independent life.

The skin and the brain both develop from the same embryonic tissue. We should think of the skin as an external brain, exquisitely sensitive to stimulation. When we stimulate the skin through touch, we stimulate brain development. In the infant, touch serves the same function as a mother bear's licking of her cub: it enhances immune function and enlivens the bodily systems into action. Antibody production is increased, a lifelong advantage conferred onto the baby. As well, touching increases the production of the growth hormone, the master hormone that regulates all endocrine functions of the body.

Today, in spite of the many life-long advantages of immediate mother to child tactile contact, childbirths are routinely performed in ways that maximise rather than minimise the traumatic effect of birth separation to both Baby and Mother. It is standard practice in most hospitals to quickly sever the one remaining biological tie of mother to infant, the placenta. Immediately post-birth, Baby is usually swaddled in blankets, presumably to keep its body warm. Most hospitals and birth centres limit the initial time for bonding to one hour. And then Baby is wheeled off for its various tests. These procedures have the disadvantage of decreasing the mother's responsiveness to her child, interfering with her ability to be emotionally engaged with her infant, and these practices impact on the overall mutuality and reciprocity in the dyad.

Instructions from a damaged self

There are various ways in which the processes of symbiosis and separation can go awry. Tragedies of neglect move in stages, and they always involve sensory stimulation—either too much or too little. There can be malignant neglect, or malevolent abuse. They occur through either the absence or an overreaching presence of the sounds and sights and touch (visual, auditory and tactile stimulation) of the mother.

A human mother's disappearance, and the infant's subsequent lack of sensory stimulation, arouses more rage and protestation in the child than does even hunger. Initially, the act of separation from the mother results in the expected cries of protest. If the mother quickly returns, the infant will regain a sense of comfort and interest in the world. Similarly, if the mother is predictable about her return, if her comings and goings are consistent, then the infant learns that she disappears and then reappears—and the child is able to accept her absences with less and less fear.

If the mother fails to come in a timely fashion, the crying resumes. Crying is Baby's first self-expression, but it is also Baby's first opportunity to learn how to take turns in interaction. Baby gives expression to feelings and urges; Baby waits for a response; and then Baby expresses feelings and urges again.

The voice sounds of a mother who is not fully engaged with her infant are different to the sounds of an active, loving mother. The voice of a depressed mother is flat and unelaborated. She has a slower rhythm, a weaker tone, and a lower pitch. These diminished and truncated sounds reduce effective interaction between Mother and child. As the infant, particularly the girl-child, searches for herself in her mother's face, she sees reflected back to her a mirror that both lacks emotional expressiveness and is unresponsive. The infant, then, is never activated into liveliness by the sights and sounds of an energetic, ever-engaging mother, and this infant can begin to mirror the mother's depression. A daughter, who through her gender is inherently more attuned to emotionality in general, and specifically to the emotions of her own mother, will be particularly disturbed. The girl-child may wonder what she is doing wrong, why she is not getting the attention (translate into "love") of her mother. This question, and the answer she finds in her own deficiencies, may be the beginning of a depression, paralleling her mother's (as well as the beginning of a later pattern of being attracted to unresponsive men).

The mother who does not feel the necessary symbiotic attachment to her newborn may not provide her infant with the experience of creating a conversation through their interactive vocalisations (as Molly and I did with our screams). Or, she may not give her infant the experience of gazing into her eyes such that the infant is enabled "to find (her)self therein." The mother who does not sufficiently touch her infant impedes the development of the child's nervous system, and the child may be handicapped throughout life in not being able to fully enjoy the sensuous pleasure at another's touch. This child may grow into an adult who fails to enjoy her own sexuality.

Such an unengaged mother does not see her child as an infant truly is—a small, helpless creature needing her love and protection. She may project onto the baby her own identity, her own fears and expectations. In this case, as psychoanalytic writer Alice Miller has said, "The child would not find himself in his mother's face but rather in the mother's own predicament. This child would remain without a mirror, and for the rest of his life would be seeking this mirror in vain."

When separation from mother is forced prematurely, or when the quality of the attachment is too slight, the state of separation—and concomitant sense of isolation—establishes a repetitive feeling in the infant. There will then be a long-lasting sense of disconnection, resulting in a perpetual yearning to re-find that place of harmony that was taken away too quickly. This developing child re-experiences the intense helplessness that was felt at birth. The child remains unable to affect its emotional environment to get needs met and desires fulfilled. Impotence and despair are learned as primary feelings, and a process is begun that leads the child away from a sense of an authentic self, away from true feelings. There comes to exist, then, a profound sense of dislocation from the inner self. The authentic "I" does not propel the life of the individual. All of the later derivatives of symbiosis—intimacy, closeness, emotional communication—become difficult because of this early wound.

Yet the infant who is often (though not always) left in a state of terror can still be coaxed, when an effort is made on the part of the care-giver, to be interested in the world. The ability, then, to forge loving relationships later in life is still retained. But always, throughout this individual's life, there will remain, ready to be re-activated, a deep sense of foreboding and distrust that has its origins in this painful period.

When separation is unduly long, when sufficient coaxing is not provided, more terror and rage are stimulated than the infant has the ability to tolerate. After prolonged crying, the infant will eventually become silent—eerily silent. Baby appears to be calm, however, only because demands are no longer being made on the people in the immediate world of the infant. In fact, Baby is in a state of deep mourning; the sense of detachment is profound. Baby has lost all interest in the world.

When this occurs repeatedly, the infant will become permanently remote. Even any renewed attempts at care-giving, at this point, will fail to arouse any interest from the infant. The child has withdrawn from a world that has withdrawn from it. In order for the infant to have reached this degree of withdrawal, Baby has to have reached a point where all hope has been lost. Overwhelmed by the sensation of defeat, too helpless and hopeless to try again, the infant has shut off all feelings of rage toward the mother. A psychological death has occurred. The infant has succeeded in killing off the feeling function of its own psyche.

Experience is the organising framework (in both abuse and love)

Most mental health professionals today accept that the premise that basic personality traits are largely already in place at a young age; and, further, that the connection between how the personality develops and the relationship to the mother is the most profound in these early years. Many of the paradigmatic ways that a person will respond to situations, most of the ways of handling and expressing emotion, will be set in early childhood, determined in part by how the mother has aided her child in handling the normal development issues.

This does not mean that changing maladaptive patterns is not possible, but the energy required to make change is greater than the energy required to initially create the pattern. It's easier when it is done right the first time with the mother, than when imbalances need to be corrected later in life.

A mere twenty years ago, researchers thought that by birth the structure of the infant's brain was genetically determined. However, it is clear now that this assumption is wrong. Early childhood experiences are powerful determinants in how the intricate neural circuits of the brain are wired. But genes determine only the basic wiring, such as the heartbeat and the lungs respiring. Everything else, fully half of the tens of thousands of genes in a human being, is given over to the formation and running of the nervous system: the building of synaptic connections. There are simply not enough genes to do the job necessary to keep the human being running. This limitation leaves experience. Experience provides the organising framework for the child. The experience of a child is, in large part, the emotional tonality of the child's inner world. Building synaptic connections is best done in an emotional context.

The downside of how influential experience is on the brain, is that our mental and psychic apparatus is acutely susceptible to trauma. If the child's primary emotional experience is fear, then the neurochemical responses to fear become the building blocks of the organisation of that child's brain. In trauma, there is an elevation of stress hormones, such as cortisol. High cortisol levels in the first three years of life will increase activity in the brain structure, the *locus coeruleus*, involved in vigilance and arousal. The brain, then, is primed to be on hair-trigger alert on a continuous basis. Later, whenever there is an experience, a memory, even a fantasy, that only remotely reminds the individual of the trauma, this region of the brain is re-activated, and a new surge of stress hormones is unleashed. When this hormone is produced over and over again, regions in the brain responsible for other emotions fail to be appropriately stimulated.

The region of the brain responsible for attachment is particularly vulnerable. Abused children have been shown to have 20 to 30 per cent smaller areas in the brain systems responsible for attachment. Adults who were abused as children have a smaller hippocampus, a part of the brain that is involved in memory, than non-abused adults. This finding gives a neurological explanation of why abuse, particularly sexual abuse, in childhood is sometimes relegated to the unconscious, not consciously remembered: it is not merely a psychological phenomenon; neurologically, there are few neural pathways set up to retain the memory.

Even with these important findings about the brain and the psyche, science is only beginning to develop measurements that assess functional improvements from resolution of psychological issues. Yet, within these partial understandings of the mechanisms of change, the fields of psychology, psychotherapy, and psychoanalysis have developed techniques that work effectively to improve how people feel and how they function. It is not uncommon for mental health professionals to see their patients reverse their lives in dramatic ways: angry people become calm; judgemental people become compassionate; insecure people become confident; marriages are transformed from acrimonious to harmonious;

children become cooperative rather than rebellious; terminal cancer patients witness their cancers disappear. Those in the helping profession of mental health sometimes feel like Rumpelstiltskin who knew the magical secret of spinning straw into gold; analysts and psychotherapists are like the medieval alchemists who aimed to pull out the gold that is inherent in all things.

Learning mother love

Mother love, as we know it today, with all the tender loving care, nurturing and understanding that good mothers bestow on their children, came about because a few million years ago, long before Cain and Abel, there evolved an animal who, for the first time in history, had more information in its brain than in its genes. Mothering may be, only at its best, instinctively intuitive, but the good news about it is that we can think, we can learn, and we can re-learn.

10

Fear and Trembling (and trauma too)

I n spite of the blissful symbiosis that Molly shared with her bio-mom, that my mother and I shared both in and out of utero, that Molly and I have shared in our first few months together, and that most mothers and children share, and in spite of the terrors of separation, closeness is never enough. The call toward separation, toward discovering one's own individuality away from Mother, and the desire to be different from her, is just as compelling as the need for closeness and sameness. They are both biological edicts built into our very cell structure.

Marching toward individuality

The stakes of how I, as Molly's mother, will manage the dual processes of symbiosis and separation, and how these will be experienced by Molly, will be no less than her full emotional health: the creation of a self. Successful separation will be a lifelong pursuit for both of us. Her first separation experience only began with her birth. Separation will continue as she, a growing toddler, will explore ways of being away from Me-Mother. Molly's desire to move away from me is not yet conscious, but is more like an imprint, a biological calling, the same as the baby bird's need to fly. Yet, ultimately, a conscious decision will be made, and she and I will separate—in fact, need to separate—out of mutual desire and understanding as well as for the physical and emotional health of each of us.

Within these processes of individuating, she from me, and me from her, we will experience conflicts that arise from similar questions and concerns: how do we separate emotionally from that which was once ourselves? As mothers and as children, we embrace the initial togetherness, exalting in the harmony of symbiosis that is the fusion of selves that characterises pregnancy, infancy and early childhood. And then, once having acquired that togetherness, Mother and child must forego the duet of togetherness in order to make the necessary separation. As children, we move ourselves away from our mother, the person who was initially our very link, sometimes biological but always psychological, to life. And yet, within this act of separation, we are driven to strive to create for ourselves a symbolic umbilical cord that will fetter us to our own life. We do this act of separation from our mothers while simultaneously marching toward our own individuality.

And, as mothers, our challenge is to open our bodies and minds to this foreign entity that has implanted itself within us, sometimes unexpected, sometimes even unwanted (51 per cent of all pregnancies in the U.S. are unwanted, and this figure is the highest of all developed countries). Then, after a period of time in which Mother and Baby-to-be, under the best of circumstances, have grown used to each other, and have come to enjoy their synchronised twosome, Mother's body must let go of this biological sameness. Mother's body must obey natural law and involuntarily conclude the very union that she has so preciously guarded for those previous nine months. This progression from symbiosis to separation is modified in adoptive mothers and children because the period of biological union of the womb has been bypassed. But, with both biological and adoptive infants, we struggle with the issue of how we, as mothers, can respect, even encourage, our children's need for their growth into their own self? How do we, as both mothers and as children, do this all and maintain wholeness for both?

Because of the biological sameness that mothers and daughters share, the separation process is more difficult—and different from that of mother and son, from father and son, and from father and daughter: different, and perhaps, more complex and more arduous. The mother/daughter relationship is defined by the fact that the process of identification never crosses the gender line. Sons come from mother first, but ultimately, if they are to become heterosexual, they make the transition of identification from mother to father. Daughters and fathers can have close and deep relationships, but the identification of daughter to father remains, always, only partial. But for we mothers and daughters, woman is from whence we come, and woman is where we are going.

For me, it has not been a seamless line, this growth from oneness with my mother into my own individuality and, finally, into my own motherhood. The awareness of the bond that tied my mother and me together has surpassed the ties of all other relationships. I have loved men and been loved by men. I have arranged and organised large portions of my life around my feelings for men. My passions have been brought to unimaginable heights by men. But men in my life have never had the same sense of constancy that the first woman in my life has given me. I counted on my mother; she was an always. My father, on the other hand, was a sometimes. Men have come and gone. There have been boyfriends, a husband, and now Gregg—my daughter's father. Indeed, there have been times when my relationships with Gregg and with my career were my ultimate satisfactions. During those times, there was no impulse, no desire even to be a mother. But then I would remember my mother, and the "us" that we had created together, and my longing to construct a similar life-experience would well up within me. At those times, there was no sensation more urgently felt than the need to be a mother myself.

Every trauma is a repeat performance

Perhaps separation between mother and child cannot happen without fear. Fear of separation is the shared lineage of all of us, our mammalian heritage—remnants of our old, animal brain that, under certain circumstances, can still be activated. To mammals, for many millions of years, separation from the mother meant death. Paul MacLean has identified separation from the mother as the most painful of all experiences to the mammalian infant. He found that the cry response of an infant mammal separated from its mother is hardwired in the brain, and that the only means of eliminating the cry response is to surgically cut the connections between the pertinent portions of the brain.

Molly's emerging sense of individuality—like all babies' growth into their own sense of self—began a renewed path of emphasis at birth. For both Freud and his protégé Otto Rank, the event of birth has primary importance in the psychological development of the child.

During the time of symbiotic union in pregnancy, that small living creature inside its mother's dark womb is a unified being. It is not just the union with Mother that causes this integration of self; there is, too, an internal unification within its own being. While the mature fetus has a rudimentary mental life, it is without the discomfort (and joy) of complex mentation that characterises post-birth.

After this relatively (and unprecedented) peaceful time in the womb, rather suddenly, from the fetus's point of view, its world begins to turn topsy-turvy. The walls that had nestled it safely and tightly begin to squeeze and vibrate; it begins sliding downward, not knowing where it will be stopped, and in one great, dazzling, terrifying tour de force, it is forcibly ejected from its sweet former home.

Freud used the term "trauma" to describe the event of birth. The word derives from Greek, meaning "wound" or "hurt." The birth trauma is the first and quintessential experience of separation, the experience of being ejected from one's home without desire and without control. Freud identified birth as the major trauma from which we spend the rest of our lives recovering. Trauma and separation, then, are indivisible. Every other later trauma, every other emotional experience that is felt as a deep disturbance, intolerably overwhelming or painful, is a repeat performance, a mere approximation of this initial prototypic trauma. In each trauma, from birth to death and all that lies between, the main emotional component is the feeling of helpless anxiety or terror.

Transformed into some unrecognisable being

However fearful and traumatic the process may be, emotional and cognitive separation from Mother is a necessary stage that we all proceed through in our journey toward emotional maturity. Although this stage in infant development, which occurs incrementally over time, is generally referred to as "separation anxiety," we may come to know that it can be more of a stark terror than a mere anxiety. As with the initial trauma of birth—the ejection from the baby's first home—the psychic separation process can be just as frightening. From the child's point of view, life can be proceeding along harmoniously with

Mother, and then suddenly and incomprehensibly this period of smooth sailing ends. It can be when the child realises that Mother–Protector/Mother–Provider is no longer there; she may be merely out of the room. Or it can be when Mother is distracted and can't respond instantly to the child. Mother Protector/Mother–Provider may lash out irritably at Baby, and she will have been transformed into some unrecognisable being who bears no resemblance to the loving mother of the moment before. In that instant, for Baby, the world changes, and danger and discomfort are everywhere. Mother may make demands that are unreasonable (she may ask Baby to stop crying); she may give warnings that are terrifying (she threatens that she will put Baby back in the crib if Baby doesn't stop crying). And these transformations happen for no discernible reason. There is no reasonable cause from the child's point of view; these events just happen. It feels like a life-or-death danger to the child. The child does not have the prescience to know that Mother–Protector/Mother–Provider has only stepped away for a moment, is only briefly irritable, and that the nightmare of aloneness will end as abruptly as it began. This is the emotional experience of separation for the infant. And it remains a memory—not a conscious memory, but one that is hidden deep within our tissues and brain matter—and it can be re-activated at any time during the course of a person's life: a residue of long-past experiences that occurred when we were helpless and in states of terror.

Fear may be the most powerful of all feelings. It grabs us and doesn't want to let us go. The persistent and ever-potent bond between mothers and their children is as much a fear bond as it is a love bond. From the birth of civilisation to post-turn-of-the-millennium America, mothers have worried about keeping their children alive and out of danger. Author and psychotherapist Janna Malamud Smith refers to this concern as the "signature virtue and vulnerability" of motherhood. It doesn't matter whether the child is a newborn, or middle-aged, or elderly. A mother gets knots in her stomach when she senses that her child's well-being is at risk. Mothers have alarm systems that are triggered to endlessly beep and buzz throughout the journey of human life that only begins in the birthing room.

Mother as sorceress

Perhaps it is at the trauma of birth that infants have their first experience with magic. People in distress generally want to be saved. We see this mechanism in the injured, the abused, and the dying. We see it in children when the only wrinkle in their lives is that they are merely frustrated or angry, and salvation is simply the rescue from their own uncomfortable sensations. Most of us want some change in our lives, and, if we do not anticipate it from reasonable expectation, then we imagine and hope that it may befall us magically.

The infant passing through the birth canal can experience itself as in distress. We even use the word "distress" to describe a difficult birth. And, then, that particular stress is over, and the next one starts. There are, then, those awful moments when the lights are too bright, and Baby is slapped on the back. But finally, there is salvation. There is a warm spot, a soothing sound, and sweet tasting nourishment. This is heaven. This is magic. This is Mother.

Mother is like a sorceress for the child. From the first contact, there is never a doubt in the infant's burgeoning mind of shadowy impressions that Mother can perform magic; she has the ability to alleviate pain and agony, and transform them into comfort and satisfaction.

The mother's first job then, after birth, is to help her infant tolerate the feelings that have been reactive to this trauma of losing its first home. She must keep her infant close to her so that she can aid in de-traumatising the sense of helplessness and fear that accompanies birth. Symbiosis was automatic in the womb; it was in the very biology of the situation; Baby and Mother shared bloodstreams, nutrients, and oxygen. Pregnant mothers don't need to know anything to accomplish the task of biological symbiosis. It is their bodies'—both Mother's and fetus's—own innate evolutionary brilliance that accomplishes this formidable task. But now, after birth, Mother and Baby are separated. Yet, in this state of separation, the infant still has the same need for psychological symbiosis as when it was inside the womb. And for this task, the mother must have a variety of qualities that may or may not be automatic: compassion, patience, warmth, wisdom, intuition—the ability to translate these emotional states into caring and effective mothering behaviour—all of what comprises what we think of as maternal: Mother Love.

In creating a psychological world of symbiosis—a world now not of biological unity but of psychic oneness—for her infant and herself, the mother enables her child to hold onto, for just a little while longer, the harmony of self and world that was experienced in her womb. The mother must establish a strong psychological bond between herself and her infant after birth so that the disruption of the biological symbiosis during birth is mastered without long-lasting damage.

Birth trauma involves extreme changes for both mother and child. But, as well as trauma causing injury, it simultaneously motivates healing. The whole cloth of the original unity of mother and child is torn asunder during birth, this primal division being mirrored in the overlap between the physical pains of childbirth and the emotional pain of separation. But healing comes about through the re-establishment of union *ex-utero*. Restorative soothing for the mother occurs symbolically through her ability to replace her trauma with the life of the infant, giving her the experience of feeling emotionally complete. Healing for the infant occurs as the mother clutches her infant into her realm of safety.

11

The Journey of the Soul
Between Life and Death

Now that Molly and I have completed the first several months of our life together, we proceed into new territory. I watch vigilantly as she throws all of her sensations into expressions of her voice. I am awaiting the first sign that our heavenly period of symbiosis is ending. I await an indicator that she shares the destiny of all other humans, and has begun the process from being perfectly unified to being internally divided, capable of conflict, ambivalence and yes, even deceit. I try to retain awareness that I, as her mother, need to help my child make the transition to the next phase of development in which the emphasis will be on her mind. I want to help her to make this transformation without her losing the memory and connection to her soul.

Learning to "deal with it"

One morning—Molly is eight months old now—I wake up to see her just sitting there. She isn't laughing as she usually is. She looks pensive. She is staring; she is quite still and is not making contact with either Gregg or me. Gregg is watching her, so I ask him, "What's up?"

Molly has got into the habit of chewing the windowsill above the bed. She'll struggle to move herself over to the head of the bed, position her little body exactly in alignment so her mouth is level with the sill, and then CHOMP. We have just begun to teach her the meaning of "no," and the lesson has been around this windowsill. Gregg has just said "no" to her. Molly isn't moving, isn't making any sounds. I ask what she's doing. He says, "She's dealing with it."

I am witnessing, before my very eyes, the formation of conscience. Or, is it conflict? Cooperation or rebellion? A burgeoning morality? The first consciously experienced anger? But the only important question is: is learning to "deal with it" a psychic process that is going to result in her not waking up to her own laughter any longer? I think that, in fact, this learning to "deal with it" is the first visible sign I have of Molly's separation from her baby-soul. I think this is the first sign of the growth of her own individuality and, thus, her inevitable separation from me.

As long as Molly is still living entirely from her soul, she is a unified being; she is whole and she is free. But when she starts living more from her mind, when she will begin to be capable of thoughtfulness and deliberation, she will become capable, too, of conflict and of things like denial, or twisting the truth, or blaming people, or self-attack.

The psychic birth

Just as biological symbiosis gives way to the separation of birth, psychological symbiosis, too, must be relinquished. Any loving mother meets the inevitable movement from symbiosis to separation—even at its first stage of birth—with conflict. The psychic birth—the "second birth" as psychoanalytic researcher Margaret Mahler has termed it—is just as fraught with danger and difficulty as is the biological birth. Some researchers believe that this second birth, which, like the first birth, is not immediate but rather takes place over time, is more significant even than the physical birth.

Mahler likens the normal developmental process of separation to a magnetic force field. I think of it as being like a rubber band being stretched out. Toddler ventures away from Mother, and then keeps returning back to "refuel," as assurance that Mother is still there as an anchor of safety, a "beacon of orientation," as Mahler describes Mother's role. As the toddler becomes more secure during this phase of development, the child gradually increases the distance between the two of them, and the rubber band is elongated, being pulled tighter and tauter.

The child's burgeoning independence is intricately tied to the development of a mind: fantasy and creative imagination. The drive toward independence begins with the infant's early experience of being alone while simultaneously in the presence of Mother. The child plays alone, yet knows that Mother is available: through this process, of testing the dual waters of separation and independence, a personal life for the child begins to be discovered. The child begins to think thoughts and feel feelings that are uniquely his or her own.

Adults as well as children often have dreams as ways to explore and master this process of separation from Mother into individuality. These dreams are often quite straightforward and concrete descriptions of "refuelling." One of my patients dreamed that she was riding in a red Volkswagen, feeling on top of the world, full of confidence and joy. Suddenly, the car ran out of gas and stopped moving. Her mood dropped precipitously from ecstatic to fearful. She realised that she was on a hill. She decided to let the car roll down the hill. At the bottom of the hill, she found a gas station where she was able to refuel, thus able to resume her journey, thus able to continue her independent life.

Womb-rituals of relatedness

The event of psychological separation holds equal importance, and equal possibility of trauma. We know from research that fetuses have a rudimentary mental life. Babies can be born ready for the event of birth, welcoming it; or, unprepared for the event of birth, seemingly dreading it.

Italian psychoanalytic researcher Alessandra Piontelli has demonstrated that the psychic life (as well as the development of the auditory and tactile senses) of the fetus, and then the child, follows a continuous pattern from inside the womb to after birth. Taking sonograms of twin fetuses during various periods of the pregnancies, Piontelli has documented that within the womb, already there are characteristic ways that the unborn babies relate to each other. In their watery first home, the twins develop paradigmatic patterns, elaborate womb-rituals of relatedness. Typically, for instance, one unborn baby will be more active than the other. Or, one will dominate the other. Piontelli observed one fetus that favoured lying regularly on its right side, spooning its twin. Another incessantly strove for the position where she could cradle her arm around her brother. One sonogram showed the larger male baby curved over the back of the smaller twin, incessantly kicking his brother with his right foot.

Then Piontelli filmed the babies' interactions with each other after birth—at three months, six months, up to two years. The same patterns of relating were observed at each stage of development. The twin who had been the more active of the two in the womb was the more active one in the crib. The twin who had been dominant in the womb was, similarly, dominant in the playpen. The girl who had had her arm around her brother still acted protectively and affectionately toward him as they scooted around the house. Even the boy who, in the womb, had kicked his smaller brother, was observed later playing in the bathtub, still curled over the back of his brother, still kicking him with his right foot. It was as though no time had passed between womb and crib, womb and playpen, womb and bathtub, womb and outside world.

The womb allows for the creation of a space in which the unborn child can begin the development of a sense of self. It is a unique time in the life of Baby-to-be in which discoveries are made about its own existence and the small environment in which it resides. This is the bliss of the womb; life is mostly sensation and pure biological symbiosis with Mother.

But after birth, infancy is still symbiotic for both the mother and child. The infant retains the same high degree of self-involvement in its own needs whether home is inside or outside the womb. Symbiosis between Mother and her infant is a psychological reality. The human baby is born after nine months not because it is finished with its symbiotic dependence on Mother, but because, among other reasons, the size of the head requires Baby-to-be to leave the once cosy, now suffocatingly small home.

Not by any means is the newborn finished with symbiosis. The human infant is born utterly prematurely in terms of both emotional and psychological needs. Baby stays dependent and emotionally attached to Mother longer than does any other animal species. For quite some time after birth, Baby still craves Mother's unconditional, undivided attention. Long after birth, Baby holds fiercely onto the infantile states of symbiosis and narcissism.

The epiphany of separateness

The major trauma, then, is not at birth, but rather at the point when children consciously realise that they do not own their mothers. And the converse is true, as well. Mothers have to undergo the same disturbing shock. Mothers must develop a life separate, away from, and unconnected to (even at times, unconcerned with) her child; and the child is, similarly, capable of having a life separate, away from and unconnected to (even at times, unconcerned with) Mother. This epiphany of separateness can take place at any time in the life of a child. It can take place, and most often does, repetitively. We, as children, do not give up our childhood narcissism without a good fight, and it usually takes many lessons before we come to understand that we are not the only centre of our mother's orbit. Birth is only the first of the many possibilities of this awareness. This change in consciousness can happen in big and obvious ways, like the first day of school for a child, or the going off to college, or a marriage. But it can happen, too, in small and subtle ways, undetected except in retrospect, much like physical growth.

I had a lightening flash experience of separateness when my mother told me that she would no longer be making my car insurance payments. This renunciation of my mother's assignment of tasks happened when I was well into my twenties and had moved away from home. Yet, I was in disbelief at her abnegation of responsibility. This was a mother I did not know, this mother of separateness. Her decision caused a profound upset in me. This was a trivial decision for her, one of mere convenience, and whose emotional impact on me she could not have predicted. But I felt wounded and frightened (and maybe a little peeved too) because I understood that we were veering away from the kind of overreaching mothering that I had been used to.

Momentary events that last only an instant, small events whose impact stretches out over a lifetime: these are the realisations that became milestones in the inexorable path toward separation and reunion that my mother and I took, that all mothers and children are fated to take in an unalterable ebb and flow of togetherness.

And now, in being Molly's mother, I know that her unfettered happiness, the unadulterated use of her voice—the absolute unity of her cries and her laughs, of her being—won't/can't last. The time will come when Molly will outgrow the time when her baby-soul defines all of who she is. Separation from one's baby-soul is natural and inevitable, and it starts when the infant begins the move away from blissful symbiosis with the mother. I know that her mind will eventually be able to do things of which her soul is incapable. This development of mind, the ever-expanding cognitive development that will mark the next several years of her life, is essential for her further thriving survival.

Leaving the baby-soul behind

Different psychoanalytic researchers call it different names: it is the period when the individual self begins its emergence. Lacan calls it the *Imaginary Order*: it is the domain of self-identity, the period of time when the child attempts relentlessly to shore up its individuality. The result is the newly acquired ability to perceive the differences between self and other. It inaugurates the lifelong quest to return to the pre-imaginary stage, Lacan's more "real" state during which there is no differentiation between self and other. Perhaps it truly is, as Lacan maintains, that the sense we acquire of a stable, whole, unified self is an imaginative construct, a compensation for having lost the original oneness with the mother's body.

There is, I think, a deeper reason than the rupturing of the symbiosis that makes the second birth so pivotal in the psychophysiological development of the infant. It is at the time of this psychic birth, when the initial awareness of separation from the mother comes into existence, that the possibility of separating from one's soul first comes into being.

It is here, generally at the age of one year, that Baby discovers that it has its own private "*mindscape*," a mental landscape that is invisible to others. The core constituents of this internal mindscape are thoughts and feelings, but included are also intentions, desires, attention, and memories. Baby's world has shifted from an almost entirely physical, immediate "now" experience to one that is laden with hidden subjective events spread over past, present, and immediate future. And, too, Baby realises that (M)Other is herself capable of having a mindscape. Baby and Mother may share a mindscape; or they may have different mindscapes. And when there is separation, when Baby's mindscape is different to Mother's mindscape, there is, as well, the possibility of mis-readings and mis-fits.

In the ensuing time, after my first observation of Molly's mind-expansion, after the windowsill chomp, I see further evidence of a departure from her baby-soul. I see a keen mind that is infinitely curious and imaginative, and I see that sometimes these qualities are infused with aspects of coyness, shyness, and embarrassment—each a sign of conflict, of a divided self. I also see signs of deeper (and thus darker) variants of this split—shame and manipulativeness. These are all mental machinations; they are the beginning of the creation of a rich internal life. The fact of a divided self also creates an unconscious that is unique, wholly that person's own, a hidden world that is sometimes filled with terrors and horrors, the monsters and goblins of childhood that convert later in the adult life to more complex mental constructions of fears, anxieties, states of confusion. But as long as we live from the soul, as long as we are still not separate from our soul-being, these mind-manipulations are unnecessary. They are not even possible.

Soul-displacement

From experiencing the grief at the loss of my mother, from having grown up with her telling me that her own mother might as well have been dead for all the good she did her as a mother, and from listening to my patients talk about their varied but often difficult relationships with their mothers, I see that helplessness and despair can be as powerful determinants of soul-loss as death itself. In sharing with my mother the process of her death, I know that the actual moment she died, life itself left her body; but I suspect that long before that one moment when death grabbed ascendancy, my mother's soul had already become disconnected from some portion of who she was. Even now, there exists a hole in me because of that part of my soul's attachment to her and its abandonment of me. Perhaps a part of my soul began to leave me even before her death, though: through our various mini-deaths, the disagreements we had with each other, the differences in choices and attitudes, the psychic separations that we took from one another throughout our lives together; and my ensuing pain—my fleeing from my pain, defending against my pain— leaving my self because of wanting to leave my pain. I know that my patients, too, often feel only half-whole, without a full soul because of pain they feel, pain that originated in their relationships with their mothers, and that now follows them in their adult relationships with their loved ones.

Rose is a patient who is a successful physician. She has, in fact, become well known in medical circles for a particular medical technique that she excels at performing. Rose knows that her mother is proud of her. In fact, her mother actively encouraged her to pursue her medical career, and has emphasised throughout Rose's life that professional success and recognition for achievements is what make a life significant and meaningful.

Rose grew up having been taught that the White family, her family, was all that counted. She grew up believing, as her mother and father drummed into her time and time again, that their family was superior to all others, and that the White children would excel in any endeavor they undertook because of their superiority. Rose never questioned these family lessons. And true to her parents' expectations, in high school Rose became a successful musician, a top athlete, and an honours student. Through college and medical school, she stayed tied to her parents' principles, unconflicted about their veracity.

But Rose became a tortured woman after she started her practice as a physician. She suffered because there was a part of her that shared her parents' belief and honoured being a physician above all other endeavours. But there is another part of Rose that was begging to be equally honoured, and this was her true love for singing and acting. For this passion, success and recognition were irrelevant to her. Ever since she had the lead in her high school play, and through her college years when she was active in the dramatics club, Rose has dreamed of performing. In her therapy sessions, she said that she felt most truly alive, most truly herself, only when she used to sing and act.

Rose suffers today because her parents, at an early stage of development, failed to encourage her search for independence. Each child must learn to say "no" to her mother in order to make the successful transition from symbiotic fusion to an independent self. Each "no" from a child represents not a negativistic reaction, as mothers often experience it, but rather a powerful striving on the child's part to become a person. Mothers should consider their child's "no" to be a priceless addition to an ever-expanding vocabulary. The "no" may be as simple as: "No, I don't want the food you are trying to give me." It may be as hurtful as: "No, I don't want to hug you."

The "no" may be said with rebellion, or guilt, or with pleasure or even sadism at defeating the parent. Yet, the mother who is interested in helping her child to develop will encourage all these various "nos," accepting her own defeat, at times, knowing that it is one step in her child's victorious march toward individuation.

Perhaps Rose's mother saw her daughter's declarations of independence as a revolution requiring immediate quelling. At critical stages in childhood, Rose should have been encouraged to express her own self, even when it went against her mother's wishes for her. She needed to develop the ability to say "no" to her mother with splendid authority; instead, she remained fused with her. And thus later in life, the point at which she should have been acquiring her own tenets and principles, her relationship with her mother remained too prominent a part of her emerging value system. Fusion was the method she had learned for being in a relationship.

Although Rose has a good, solid marriage, this issue of fusion was initially the predominant method of interaction in the marriage. Rose found herself adopting all of her husband's principles about childrearing. She deferred to her husband on countless matters, thinking that whatever he thought was the correct way of thinking. She replicated with her husband her early relationship with her mother.

Rose suffers from a condition I call "soul-displacement." Like all soul-displaced people, she has taken a side road in her journey of life and tried to make it a main avenue. But this path was never meant to be the focal road for her life. Soul-lost people often pretend that the path they have chosen is the right road, but on some level there is a dimmed awareness that it is not. They suffer for the displacement, and they suffer for their delusion. They feel separated from themselves, and thus separated from others.

Masters of adaptation

Rose is not unusual. Most of us suffer from some degree of soul-displacement. Most of us struggle, in varying degrees, with living a life that is altogether true to our natures.

Each of us incorporates aspects of our parents, internal images, in our journey toward maturity. These internal images serve as ways that we find to define ourselves. Normally, we incorporate those aspects of our parents that we like, and reject those characteristics we don't like. But when people leave their souls, or when they are out of sync with their souls, they have made these images all of who they are, rather than part of who they are. They have incorporated, without discrimination, both good and bad parental aspects.

Soul-displaced people live as though they have no independent self. They have not become who their inborn natures would have led them to become. They have been dislodged from the people they should have been. They live their lives in the body or mind of someone else. Often, that someone else is their mother. Their growth comes in casting off inauthentic selves, in re-finding the original self that had been discarded, and in erecting an ego structure on this now solid foundation.

We humans are masters at adaptation. I see the ways in which we continually compensate for our half-wholenesses, our soul-dislocations. Linda is a patient who struggles valiantly with feelings of isolation. She says that the way other people feel about spiders, tarantulas and rats, which she collects as pets, is the way she feels about other people. She presents herself as angry and embittered, a woman alone battling the rest of the world. She knows her soul only through her art. Her art is childlike and colourful, full of spontaneity and joy. It is only when she creates her art that she finally comes to feel at peace, free, and connected to something outside herself.

The neurologist Oliver Sacks has found a similar phenomenon in his patients in relation to music. He has found neurologically impaired patients who cannot walk, cannot take a single step, who stay motionless for hours on end, but who, through a neurological malfeasance, a brain quirk, can dance through the night. And he has found patients who cannot talk, cannot utter a single word, but who can sing like larks. We have seen this phenomenon, too, in some autistic people. They are geniuses at creating music, yet have almost no language. Sacks describes these individuals as being "activated" by the sound of music. The phenomenon is explained by a unique conjunction in the human brain between the auditory parts of the brain and the dorsal pre-motor cortex, which controls aspects of our motor/movement ability. And because of this particular circumstance of brain neurology, music is helping these afflicted individuals to re-find their souls, even when access to basic mental functions has been hampered by neurological damage.

In search of a queendom

Because soul-displaced people do not live from their souls, they are not able to live fully from their bodies. Many of my soul-displaced patients have actual bodily disturbances. One of my patients, Harriet, has panic attacks. These are absolutely debilitating to her. They come unpredictably and exhaust her for hours afterward. She may have just finished her lunch; she may be at home relaxing with her husband and children. Then out of the blue, for no apparent reason, her heart will start beating wildly out of control. She gasps for breath, and she is utterly convinced, without a moment of doubt, that she is dying. It feels to her as though she is dying. Because these attacks spring up on her unexpectedly, she lives every day under a threat. Sometimes the anticipation itself is more than she can bear.

I asked Harriet the meaning of her body swinging wildly out of control. She told me that she had been raised according to the principle that only silk was good enough to touch her skin. Her mother raised her to be a queen. To her mother, she was a queen, and their home was her queendom. Her problem in life, now, as Harriet explains it, is that once she left the castle of her childhood, her mother did not provide her with another kingdom to rule.

Imagine the frustration of being a queen in search of a queendom: your talents are not being used adequately; you are not heard, for the world is not listening to you, a world that would be infinitely better if only it would hear what you have to say. There is no venue in which to spread out your riches and generously share your wealth. Being a queen without a queendom is surely an excruciatingly painful position to be in. Such is the life, from moment-to-moment, of Harriet. She rails at her impotence. She rages at those who do not listen to her. She hates those who stand in the way of her expressing her goodness and essential generosity, and, most of all, she cannot stand her own railing, her rages and her hatred.

Harriet is displaced from her soul because she is not living her own life. She is still living her life as though she were living with her mother. She is living out—or trying, at least—to live out her mother's plan for her.

Cancer as soul-displacement

Cancer, too, is not uncommon in soul-displaced persons. In my work of treating cancer patients, I have listened to people who are dying. They are terrified of the process of being in their bodies and suffering the pain from their disease. They are equally terrified of being out of their bodies, the release from their bodies that is the meaning of death. But accompanying those fears is the dread they have of continuing to live a life of soul-displacement, feeling hopelessly disconnected from themselves. Perhaps one of the lessons to be learned from cancer and other life-threatening illnesses is about re-finding one's lost soul.

Marsha is a patient who came to me shortly after a cancer diagnosis. She was interested in exploring whether her cancer was related to her psychological state. She suspected that she had got sick because of the toxic nature of her relationship with her mother.

Marsha is the child of politically active, liberal parents. Her father was active in the civil rights movement in the sixties and protested against the war in Vietnam in the seventies. Marsha has a younger brother who has followed in the footsteps of their parents, and who has been jailed on numerous occasions for his involvement in political protests.

These are Marsha's words that describe her discovery of whose life she was living before her cancer diagnosis:

> *My mother was a very intense, but emotionally withdrawn woman. She clearly had an easier time being loving to my brother than she did to me. I remember her saying to me repeatedly throughout my childhood: "Stop torturing me." I can still remember the feelings when she would say that to me. It was always when I could no longer be the "good girl" and my jealousy at my younger brother for her affection toward him got overwhelming. It took some years of training to bury my poisonous feelings in my body and put on the act of the perfect girl. But what a tender nerve that left me with.*

Marsha described to me the way she dealt with the unlove she felt from her mother:

*My mother had always taken for granted that everything
would go well with me, and had given me the message:
"You can do it on your own. You do not need me as much
as your brother who is weaker and more needy." Again,
I went along with her communication, but I found a
loophole: sickness. Being sick was a sure way to get her
attention. Being sick made me important.*

And, once Marsha developed this pattern of sickness as a way
of dealing with feelings that were too difficult, too painful for
her to allow into conscious awareness, her plan began to take
on a life of its own, independent of her conscious control:

*When my brother was jailed for his political activities,
I felt so guilty that, for a long time, I had difficulty
doing anything that he himself could not have done in
prison. And when I did do something that I considered
pleasurable, I would think of his not being able to do it.
It was as if I had gone to prison with him. But at the
same time, I felt that my mother had gotten what she had
bargained for—having a hero for a son, the right kind of
hero, one who sacrificed his life for the right cause. She
was so proud of him.*

*I developed bleeding colitis right after he was arrested, and
continued to suffer from it on and off for years after that.*

*This conflict, between my brother's life or my own, repeated
itself again, years later, when a campaign was begun to
release him from jail. I was supposed to be helping out
with this. I was holding a full-time job and was studying
full-time for a master's degree. I remember my bodily
sensations during this awful autumn. It was like my*

body was stiff from tension, and the despair of constantly choosing his life over mine was just unbearable. It was about four months into this campaign that my cancer was diagnosed. I remember saying to myself before the diagnosis: "What I need now is some horrible disease." In my mind it could not have been anything else but cancer.

Marsha presents a clear picture of a child who longs for the love of an emotionally unavailable mother. In reaction to this deprivation of maternal care, Marsha forged an identification with her brother, living out the life she thought her mother wanted her to live, abandoning her own true self.

The whispering of the walls

Because of the original symbiotic relationship between mother and child, the child is particularly sensitive to the unconscious or unspoken wishes, fears and feelings of the mother. This is truer for mothers and daughters, who share a biological sameness, than it is for mothers and sons. Jung commented that nothing influences children more than the "silent facts" of the home-life, or the "whispering of the walls"—what is palpable but remains unarticulated in the lives of the parents. More than anything, this whispering is found in the facts of the mother's life that prevent her from being satisfied or from pursuing her own fulfilment—her "unlived life," as Jung refers to it. The child senses the unhappiness of the mother, and desperately wants to right things, going to extraordinary lengths to please her. Yet, the child doesn't possess such power.

A sensitive child who is able to read the unconscious of the mother will try to fulfil the mother's unconscious wishes. It is out of love for the mother, or from the child's own wish to be loved, that the child will attempt to rescue the mother, save the mother from the self-hatred incurred from her unlived dreams of her own life. Rescuing another from misery is, of course, not a task that one human being can fulfil for another. But it is particularly burdensome for a girl-child, who is identified with her mother, and still subject to the magical thoughts of childhood that delude her into thinking that she might actually succeed. The child, then, has taken on the shadowy aspects of the mother's unconscious, unaware that the life she is living is not, in a sense, her own but her mother's.

A long lasting disconnection

Separation from one's soul comes about most often when either the original union with the mother is inadequate, or when the process of separation between mother and child is mismanaged. In these cases, there can be a long-lasting sense of disconnection, a split separating mind and body from soul. Each of these divisions within the self is like a mini-death. The physical process of soul-separation that takes place at the point of death—separation from the body—is, then, sometimes only the ultimate expression of a psychic process that began long before—a long-standing disconnection from the true self, sometimes experienced as a living-death.

Most of us suffer from some degree of soul-displacement. Most of us struggle, in varying degrees, with living a life that is altogether true to our natures.

Each of us incorporates aspects of our parents, internal images, in our journey toward maturity. These internal images serve as ways that we find to define ourselves. In healthy states, we incorporate those aspects of our parents that we like, and reject those characteristics we don't like. But when people leave their souls, or when they are out of sync with their souls, they have made these images all of who they are rather than part of who they are. They have incorporated, without discrimination, both good and bad parental aspects.

Soul-displaced people live as though they have no independent self. They have not become who their inborn natures would have led them to become. They have been dislodged from the people they should have been. They live their lives in the body or mind of someone else. Often, that someone else is their mother. The antidote comes in casting off inauthentic selves, in re-finding the original self that had been discarded, and in erecting an ego structure on this now solid foundation.

Soul-displacement begun in childhood becomes a chronic and painful condition in adulthood. These are wounds, insufficiencies that exist in the adult personality but have their origin in early childhood. Louise Kaplan, Director of the Mother-Infant Research Nursery at NYU, concludes that inadequate separation results in the person having difficulty "loving others, nurturing the young, taming his own aggression, knowing the boundaries of immediate time and space, mourning the dead and caring about the destiny of the human species." Meeting the challenge of separation is part of what enables us to become most poignantly and profoundly human.

The long journey of growing up

After that first anguished cry of birth, growing up is a long journey of learning to use our voices, our minds, and our bodies in more effective ways. In this journey, the mind becomes much more complex than the pureness and simplicity of the soul. The mind is what gives us the ability to think and feel one way, and yet to present ourselves differently. Unlike the soul, the mind is capable of defending itself against truth.

In this long passage away from Mother and toward individuation, the child remembers the honesty, pleasure and depth of true feeling that comes from soul-living. But the child also learns to conceal. The human being can hide in ways that no other animal can. An infant—even a month-old infant—can already, at this early age, learn to hide discomfort if its care-giver responds punitively to cries of distress. Or, infants can hide not only from the care-giver, but also from their own selves; they can learn to disconnect from knowing what they want and need, and from their true sense impressions—their pre-thoughts and pre-feelings—in order to accommodate themselves to the world. It is only a short step, hiding from another to deceiving one's self, forgetting the true nature of one's self. Even infants can learn to be depressed. It is this deceit, an internal hiding that represents our journey away from our centre that will cause the separation from our innate essence of our being.

I have had patients begin their analyses by telling me that they adored their fathers and abhorred their mothers. By the end of their analyses, they came to understand that the love for the father was a defence against anger at his emotional distance, and their own feeling of neglect from him; and they have learned that the hatred of the mother masked an appreciation of her true and unswerving involvement, and their own feeling of vulnerability from the deep love they felt toward her. I have had patients come in stating their intent to leave their spouses, only to discover that the rage against the partner was misdirected, and originated from held-over fantasies of revenge against an absent parent. And, I have had patients proclaim that they have a perfectly satisfactory marriage, who mature into the understanding that the foundation of the relationship was soft sand, ever shifting, dangerously unstable.

The soul cannot lie and it cannot be deceived. It is true, and it demands truth. It has a sensitivity to purity and honesty that the mind may not have. We are only born into our souls; then the stings of early maturation can cause us to swerve away, at times, from our souls. Perhaps growing up necessarily includes a search back to that soul-state of completion and wholeness.

Conferring whole-self integration

I share with all mothers the responsibility to confer whole-self integration onto my child. Molly's innocent, trusting spirit is nowhere more evident than when she tries to go to sleep. Molly never wants to go to sleep. So entranced is she with the glorious new world that she is beginning to get a taste for, that the idea of missing one precious single moment of it is troubling to her. And, because in this stage of our ever-evolving relationship, I *am* the world to her, she doesn't want to miss one precious single moment of being with me.

Every night it takes about an hour, no matter her level of exhaustion from the day's events, to get her to settle down enough to close her eyes and let sleep overtake her. The last few minutes involve a game. I say: "Good night Molly. I love you. See you in the morning." And she obediently closes her eyes, breathes deeply, only to open her eyes widely a moment later with a big fooled-you smile on her face. We repeat this little drama five, six times. Sometimes it goes on for fifteen minutes before she will cooperate and leave her eyes closed long enough for sleep to come. I play this game with her because her spirit is energetic and amusing. It is her sense of humour—a little game that she invented, and of which she is, in her own childlike way, proud. And maybe, too, she doesn't want to say good night to me because, in her sleep, she is leaving me.

When Molly gets older, she will confer on me the power of instructing her, of giving her orders about what to do, what to say, even what to feel. Up to a certain age, she will, likely, do whatever I tell her to do. I might tell toddler Molly to go across the room to get her doll. She will do this obediently, willingly, happily. It will never occur to her that she should object to doing this. How easy it would be to tell her—just as rationally and just as calmly—to engage in some act of destruction. I could give her permission to be cruel to other children by not intervening when she is; I could communicate to her that she should honour her mother, but not her father, by constantly criticising her father and showing him no love. It is in my power to construct this child in a million different ways. And she would let me. She might develop a stomach ulcer in order to let me; she might live a secret life that would give her nightmares and fear of men or women for the rest of her life. But she would let me because I am her Mommy and she trusts me.

I have the power to subvert this child from living from her soul. It is because of her love/need (the two are not yet separate) for me that I have this power. Right now, at this period in her life, instead of playing her go-to-sleep game with her, I could become irritable or forceful and demand that she go to sleep immediately. Indeed, there is nothing more I want in life at these fatigued moments at the end of the day than for her to go to sleep immediately. But this would not be fair to her. This would curtail the expression of her spirit.

When the soul remembers its original intent

Perhaps all of life, between birth and death, is an attempt to regain our first experience of harmony, the living from the soul that characterises the newborn. Perhaps it is our mothers who, most of all, grant us the power to live from our souls, or force us to depart from our souls.

The Greek goddess Mnemosyne, goddess of memory, was the mother of the Muses. All creativity flowed from Her, from the remembrance of Mother. Trauma is often accompanied by loss of memory. Perhaps birth traumatises the soul (as well as the psyche) of the infant because leaving the realm of the ethereal and entering into the realm of the physical results in memory loss. The soul forgets what it is and where it came from. But the pain of the wound instantly re-organises the entire inner world of the infant in order to bring about reduction of the pain. A primary homeostasis is then able to be re-established through the embrace of Mother. Perhaps it is, as Plato says in the *Symposium*, that we spend the whole of our lifetime in the process of remembering—searching for lost memories, searching to re-unite with our lost souls. And perhaps, too, it is only through our unique experiences as an individual, and from the accumulation of the scar tissue of defences against pain and injury that we are able to cover over the traumatic wounds of birth, of soul-separation, and of all other wounds. And having accomplished that, the soul can finally remember who it originally was and achieve its unique identity. And perhaps it is at the time of death that we return most wholly to the "actual me"—the Lacanian "real" that we were born into.

12

The Pas de Deux of Anxiety

his love thing that I have for my daughter is like a duet; it needs both of us to participate. I am exhilarated in our togetherness, that out of all the babies in the world and all the mothers in the world, we two have found each other.

Yet, in the midst of all this togetherness, this love *pas de deux* that Molly and I perform, there is a deep anxiety. My fear comes to me only in the dark of the night. It is only in my dreams that my anxiety is allowed to seep out. My dreams tell me the origin of my fear: it is separation. My dreams reflect my terror of my daughter's leaving me, of my continued existence without her.

A safe voice of many dimensions

Molly and I have developed the same routine every night. This feels important to me because everything has become so different for Molly, so sudden, so unexpected, this new life I am giving her. I know that even if I am vacuuming my house as often as her bio-mom might have done when she was pregnant with Molly, I am using a different vacuum cleaner, and the whirring sound may not have the same familiar whirring sound that Molly had grown used to; it might be more deep throated; or it might stutter when the other one was going along like smooth sailing. And my voice is not the same voice Molly heard for her first nine months during her in utero life; I lost my southern drawl many years ago when I left the south to go to college; I am sure, however, that Molly's bio-mom, also southern born and bred, still retains her thick Louisiana accent.

I do the same routine every night because I want Molly to know that, despite all the dramatic changes she has experienced, she is safe. And I repeat our little nightly routine for the sheer pleasure of the togetherness experience. I make sure that she hears my voice—the new voice in her life—every night before she goes to sleep. I either make up my own stories—mini fairy tales about Robbie Rabbit, or Debbie Deer, or Freddy Fish—or I read the classic fairy tales and myths to her. I especially favour the story of Rapunzel, whose golden locks were so legendary in her time. It is one of the stories that my mother and I shared more days and nights than I can count. The story came quite naturally to us because, like Rapunzel, I had long blonde locks as a child.

I know that Molly doesn't yet understand the words or the meaning of what I am saying to her, but I know that I am creating an experience for her—a repetition of behaviour that tells her, on a level that she cannot yet articulate but is processing viscerally, that her mother has a voice. The lilting quality of my voice is heard by Molly as either soothing, or excited, sometimes sad, perhaps even theatrically fearful, or dramatically angry (reflecting the tone and meaning of the story). These tonalities and meanings of the stories are all heard within the safe containment of our home and our togetherness, and this safe voice that she hears is a voice of many dimensions.

I read the fairy tales to Molly not only for her sake, but for mine as well. It is not just that everything is different for baby Molly; everything is different for me, too. I am having feelings that I never had before. I resort to the fairy tales, at times, because I want to be reassured that my struggles/anxieties are the concerns of all women—that I am not some quirky, odd anomaly of a mother. I want to connect with women and mothers from time immemorial. I retreat to myths and fairy tales because they are the universal elixir for reconnecting with all humanity, ancient and modern, dead and alive.

Fairy tales are magical because they accept and address the problematic nature of life without defeatism, without meaningless or irrelevant escapism. Unlike the safe and pleasurable experience of a mother and child reading and being read the stories, the actual contents of fairy tales and myths are never entirely "safe." They often begin with the death of a mother or father, or the kidnapping of a child. There is always a loss, a separation, and then a determined effort to re-find, reunite—with others, and with self.

And I read the fairy tales because they are stories about confidence. I want my daughter to become a person who believes in herself, who lives every day of her life with a sense that she can be and do whatever she desires. Fairy tales aren't, for the most part, stories about morality. They aren't about being a good or bad person, a rich or poor person, or a powerful or insignificant person (though all of those themes appear in the tales). Rather, the question all fairy tales ask is whether one meets life's challenges with the possibility of mastering its difficulties. After all, what's the use of being a good, rich or powerful person when one *feels* insignificant? Because separation is the very first challenge we meet in entering life; it is primary in our successful development toward a secure sense of self. The extent to which a child masters the challenge of separation depends on the mother's commitment and skill in helping her child to handle the conflicting and simultaneous urges to stay close to her and to move away.

In Rapunzel's case, her parents have stolen food from a sorceress. They make the reprehensible agreement to pay penance for their thievery of the sorceress's rampion plants by giving to her their own daughter, Rapunzel. And for many years Rapunzel seems entirely content despite her being traded as a punishment, despite being separated from her biological mother. Like my baby-Molly, for a few years Rapunzel remains blissfully unaware that the woman she thinks of as her mother, is not her "real" mother, not the mother she was born to. Like my own adopted baby-Molly, Rapunzel seems not to (consciously) miss her biological parents. Like my baby-Molly, Rapunzel seems to have no apparent need for anyone other than her adoptive mother, and embraces her singular relationship with her non-biological mother.

The disappearing children

I have heard over the years from a great many of my mother-patients that they suffer most intensely from fears, anxieties and nightmares immediately after the arrival of their first child. In the dreams of these mothers, their newborn children frequently disappear: they vanish suddenly or gradually. One of my patients had a recurrent dream about losing her child at the shopping mall: one moment the child was there holding onto her skirt; the next moment, she was gone, spirited off in some enigmatic way to some mysterious place. Another patient dreamed that her child was gone for a day, inexplicably came back for a week, then was gone again. In mothers' dreams, children disappear in all manner of ways: some disappear as the newborns they are, never to grow, always to be memorialised as they were—eternal infants. They perish in fires, and they are kidnapped. Others are projected into some hypothetical future and disappear as the people they would have become. As dream-imagined teenagers, they run away to live on the street and become drug addicts; as adults, they die inexplicably from terminal diseases for which there are no names and no cures. Dreams can reveal to mothers their concerns about their most terrifying fears related to their children.

And so I join the ranks of mothers from time immemorial who, like myself, have been busy mothers at night. Everyone else in my household—Gregg, Molly, the nanny, poodle-dog Oscar, brown and white guinea pigs Chocolate and Vanilla—all are sleeping peacefully. For the first six months of Molly's life, I have a multitude of dreams of her near-death. It's like a never-ending movie—one nightmare-night picking up where I left off from the previous nightmare-night. Molly is lying at the bottom of a swimming pool, and her body is lifeless. I pull her up, and I breathe into her mouth, but she remains immobile. I know that she is dying. This thought is intolerable. It cannot be and it will not be. I scream at her; and then I scream again. It is the intensity of my screams, and the force of my not accepting that she is leaving me, and the concomitant loudest scream ever created on earth, that brings her back. "Molly, come back. Come back," I cry out, vigorously, vehemently, violently. And she hears my agonised plea to her, and thankfully comes back.

Or she is falling down the banister and, at the very last moment, I am able to perform a miraculous twist of my body, like a trapeze artist, and catch her before she hits the ground.

Every nightmare—a different miracle, a different death-defying feat occurs. I wake up to check on her breathing to make sure that night is night and day is day.

When morning thankfully comes, I am able to be clear-headed enough to understand that my dreams of Molly's death are symbolic communications from my unconscious. I know that my dreams reflect my anxiety about separation. After all, what is death but the most final of all separations? In my dreams, our separation always comes about through some unfortunate circumstance, some event beyond our control.

I know that this anxiety is deep and old for me, as it is for many of my patients as well. I know that my anxiety has to do with my own childhood issues about closeness and separation. I know that it started with my relationship with my own mother, my intimate connection to her, and my fear of being separated from her. And then it travelled to my relationships with men. It has been my lifelong pattern of falling in love, as I did with my mother, as I did with my men; becoming attached, as I was with my mother, as I was with my men; and becoming fearful of loss, as I became with my mother, as I became with my men.

And now, this "thing" that I have with Molly—the depth of the love and the attachment as well as the anxiety and fear of loss of her—feels the same as it has always felt to me—a feeling that is so intense that it threatens to wash over me like a great tsunamic wave. Most mothers who have successfully bonded with their infants say that they feel the same thing: they say they have "fallen in love" with their child—a free fall, hoping against hope that it will be a soft landing on a sandy beach.

Nurturing, obsession, intoxication

When thinking about the concept of "maternal instinct"— innate or learned—it is helpful to recognise that scientists have isolated a hormone, prolactin, that is associated with promoting nurturing, defensive, and protective behaviour (even in males). But we should also be aware that the presence of prolactin in the body is correlated, as well, with other emotional tendencies, including aggression, and post-partum depression. The state of being "in love" with a newborn child is not just emotional; it exists in the mother's body, in her hormones and in her brain chemistry. When we want to understand the anxieties that accompany motherhood, it is useful to remember that biochemical study of the brain shows that the brain state that is reflective of chemical, raw emotional attraction—be it lover love or mother love—shares the same brain circuitry with states of obsession, mania, intoxication, thirst, and hunger.

13

An Affliction of Muteness

know that with my new daughter, I am an exemplary mother in a thousand ways: I behave with this child as though she is the light of my life. I coo; I hold her affectionately and lovingly; I read to her; I play with her; I sing to her. I do every joyful activity that it is possible to do with an infant. And yet, with all this love, with our exquisite togetherness, I struggle: not just with my anxiety about potential, fantasied loss of my daughter; I suffer, as well, from a terrible paralysis of expression.

An inhibiting indifference to expression

This muteness is an old story for me. It's one of the reasons why I entered my personal analysis. Until I began therapy, it was hard for me to find justification to talk. One of my family's favourite stories of my childhood is of the time I went to meet our new next-door neighbours. I was about five then, and my brother and I walked over to their house to welcome them. We stood at the screen door, and the lady of the house came out. My brother—all of seven years old—said rather heroically, "My name is David." Then the neighbour turned to me and asked sweetly, "And what's your name?" I stood there, not answering, not offering even a glimmer of recognition that she had spoken to me. Then she said (again, seemingly sweetly, but perhaps with a slight edge of impatience), "Oh, you must be bashful." At that challenge, I found an overwhelming urgency to express myself. I exclaimed defiantly, offended at this misidentification of my identity, "No, I am not Bashful, I am Jane."

Even as a newly-qualified analyst, I was afflicted with this inhibiting indifference to expression. I remember one of my patients complaining about it to me. Until she lodged her grievance, I didn't even have the recognition that my behaviour was a bit off-putting. Effervescent and always excelling at emotional communication, perky Judy, also an analyst, would ring the doorbell, and I would say into the intercom "Who is it?" and then she would answer, and it was always a friendly answer, not just announcing her name, but with a cheery "Hi" first or "Hi, Jane, how are you?" Then I would buzz her in. I never said, "Oh, hi, Judy" or, "Come on up." I never said anything. Just the harsh, electronic BUZZZZZ as my response.

Perhaps I was even drawn to being an analyst because it is a "listening" profession. (The word "listen" is anagrammatically the same as "silent." Analysts actually have theoretical justification to not talk. However, I learned early in my career that sustained not-talking is one of the best ways to lose patients. Patients are like infants and children; they need and want verbal and emotional contact that is feelingful language-food, and they don't flourish without it. When the feelingful feeding is not forthcoming, the smart ones leave.)

But of course, that sardonic stance of mine, my stronger desire to listen rather than to talk (even, I guess, my defiance in not being Bashful) was an elaborate defence, a ruse to make myself feel okay about my silent inadequacy. Except with my mother, I just was never very good at expressing my feelings in words. I hid the ones that were embarrassing—the hurts and angers—and the love ones seemed too obvious to have to say.

A long sojourn

Amongst the various reasons that we humans invented language—from our earliest primitive grunts and screams as well as from our coos of pleasure and our whimpers of pain— was the need to be "seen" or "known" by being "heard." In ancient Greece, philosopher Heraclitus used the word *ksuniemi* to mean "to know;" but its earlier meaning was "to know by hearing." Perhaps our ancestors who developed sophisticated vocalisations collectively decided that there was no thought or feeling that was undeserving of translation into words—to be heard—and language became elaborately exquisite in describing our inner worlds. We attach sounds to our inner processes precisely so that we may render our internal experience accessible—seen, heard and known—to others.

One of the things I do with my Molly is to give her the experience of hearing about my inner world in relation to her. I know that in sharing this with her, I am giving her an experience that has the effect of constructing our bond: "audible glue," as author (and mother) Anne Karpf refers to speaking from mother to infant. This glue-like feeling that I have toward Molly must be heard and seen, but also felt. The feeling of my inner experience has a name; there are words that define its meaning. I know the words; I want to say the words; I want to own the words as mine, as the feeling that I am embracing toward this child of mine. Yet, I am unable to tell my beloved daughter that I love her.

I open my mouth to say the simple, time-honoured words, "I love you." And there it is: the old/new story; my lifelong throat constriction. The words do not emerge. I can almost get them out. I accomplish a facsimile. I get so far as to say, "Mommy loves Molly," or I ask, "Does Molly know how much Mommy loves Molly?" And I stretch out my arms as far as they each will reach, seemingly including the whole world in my scope of influence. But I have not yet been able to say, the no-holds-barred simple statement of "I love you."

I want to utter these words—desperately. I try to will myself to say the words. I rehearse when I am not with Molly. (I don't go so far as actually muttering to myself for fear of looking like a cracked person worthy of institutionalisation, but I say it internally to myself, over and over again.) And then when the opportunity presents itself, when we are lovingly together, the words stay inside, stuck deep in my throat. It's as though there is a song that wants to come out from my unconscious, and I can remember the lyrics and the words but I've lost my ability to sing. No matter my effort, I cannot eject those words, the verbal representation of my feelings, from my body and from my soul out into the air, for those words to travel to Molly's ears—for her to hear and to "know."

Perhaps with Molly I am afraid that, as my mother was with me, if I let myself grab onto this child, I won't be able to let go. I think it is the anticipation of the dreaded separation that is so daunting to me. Perhaps the words of love are the last needed bastion against separation between me and my daughter, my last defence against falling hopelessly in symbiotic love with her (as my mother did with me).

I have sojourned with this throat constriction all my life, starting with my mother and the rest of my family, then through boyfriends as well as girlfriends, with Gregg, and now with Molly. My best friend from high school, Cynthia, noticed from practically the first day we met. I have a wonderful, warm and loving relationship—genuinely loving—the best that there is, with Cynthia. But I do not spontaneously hug her, as she does me, and I do not say nice things to her like: "It was great seeing you," or "I can't wait to see you," or "I love you," as she does with me. Part of this habit comes from having established a relationship in which we have talked weekly, daily, sometimes three or four times a day for the last thirty-five years. I rationalise that it gets kind of absurd to say, "I love you" when you know you're going to talk again in a few hours, or the next day. The point, though, isn't that I *don't* say it. The point is that I *can't*. Even when I know I won't see her for a while, I don't/can't hug her good-bye. I have seen her hug other friends in front of me, and then when it comes to our turn, I stand there, arms dangling at my sides (a precursor of my "paralysed arms" when Baby Molly was first stretched out to me to receive her), helplessly waiting for her to go first, for her to break this endless cycle that I am trapped in.

Cynthia has truly tried, over the years, to help me with it. She tells me she loves me, and then tells me that now it's my turn to tell her. Of course, I have to say it at that point. Sometimes I try to get away with a lame "me too." But she doesn't let me off the hook, and she says, "C'mon Jane. Tell me." The words catch in my throat, and whatever feeble attempts I make, it all comes out sounding pretty stilted. Well, it's a start.

Fluency in the language of love

This muteness is not a new affliction in my family. It can, of course, be traced back to my mother. Even as old as I am (ridiculously past child-bearing years when Molly came to me), as cognitively trained (both a master's and a PhD degree as well as psychoanalytic certification) and emotionally developed (thirty years of my own analysis) as I am, I am still embodying so many aspects of my own mother. Even with all the progress I have made—personally, professionally, emotionally, spiritually—in this one way, this inability to straightforwardly declare my love, I am still imitating my mother, still being limited in the same ways that the togetherness we had was limited. Though I know my mother loved me madly, wildly, perhaps even as she loved no one else, the fact is: she never told me. Those words were simply not in her vocabulary, as they were not, I am sure, in her own mother's, and her mother's, and so on. It is as though it's in my genetic code, the DNA that's inside of me, and the same DNA that's been inside every living creature on Earth for time immemorial. Many mothers, over the three and a half billion years to which we trace our collective human DNA back, have learned the language of love-speak. But for all those Madeleine Malvinas who were my direct ancestors, for all those generations back, we of the Madeleine Malvina stock never mastered this simple task, and we have been handicapped ever since that first, long-ago Madeleine Malvina never learned to say, "I love you." And so, neither can I.

I think about this incapacity of mine only half-seriously as my "affliction" (as in having a terrible disease), or as a "handicap" (like in golf—"please allow me a head-start"), or a "complex" (a term Freud used to refer to a constellation of unresolved issues). Its impact on me has become much more apparent now that I want to have words to say to my own daughter that I didn't learn to say. I learned the feelings; I learned the commitment and devotion and mutuality that are concomitant with the feelings. But I didn't learn the language. That's how I think about my "affliction." It is a foreign language that my mother didn't learn to speak, and she was unable to pass on fluency in this language of love to me.

And so, with Molly, here I am in the same paralysed-throat place I inhabited for all those previous years. Molly doesn't know that I'm not saying "I love you" (as I never noticed it with my mother until about midpoint in my own analysis), and she's hearing that I love her in everything else I say and do; in the caresses, the gleeful meeting of her gaze, the interest and availability, the emotional activation when we are together. And she knows it from the tone of my voice, the pre-words of the oohs and ahs—the language of infancy—the language of "motherese," the true "melody of intimacy," as Anne Karpf refers to it.

But Molly has changed the structure of the world for me. "Implicit" is no longer good enough. I know that I must be able to proclaim my sentiment in word as well as in feeling and deed. I know that I need to teach Molly the adult language of love that comes in words as well as the baby language of love that is conveyed in the display of feelings and in tone of voice. I know that if I am going to raise this baby to be a healthy, loving, productive stalwart member of society, I need to be able to tell her I love her. The words themselves (as well as the feelings) count, and the words will give Molly an extra sense of security about her relationship with me which will then, later in her life, carry over to her feelings about her place in the world.

I need to be able to tell her because there are two pronouns and one verb in the sentence "I love you." The verb means that my love for her has a humming, buzzing, bustling meaning; it means that I have moved from the infantile passive position of "being loved" to the adult active posture of "loving." The pronouns "I" and "you" will tell Molly that she is not I, that we are separate. And the whole sentence—verb and pronouns together—will tell her that our separation is safe.

I need to tell Molly that I love her with ease and feeling because it is through experiencing me that she will model herself. I need to be able to do this because the most compelling lesson I have learned from being a psychoanalyst is that the feelingful use of language represents we humans at our most profoundly high level of achievement. Without language there is no mature self, there is no integration of thought with feeling. Language is what enables the self to have a solid foundation; it is what allows us to digest feelings throughout the psyche. Language integrates body, mind, and soul. It can be like glue and it bring us together, but it is also what separates us into our separate selves.

And, I need to be able to tell Molly I love her because I need to be able to separate myself from my own mother. I need to divest my long-dead mother of the overarching power she still holds on me. I need to see her as a woman—a mere woman, limited by her circumstances, her upbringing, and her character. I need to see her as something other than the mother of my infancy, the source of all things, the mother who defined for me the way things were. I need to be able to separate myself from my mother in order to be separate from my child.

If I can get myself to say these words to Molly, then I will raise a child who not only knows that she is the light of her mother's life, but who can say, "I love you" to a man should she choose to be with one later in life, or to her sister should she have one, and, best of all, to her mother. I need to be able to do this for Molly. And I need to do it for myself so that my throat can become unconstricted and I can be free.

For all those reasons, the words I use with Molly, and precision in their use, are important and their effect large. As Mark Twain said, "The difference between the almost right word and the right word is really a large matter—'tis the difference between the lightning bug and the lightning."

14

Recognising the Squeezed Tightening in Another

H aving this affliction of a strangulated throat—this constriction that prevents the free flowing of words of love—means that I can recognise this squeezed tightening in others: like Jews finding their fellow Jews anywhere in the world; like shy people recognising their fellow loners at a singles dance—I notice a fellow sufferer.

Times of stops and starts; periods of talking and non-talking

I see that one of my patients, Marnie, suffers from this same throat paralysis as I. Marnie first came to me as a forlorn teenager: suicidal, desperate, unable to talk. We began her treatment with my asking her questions that she either could not or would not answer. She had the habit of turning away from me in disinterest, or perhaps even disgust—it was hard to read her in those early days of treatment. We suffered in silence together for agonising, unfulfilling, silence-filled sessions. And then, finally, words come: she tells me, not unexpectedly, that she will not be returning. I surprise her with my response. I tell her what a good patient she has been. She laughs.

Her laughter is the first expression of feeling, the first sign she has had since first coming that she is not a concrete block. She has laughed in dismay, and in disbelief and probably also in contemptuousness or disdain. She thinks I am joking at her expense. And, just as being so roundly misunderstood at being Bashful had impelled me to find my voice so many years ago, telling Marnie that she has been a good patient compels her to speak: her first words. She asks how I could say such an obviously ridiculous thing since she has not uttered a word. I tell her that she has come on her own free will, and that, at her age, that itself is near-miraculous. I tell her that she clearly has a great deal of pain that she wants/needs to talk about. And, that if she ever decides to privilege me with her pain, I would like to listen.

Slowly, over weeks, months of stops and starts, periods of talking and non-talking, Marnie unfolds for me her past. Marnie's early history was that she was placed in an orphanage shortly after birth. She never had the benefit of a warm and receiving hello as her first contact with the world. Rather, her first emotional experience in life was rejection, as I believe it is (at least on the level of the unconscious) for all adoptive children. And then, unlike my Molly who found me and Gregg, and Oscar and Chocolate and Vanilla, Marnie didn't find a replacement home that gave her the recompense feeling of being wanted and loved. Her next mother, her adoptive mother who brought her home when she was six months old, replicated the same rejecting emotional experience for her as her biological mother had created in giving her up. These two, adoptive mother and adoptive child, were not a good match. They never developed an emotional resonance between them that might have helped to heal the wounds of Marnie's initial rejection. Marnie grew up feeling alone, unloved, untethered to a primary relationship, and thus undeveloped as a full self.

We have a good run at it. Years go by. Marnie becomes "normal." She comes to know herself—her own thoughts and feelings, as disturbing as they are. She develops the ability that all analysts aspire to for their patients—the skill to put her thoughts and feelings into words with relative ease. Marnie has productive relationships; she gets close to her brother (also adopted); she shares meaningful moments with her father; she develops friendships with girls. She meets a good man, a detective, marries, and has a good marriage.

But now her throat constriction that she came into therapy with has returned; she wants to solve this affliction once and for all. She confesses that it has become important to her to tell her mother she loves her. Her inability to say these words to her mother has been plaguing her because she has just given birth to her first child, and her mother is now aged, presumably soon to die. In spite of many past battles, misunderstandings and antagonisms between them, Marnie wants to accomplish this task of telling her mother that she loves her for the sake of the young (the just-born) and the old (the about-to-die).

We are forced, then, to return, years later, to the discussion of Marnie's verbal paralysis, an affliction she had thought she was free from, but which is now in full dress regalia, torturing her once again. She wants, more than anything, to be able to complete her relationship with her mother, and to be able to begin her relationship with her daughter, with these words of love having been said.

I ask her what the impediment is. I ask, already knowing what her answer will be, because she is no different from I in this. "There is no impediment," she says. "There is nothing to say about it. The words just don't/can't come out. It is an unfixable problem."

I want to cure this woman of her "problem" as badly as I want to cure myself. I think that if I can cure her, then maybe in some osmotic way, I too will reap the benefit. We discuss all the permutations of her relationship with her mother. Here, we part company. Her mother was demonstrably angry a lot; mine wasn't. The frequent outbursts of rage frightened Marnie. She attributes many aspects of her life to her mother's rage. She retreats into fear whenever her boss criticises her performance. She is afraid to speak her mind, at times, out of fear (as she has demonstrated with me in our first sessions). But, she still insists that her ill mother's rage is a thing of the past; her mother is half-blind and arthritic now, capable of no damage, and Marnie has forgiven her. Yet, with these insistences that bygones be bygones, Marnie still cannot bring herself to utter the unspeakable words of love.

I am so identified with Marnie that I wonder to myself if I can even help her. In hearing about her vocal paralysis, I start to feel impatient with my own affliction, and my impatience with myself begins to manifest itself in relation to how I think and feel when I am with her. I start to feel impatient, even bossy, not just with myself but with her too: I want to point out to her that she *has* to do this. I want to say it to her as an accusation: "How can you be so unloving? Get it together before the poor woman expires." But even if a glimmer of my impatience seeps through in my instruction to her to just "do it—take a deep breath and tell your mother you love her," I am careful not to reveal my secret—that I am the pot calling the kettle black. I only feel a little bad that I am telling her to do what I myself cannot (and I reassure myself that sports coaches do it all the time with their players).

Marnie rebels against me (as she should; orders to make behavioural change rarely work in therapy—or even in mothering for that matter). Now, every time her mother comes up for discussion in the sessions, Marnie falls asleep. We decide to put her mother to sleep for the time being in this therapy in order to keep the patient awake. I instruct her to stop talking about her mother. And, as she comfortably describes the miracle of her new-born daughter, she becomes alive once again.

Moving me off my perch of immobility

It is my new Molly herself who, finally, is able to "cure" me of my "affliction," enabling me to love her with language, and, as well, enabling me to help Marnie with her own vocal strangulation. It is Molly's modelling for me how to love, and the inspiration from her assumption of her right to be loved, that changes me.

I know that my affliction of muteness has to do with my deep-seated struggle to feel that I belong to someone. Since my mother's death, I have never really felt that anyone was solely mine, nor that I was solely anybody else's. Even when I was married briefly, my sense of my not belonging to the man I married and his not belonging to me was so powerful that I couldn't even refer to him as my husband. I heard him refer a few times to me as his wife. It was the kind of thing where you look over your shoulder to see who the person is talking about because you know it's not you. I never felt married to him, so he was never *my* anything.

Except for my mother, no one has felt entirely secure or solid in my life. If we human beings move in orbits, I have felt my orbit to be a solitary journey, and only on occasions, only for moments (even if those moments have factually stretched out to be years) have I intersected with someone else's orbit.

No one has given me the feeling that my mother gave me: that my existence is essential to them; that our orbits intersect because life would be intolerably dreary otherwise. I feel liked and even loved at times, respected, honoured, looked up to, but not *needed*. Since my mother died, I have missed feeling needed.

I think that in order for me not to feel anxious about my daughter and to unconstrict my trapped throat, I need to feel that Molly and I belong together—that she is *my* daughter, *my* child, *my* baby and that I am *her* mommy, and that there is no one else for us at this time—the brief time that she and I enjoy living together as almost one. I need to feel that we two are alone in our orbit of union (even blocking out Gregg at these times of symbiotic oneness). I need to have with my child the same feeling that my mother imparted to me—that it is our cosmic destiny to be together.

Entitlement to the privilege of love

Scientists have studied the love duet that occurs between mothers and infants. Through analysing interactive patterns, researchers were able to predict which babies at four months old would be the most securely attached at twelve months. The key component is not, as one might expect, a continuous synchrony of interaction: rather, the infants who developed the most secure attachments to their mothers were neither those who were exposed to the most synchronous interaction, nor the least synchronous. They were the ones who had a variety of interactive exchanges. There was predictability as well as variability; there was safety in sameness as well as excitement in novelty.

But scientists have not studied as much the sense of security that babies confer on their mothers. (The expectation perhaps is that we mothers—presumably paragons of maturity—already have it.) No research study could have predicted the change that came over me from being Molly's mother.

Molly is the best teacher of how to love—and the assumption of love that comes with a sense of belonging— that I could have. She takes my hand and places it on her cheek, in just the right place, in just the position she desires.

Then when she's had enough of this little exchange of love, she deliberately and knowingly removes my hand. These small acts between us arise from her having the surety of my love; she never doubts that I will want to perform these acts of loving togetherness and loving separation. What is assuaging my anxiety is Molly's assumption of her right to want my love, to ask for my love. Although I may not have been able to come to a sense of our belonging to each other all on my own, of our counting on each other's love with the same level of assurance as night following day, she is telling me that it is so, and I am believing her. She never imagines that her lot in life is/was/will be anything other than being my one true child. And through this process, through her knowing that she is mine, I come to know that I am hers.

It is remarkable that even as a baby, this child—like all children her age, before the acquisition of language—has enough of a self to know what she wants and enough drive to seek what she wants. I know that my job as her mother is to ensure that this sense of entitlement stays with her, that I do not do anything that will take her away from this place of privilege of love. My job as her mother is to follow her innate, healthy instincts about the kind of mother she needs.

And so, Molly does, in fact, "cure" me of my fears, anxieties, and insecurities as her mother. Molly's assumption of her rights as my daughter, her absolute assurance that she and I are meant for each other out of all the children and all the mothers in the world gives me a breakthrough of voice. She has shown me, more forcefully than all the therapy/self-healing/instructional videos in the world could have, the illusion of the life story I have been living: she proves to me that I, finally and irreversibly, belong to someone. And so the words finally do come. It is day 182 into my being Molly's mother, and before the day is over, she has heard ninety-seven times from her mother's own lips that her mother loves her. Once I grasp how to do it, I can't stop, it feels so good.

Dispelling the illusions of her life story

And then I know what the cure for Marnie is. Her cure is my cure. She needs to hear from me that I love her. She needs to have the illusion of her life story dispelled. She needs to know that just because she has never been told that she is loved, she is not unlovable. Now I am an old pro at this. The words fall from my lips as I tell her that I love her. It is easy to tell her honestly and authentically because, after the years of our being together, coming to know all of what lies inside her, love is, indeed, what I have come to feel for her. She really is quite lovable. She cries from relief at having been told, for the first time in her life, that she is loved.

In her next session, Marnie describes the experience she had of observing her mother holding her child for the first time. She says that the phone rang, and she had to run into the other room to get it. Without thinking, she thrust the baby into her mother's arms. She saw how tentatively her mother held the baby, and, at that moment, it seemed inconceivable to her that this woman had raised her and her brother. Her mother seemed as vulnerable, as frightened, as the newborn.

Then the baby began to cry. And Marnie witnessed the transformation in her mother's face. She explained that it was the face she grew up knowing, the face that she was afraid of: her mother's fear had turned into anger.

For the first time, Marnie had an understanding about her mother. She understood that her baby's crying was inducing in her mother old and painful feelings of inadequacy. And in that moment, Marnie explains: "I was filled with wholeness." She understood both her daughter's feelings of insecurity at being in a strange person's arms, and simultaneously, her mother's rage that she was ineffectual in being a good-enough mother. For that instant, Marnie became both her mother and her daughter, and in identifying with both of them, she was able to love them both and feel whole within herself. And from that place of wholeness, Marnie was able to tell her mother, finally, that she loved her.

Molly has lit a candle that I now hold. And then I lit a candle that my patient, Marnie now holds. And Marnie will light the candle that her own daughter will hold. And so on. Candles are lit now in places that were dark before. Molly has broken the grip of the inheritance of mute mothers that has gone on for I know not how many generations back.

15

The Loss of the Omnipotent Mother

Now that Molly is a toddler, I see her struggling with taking beginning steps to move away from me in order to establish a tiny bit of independence. I see her frustration as she tries to take on her small world. She marches out into her small area of the universe with great confidence. She may want to try dressing herself, or getting some food for herself out of the refrigerator, or try her hand at ping-pong. And then for some reason, it doesn't work out. She puts her left arm in the right-armhole; she drops the egg on the floor; the ball whizzes past her. Her frustration, and then the rage that follows at the failure, is never directed toward herself. It's always enthusiastically directed toward me. Even if I am nowhere around, and I have had nothing to do with the situation; it is still all my fault. Everything that goes wrong is my fault. I know that her blaming me represents a directionality of emotion that is healthy and appropriate at her age: she is angry at me rather than the worse alternative of turning the aggression against her self—a psychic mechanism that would, conversely, be the beginning of a lifelong struggle with feelings of incompetence, lack of self-worth, and fear of failure. I know, too, that at these times of her rage at me, Molly is confronting a sudden realisation: the awful truth that I am not omnipotent. It is her powerlessness as a child in the face of my powerlessness as her mother that is the cause of her wrath. I can't say that I blame her entirely.

Powerlessness is a gradual awakening

I think that of all the stages of separation between mother and child, it is the loss of the omnipotent mother that hurts the most, the one that is the most frightening, as well as being the most enraging to the child. The child comes to understand that the mother is not all-powerful, cannot take away every pain. She cannot protect her child from every contingency. The world intrudes, and the mother is not master of the world. In fact, her domain begins to seem smaller and smaller to the ever-growing child, until the child understands that sometimes the mother's domain is primarily just about them and their family. She doesn't rule the classroom where the child spends time away from her; she doesn't control all the other children at the playground who engage in unpredictable, sometimes even cruel, behaviours. And some times, some awful times when the child is still young, she disappears forever. She dies. She has lost even her power to live.

Simultaneously, as children begin to divest their mothers of the power of omnipotence, the process of the children shedding their own sense of grandiosity ensues. Like the mother, the child does not rule the universe. There may be times when the child can direct Mother, but it's never a sure thing; it is only at the mother's discretion. Normally this sense of their mutual powerlessness is a gradual awakening, and the ever-expanding identity of the child grows concomitantly to meet the pain of the realisation. Later in life, then, the adult child is enabled to meet Mother as another adult rather than as the all-powerful (and disappointing) mother of childhood.

One more awful blow to symbiosis

I remember an experience I had as a teenager when I was taking the bus home from school one day. I had to change buses, and at the intersection where I stood waiting for the second bus, I unexpectedly saw my mother driving through the intersection. I called out to her; I even began to run furiously after her car. But she didn't hear or see me, and she kept right on driving her sure path toward home. I was too experienced a bus-taker, and I was too old to logically have this reaction. Nevertheless I found myself standing on the street corner of Carrollton Avenue, across from the Gus Mayer store, as a well-seasoned teenager, weeping like a child with the pain of abandonment. It was somehow strangely not possible to me that my mother could not know of my existence—that I could have remained invisible to her. It was hard to believe, and not without an emotional ache that I was forced to accept that she actually had an existence separate from me, a life that did not include me.

Having grown up with the certain knowledge that my mother adored me, even with all that love, for that one moment as I watched my mother's car vanish as she pulled away from me, lost into the anonymity of traffic, the sting of recognition of our separateness was searing. This was a pain originating in her not knowing that I was there, in our union having been dissolved, in her not knowing absolutely everything I wanted/needed her to know, without words, without communication. This was a pain originating in the realisation that we were no longer as one, that I could no longer have confidence in my mother's omnipotence, one more awful blow to our symbiosis.

My work with patients shows me that the trauma of the loss of the illusion of the omnipotent mother, and the rage that ensues, can keep mothers and children tied to each other long after they should have let go of each other.

All my patients talk about their mothers. All my patients who are themselves mothers talk about their children. It doesn't matter whether they are eight or eighteen or eighty. Mothers are devastated by their own confrontation with their helplessness in the face of their children's individuality, the ways in which children swerve from the course that their mothers would have them take. And conversely, children are devastated by their ultimate recognition that their mothers do not, cannot always control or protect them, in spite of their protestations to the opposite.

All children are angry, in some ways, at some times, with their mothers. Their rage can reach an unreasonable level of intensity, unrelated to the actual "deservedness" of the mother, unrelated to whether the mother is a good mother or not. When this irrational rage occurs post-childhood, often the origin of the rage is not situated in whatever present situation appears to have stimulated the feelings, but rather has brought us back in time to early childhood. When anger about the loss of the omnipotent mother is not worked through and let go of in childhood, then, as teenagers and as adults, we find ourselves still reacting to this struggle, still placing the blame on our mothers. It is a difficult process for all children to recover from the disturbing realisation that Mother cannot leap over tall buildings, cannot fly through the air, cannot perform the acts of a Supermother.

Opposing desires to proceed onward

Mothers give; mothers withhold. All mothers do both. The infant does not yet have the psychic apparatus to experience the gratifying mother as the same person as the frustrating mother. Thus, the mother is split into "all-good" and "all-bad"—separate mothers from the point of view of the still rudimentary sense of self of the infant. As a child becomes older, a process begins of integration of part-mothers into a perception of a one-and-whole person. Mother can then be seen more realistically and with less idealisation. She serves as an emotional container, holding safely all the feelings and impulses of her child. When this realistic view of mother is adopted, the child can begin to let go of the need for magic, and can see, not only Mother, but the world, too, in realistic, ambivalent, ambiguous, and conflictual terms.

Now, with Molly, the symbiosis that we once enjoyed so blissfully with each other is a thrown-away relic, relegated to psychic history. Now, conflict accompanies the opposing desires to proceed onward with separation and, simultaneously, to return back to our discarded symbiosis. I saw this in my mother in relation to myself. I saw it in myself in relation to my mother, and I see it now in relation to Molly and me. As separate selves, Molly and I are not identical, no longer fused. We find ourselves, on occasions, feeling angry, annoyed, impatient, and otherwise discontented with each other.

My anger toward Molly, as well as hers toward me, is almost always about separation. There is no other issue between us that evokes the same level of dissatisfaction with each other. I am angry because I depend on her (I ask her to clean up her mess), and she shows me she is undependable (as any young child is, at times and in some ways). She is angry with me because she depends on me (she asks me to play with her), and I show her that I am undependable (as all mothers are, at times and in some ways). Sometimes it is Molly's insistence that she is not I, has entirely different wishes or plans than I, that disturbs our equilibrium. I want to scoot out of the house quickly while she wants to continue rearranging her Barbies. She is hungry at just the moment I need to take a phone call. When this anger comes within me, it almost always reaches the heights of wanting her to just go away, to leave me alone, to disappear. It may have nothing to do with her; it may be because I am just plain dog-tired and can't listen to one more demand or question or whine. Sometimes my need to be separate from her comes at the very moment that she wants most to be close to me. It may be when she is her most sweet and lovable self, but I want nothing more than to experience my own body and mind as belonging again to me, as they were before she came along.

The anger is always suffused with guilt. We are both guilty in our negative feelings toward one another because we know (I, consciously, and Molly, not yet consciously) that the severing of our infant/mother emotional ties can feel, to the other, both disconcerting as well as painful.

None of this should surprise me. As a psychoanalyst it has not, but as Molly's mother, it always has the power to spin me around. As a psychoanalyst, I would have expected it, even predicted it. In working with patients, it becomes clear that the relatedness of the feelings of love and aggression is deep. But as a mother, the love supersedes all other feelings; and it is always the other feelings—the negative ones—that creep up on me. They're not there; and then suddenly, they are—loudly and explosively.

The other mother

Adoption—the acquisition of another mother—gives us one of the most powerful lessons in the failure of the mother to be omnipotent. The biological mother who gives up her child says, in effect: "I cannot be your mother." Many women give up their babies because they feel they lack the support and resources to care for the child. Some respond to religious or cultural objections to having a child out of wedlock. In each of these cases, the mother is faced with her own powerlessness to be an adequate mother.

I see a possible future of Molly's in the work I am doing with Marnie. Marnie's present may represent Molly's future. I know that, at some point, Molly will have to confront her biological mother's decision to have given her up. I can't know what that will mean to Molly. But I fear the process; I fear that no matter how embraced she has felt by her new family, there will be, still, a residual wound, the distress of two traumatic separations in the first few days of her life: separation from the warm enclosure of her bio-mom's womb that she shares with all newborns, and, as well, the separation from the actual person of her first mother. I fear that one of the selves that Molly will have a life-long struggle with, as Marnie has had, is the self that felt abandoned.

The wound of aloneness

Marnie still battles in her therapy sessions with me, feeling her aloneness, her isolation and her essential strangeness to the rest of humanity including to me. Now that her mother is dead, she has returned to her stance of silence. She feels she and her mother were never able to get it right, and the same feeling of hopelessness about our relationship envelopes her. She struggles, once again, to talk to me, feeling that words themselves, communication meant to be heard by another, only make her feel more alone, more empty. She wonders whether I care enough even to listen.

The words the analyst gives to the patient are like medicine in that the dosage has to be correct: too many words are over-stimulating, and too few are under-stimulating. I noticed with another of my patients that every time I spoke, she would fall into a psychotic state. She would become confused and disorganised. I stopped talking, and we proceeded along nicely for five years. She announced she had decided to leave, and told me how grateful she was for how much help I had given her. I was curious that she perceived me as helpful since I had barely said a word in all five years. She explained that she really appreciated my *not talking*—which gave her a chance to work things out on her own. She then told me that she had seen another therapist before me, and that that therapist kept trying to explain to her what was wrong, and that she resented the intrusion.

So, with Marnie I follow the directions for contact that she asks for. She won't/can't talk, so I will/do. I talk about anything: I tell her about my day; I tell her about world events; I read stories to her. I do what any good mother does with her infant; I teach her to talk by talking to her.

Then Marnie finds a new way to talk. She starts writing me letters between sessions. Although she is barely able to get herself to utter a meaningful word when she is with me, between sessions I get long, heartfelt, anguished letters detailing as rich an internal life as any I have ever encountered. Though she may be mute on the outside, her letters show her to be a seething cauldron of feelings and conflicts on the inside:

> *Dear Jane,*
> *I called you on the way home from my last session but you were already with another patient. I was thinking that if you handed me a gun I would have shot myself, and then I tried to figure out why I hated myself enough to even think of such a thing. Before the session I was sad. During the session I was on the verge of tears. I didn't know why I was feeling this way. Now I feel powerless, like a freak of some kind. I can't make myself do what I really want to do. I want to be with you and to let you see me. But I think it is impossible. I try to think of what to say, I try to give you the best of myself but there is nothing worth telling you, and somehow I reduce myself*

> *to nothing, and that's what you get. I am trying to take*
> *care of myself. I am pushing myself to be with other people*
> *to give them a chance to know me, even when I feel like*
> *crawling under a rock. I thought things would be better*
> *between you and me by now. I hate myself.*

Marnie's letter reveals that she is living in the underground of her psyche, the land of self-hate. It is her self-hatred that is paralysing and silencing her.

With her history of early abandonment, and her feelings of not being wanted by either her biological or her adoptive mother, Marnie's primary conflict, a lifelong vulnerability, has been around the issue of separation. Her wound of aloneness has been with her for as long as she has memory. With this emotional lesion, Marnie has lived every day of her life feeling that she was not lovable enough to be loved, not lovable enough even to be kept. Separation has been, for her, both a terrible fear as well as an unremitting desire. It has been her hope for rescue and salvation as well as her most painful curse. It has been what she has run from, but it has been what she has embraced.

So much trouble

Marnie has struggled against her impulses to stay separate from me through silence or through leaving. She has wrestled, for all these years, to talk and to stay. She has fought me and resisted me. She has left me for stretches of time. And I have struggled just as mightily as she against my own induced impulses to throw her away, cast her out, as was done to her originally. I have had, on occasion, the same feelings that I believe both of her mothers must have had toward her—that she was too much trouble, that she made my life too difficult, that it was better to just expel her and be rid of the problem. I have struggled to not act out these impulses, but rather to keep her, using my words to persuade her, assist her, even coerce her to continue this process of self-exploration that we have embarked upon.

Marnie's lifelong open wound around the issue of separation means that the very slightest intimation that I want to leave her devastates her. She has imbued me with the power of a carnivorous, omnipotent mother; I have the power to destroy her, to take away any vestige of hope that she may have. With this as her emotional home base, the mere process of ending the session is a trapeze act. I know that if she senses that I want her to leave, or that I am relieved that the session is over, or that I am in a hurry to get on with the rest of my life, even to see my next patient—I know if she feels these feelings coming from me, she will never come back. I cannot leave for vacation, I cannot innocently change an appointment, I cannot let her pass in the hall the patient before her or after her, I cannot have any distraction from her when I am with her (such as the phone ringing or my becoming aware of traffic noise outside the office)—none of these things can happen without her sinking into her regression, falling down into that psychic space where she once again feels unwanted, cast out, lost. This is the power over her that she has granted me.

Her response, always, is to leave. The pain of her feeling unwanted is so deep that it is intolerable to her. She leaves frequently and she leaves for long stretches of time. There are a host of stimuli that cause her to leave the analysis. She leaves when she feels better and she leaves when she feels worse. When she cannot bear for one more moment the idea that she is "sick" for putting so much into our relationship, she leaves. When she feels grateful for my attentions and care, she leaves. There may be no stimuli other than the demonic images within her mind of her own revulsion that impels her to leave. She tells me that I will be a free woman without her, as though she has chained me, forced me against my will to tolerate her presence. Her imagination refuses to conjure up any reason at all for why I would want to be with her, and she concludes that I have to be doing it only for the money.

But she always comes back. I always take her back. More often than not, I pull her back—I chase her down, make her come back. We follow this pattern of leaving and coming back, struggling to find a voice, for years. I watch her give birth to two more children, and embrace these roles with real joy and satisfaction. Her life outside of the analysis has become rich and full. She has matured into an independent, productive woman, wife, and mother. Yet, inside the analysis, she stays regressed to the place of her open wound. As she says, "I save the sick part of me for you."

Tricking me into rejecting her

Most patients in analysis become interested in their own personal history. Often, once the analysis has begun, previously lost memories will emerge. Dreams will become more vivid. The psychological tone of the person is both widened and deepened. It is as though one's emotional life moves from black and white to technicolour.

It is Marnie's search for her early history that begins to absorb her in her analysis. In exploring her past, Marnie reaches a point where she comes to believe that finding her biological mother will fill her emptiness, will satisfy the perpetual longing for union that has taken residence in her psyche. We explore this idea. We discuss every possibility—that her mother is dead, that her mother is a prostitute high on crack/cocaine, that her mother is fat, ugly, or disgusting, that her mother rejects her once again. Marnie is like a pit-bull once she has got hold of this idea of re-finding this mother. It's all she can think about.

She has become brilliant at the endeavour of archaeological soul-searching. At times, she is a model patient, exploring, inquiring, interested. For moments, sometimes for weeks on end, she is actually able to forego her obsession about her long-lost mother and concentrate on the relationship that is alive, the one with me. It takes me a while to catch on, but I eventually realise that many of her questions are manipulative tricks (albeit unconscious) to get me to reawaken in her the same feelings that she has had in relation to her biological mother. It's not enough that I end the sessions, not enough that I leave her to go on vacations—not enough that my "rejections" of her are incidental to our analysis, manifestations of my life independent of her. She wants me to actually— deliberately and consciously—reject her. She wants (in that silly sense of the word "wants" that psychoanalysts use, which actually doesn't mean "want" at all, but rather suggests the opposite—not wanting, but not being able to do, or think, or feel otherwise) to re-experience the same pain of disregard and indifference with me that she felt from her mother. This is the brilliance. This is what every analyst waits for, prays for: the patient brings into the analysis, and, indeed, into the analytic relationship itself, the core conflict—the issue that has plagued them, the concern that cannot be shaken. Without that re-experience, without Marnie going through the same pain now with me that she had initially experienced with that first (or second) mother, there is no hope for resolution, no hope for freedom from her pain.

She spies my cleaning man. He is young and handsome. She asks, tentatively and fearfully, if he is my son. At first I am offended. I do not consider myself old enough to have a son his age (roughly her age, as well). Then I wonder if she wants him to be my son. I ask. She roundly denies that her fear is an unconscious wish or that her question has any unconscious meaning. She does not admit the truth that I suspect—that she "wants" him to be my son because she "wants" to feel (can't help herself from feeling) envy/pain/rejection that I have a child who is not she.

Yet she understands that the battle she is fighting is the struggle to re-find her lost self, and she knows that this struggle is entirely related to her early mothering experience. She understands, too, that she has transferred onto me all of her conflicts about this early mother(s). She writes:

> I am trying to grow, trying to become the person I was meant to be, whoever that is, but I don't have the right tools. I had two mothers and neither one could love me. It's like I have a hole in my heart and in my soul and nothing can fix it. I don't want to let it defeat me, but somehow it does. I feel I am fighting a losing battle. I need someone who is always on my side, someone to turn to for comfort and support. I am trying my best to keep you separate from the other women who have hurt me so deeply—it's easier to just mistrust all women. In so many ways, I am an orphan and think it would be more truthful if everyone behaved that way. If I could just say that my life began when I met Charles (her husband), there would be no confusion.

This growing process, returning to the original pain that felt so devastating to Marnie, and the growing up that ensues, takes her and me longer than either of us could have envisioned. Slowly, cautiously, she begins to allow herself some trust:

> After our last session, when you blindsided me with that question about my biological mother, I didn't want (for the first time ever) to vow to never speak to you again.

I think maybe things are finally beginning to change for us. I wanted to understand what was happening and I wanted to reach that understanding with you. Thank you.

Marnie assures me that, with me, she is ready to confront her past, to find this first mother who abandoned her. She has decided that whatever the truth, it will be better than the perpetual wonder, the endless longing to know. She embarks on her search. And, indeed, she finds her long-lost biological mother.

Hope but not confidence

I have confidence that Molly, like Marnie, will come to the point of maturity when she will have a multi-layered processing of the meaning of her adoption. I believe that Molly will come to know that there were good and rational reasons why her bio-mom gave her up for adoption. I have no doubt that she will even come to feel that her coming home to me served her better in the end than staying with her bio-mom would have. But, these will be rational thoughts, and they will not eliminate the existence within her unconscious of a self that was suddenly no longer hearing, feeling and sensing the familiar environment that was her first nine-month home within the womb. I think that many adopted children live with a life-long scar of fear of loss as a result of their first experience in the world, their loss of all that is familiar.

I have hope that Marnie, too, will come to a point of resolution—that she will find a place in her psyche that is strong and calm and not tortured by her past loss, her long-ago abandonment. I have hope, but not confidence.

16

Dreams of Flight (and other desires of the soul)

With Molly now, as she grows, every day I see remnants of her original self—the baby-soul-self that will serve as the foundation for all that will come next in her; and the self that she will want to periodically return to as she moves into farther and farther separation from that self. And, ironically, the farther she moves from her original soul-self, the more she will become interested in the exploration of that original self, even as the new selves are all cropping up, vying for existence.

Voyaging through elemental homes

The process of self-discovery points us in all directions: the present, which we only sometimes embody while having both feet solidly planted in it; the future which we are hurtling toward; and the distant past, backwards in time, when we still embodied the wholeness that is the purview of infants and which often feels more real, more present, than the present itself. Interest in our past allows us to develop a map for the journey back to the period of development when we first began our progression away from the unified self of infancy, and into the various selves that are the natural consequence of maturation—selves that we may have disclaimed, abandoned out of shame perhaps, or discarded as useless.

Practically every ancient and medieval culture—from 5,000-year-old yogic science to the late Renaissance medicine practiced by the physician Paracelsus—has defined balance through the proportionate composition of the elements: earth, water, fire, and air (also called "ether"). Within these cultures, the elements have symbolic connotation: earth, the ground upon which we walk, represents the foundational energy of Mother; water, in its fluidity without boundaries, represents the Unconscious, deep, dark and mysterious; fire, spewing out from our Sun, self-generating energy, represents our largest home, the Cosmos; and air, diffuse and invisible, represents the energy of Life itself.

Perhaps one of the missions of the soul, and the body, too, in the pilgrimage through time, is to inhabit and bring into harmony these elements that comprise the universe. As children we voyage through these elemental homes. An infant's first environment is a watery, wet solution, the embryonic fluid that surrounds it. Here, then, within the womb, Baby-to-be has its first swimming lesson, its first, and last, experience of breathing underwater. Many of us find ourselves, as was my own family, drawn to the water element instinctively, perhaps because of its being the first experience of the sensate being in the womb.

Molly has learned to love the water as all of us in her new family did at the same age. It was the first experience I gave her when she came home with me to our New Jersey home. My house is on a lake (replicating my experience of living near the original lake of my childhood—Lake Pontchartrain). It was early June, and the water was comfortably warm enough to swim. Like a baptism, the first experience Molly and I shared, upon our arrival at her new home, was her first out-of-the-womb swimming lesson. We joyfully paddled around, as my mother and I had done so many years ago.

Normal developmental progression leads children to continue their journey through the elements: they come to know earth through the solidarity of the ground that they lie and crawl on, and then, as toddlers and beyond, walk on. If the earth element is not a sufficient part of the infant's experience, the infant suffers long-lasting damage. We know this from studying certain primitive cultures. In the Amazon jungle, in one locale, the environment was so threatening that the children were not permitted on the ground until they could run; crawling was by-passed as a developmental step. Because crawling was interfered with, these children became, as clinician of early childhood disturbances, Bob Doman, has termed it, "neurologically inefficient." Peoples from these cultures acquire deficient verbal skills, poor conceptual skills, and no written language.

Infants feel the energy of fire every time they nuzzle against their mother's breast, and the warmth of her body radiates over to Baby, warming Baby too. Unlike the other elements, fire cannot exist with the companion elements of earth (wood to instigate the flame) and air (to feed the flame). Thus, fire is seen as the element of relationship: Mother to child.

Sky Walking

But now, it is the pure air element that has Molly fascinated: air—the medium of travel for butterflies and for souls; the medium through which we learn to move gracefully and effortlessly; the element of transcendence.

Molly first flew when she was only a few days old: her flight to me, her true Mother, her true home. After she came home to Gregg and me, we took her frequently to Puerto

Rico. She spent her first six years (until she was in school five days a week) travelling between our farm in Puerto Rico and our home in New Jersey. Artificial flight has become a means of movement that Molly knows as well as she knows the water element.

The sound of aeroplanes flying overhead is one of the first outside sounds Molly recognises. She looks up at the sky and watches the motion of the plane as it glides through the clouds, and I know that she wants to glide through the clouds too, to have a winged existence. Molly will fly when we jump on the trampoline together and I will throw her up into the air and for just that instant before I catch her, she will be airborne. She will fly when I lift her and propel her as though she were an aeroplane or a bird or SuperGirl. She will fly when I lie down on my back and raise my feet in the air with her on them, spreading out her arms and legs as though she were a flying angel. And when Gregg and I walk with her, he holds one hand, I hold the other, and we pull her up into the air so she swings between us as we all sing together: "Flying Molly." Molly wants to be like Peter Pan and Wendy and Tinker Bell and learn to fly from the sheer power of wishing. She wants to skywalk. I do think that these joys of flying are not merely physical for Molly. I believe that there is a part of her soul that is free and not bound to the earth. This is a connection to the soul that all children her age share.

On one of our trips to Puerto Rico, we pass through the old (now defunct) TWA terminal at Kennedy Airport. Molly spies it first: she points her small finger upward, and I follow the line of her direction. It is a large hanging sculpture, gold and gorgeous and suspended high up, travelling, seemingly, toward the high vaulted ceiling of the building. It looks, at first glance, like an archangel flying to the heavens. But it is, in fact, a mere mortal. It is an artist's creation of Leonardo da

Vinci with his winged machinery attached to his arms—the flying man—mortal man, not eternal angel, striving to reach the heavens. Molly (and all other young children) still knows that it is possible to fly, unimpeded, without restraint.

Perhaps Molly's and my misperception in mistaking a man for an angel is just the point: it is those who are newly born—and often, too, those who are imminently dying—who remain closest to their souls, closest to the place from which we all come and the place to which we all return. Our children are the best teachers we have of what is possible for the human psyche: absolute, unambiguous and unequivocal freedom.

The unconscious is our inner speech

When Freud began his study of the human psyche over a hundred years ago, he was expanding on a long history of words as healers. The Greeks recognised the immense healing power of words. Revered even more than the physician, who could heal the body, was the person who could bring "cheering speech" to the soul. The Judeo-Christian culture tells us that first there was light, but after that, the whole of the rest of the world was created through God's speech: "In the beginning was the Word." Words are divine; words give birth to life. Freud was also drawing on the ancient tradition of storytelling. People had been singing, telling, and acting out stories for thousands of years. For much of man's history, the vast majority of people couldn't read. Folk tales, ballads and theatre were a primary means of addressing the fears, frustrations, and horrors of life. Perhaps we could even say that the minstrels and actors were the world's first "therapists."

Freud was interested in the unspoken word even before he began his investigations into the unconscious and formulated his theories of psychoanalysis. His first interest was in aphasia, a breakdown in the accessibility of words because of damage to the brain. When he later utilised Carl Jung's method of free association, he discovered another kind of unspoken word. He found that if we silence the normal operations of our everyday conversational speech, when we temporarily cast aside reason and logic and our almost instinctual inclination to judge our thoughts and feelings, another language presents itself to us. This is the language of the unconscious. The unconscious is our inner speech. And this inner speech is most often expressed wordlessly and even noiselessly: "*Pianissimo*" as early psychoanalyst Theodor Reik referred to it.

When the unconscious is accessed, it appears that magic has been performed. The magi of ancient Persia were skilled in the art of enchantment. The individual who is skilled in the ways of the unconscious knows, like the wise magi of olden days, how to cast a spell. Modern-day magicians—psychoanalysts/psychotherapists/hypnotists (and all other professions that are knowledgeable in the operations of the unconscious—e.g., the Mad Men of Madison Avenue advertising, a profession that was established in the 1920s by Freud's nephew, Edward Bernays; medical researchers using the placebo effect; interior designers who chose colours to influence moods)—have the ability to create mysterious and baffling effects. This is, of course, because those in these professions are skilled artisans who know how to work with and read what lies behind conscious awareness and deliberate intention. In the world of the psyche, all magic derives from the unknown arena of the unconscious—that which we can't see, hear, taste, smell, or touch.

Things spew forth from the unconscious unpredictably. Freud referred to dreams, jokes, and "slips"—words unwittingly substituted for others, or behaviours that slip out, without conscious awareness,—unconscious manifestations that arise out of the deepest core of our being.

Plunging into the memory stream of time

In the process of re-visiting the past, it doesn't matter what the patient talks about. Patients can spend their whole time talking about their mother or they can never mention her. I have an eighty-year-old patient who still talks nonstop about her mother, a mother who has been dead for fifty years; the subject of her mother is the only thing my patient cares to talk about. Patients can talk about the first six months of their lives—which they have no conscious memory of—or their anticipation of the next six months—which may be filling them with a lurking dreariness. One of my patients refused to talk about her past or her family at all. She said that her parents were old and fragile. She didn't want to uncover any unresolved angers for fear of unwittingly communicating these feelings to them, and thus damaging them, hastening their deaths. It doesn't matter what the patient talks about because in the unconscious, there is no time: past, present, and future all coexist. We dip into this stream of time sometimes without even knowing where we are, which section of time we are stepping into. We live in the present as though it is the past. Or, we are convinced that we are seers, like the ancient magi, and can predict our future. We live with anticipatory anxiety in the present as though the present were, already, the dreaded future.

Unconscious memory determines, to a larger extent than most of us are aware, who we are, how we behave, what our fears are, what we avoid and what we are drawn to. I had a psychoanalytic teacher who told me that her first attraction to the man who became her husband was the way he held a pencil. She said it took years for her to uncover the memory of her father holding his pencil in the same position.

In analysis, we learn how to capture the energy of the unconscious, and to transform it into a force for healing. Analysts cast their spell over the patient through the primary assumption that the unconscious is all-knowing and all-powerful. The unconscious is like the sorceress who has magical powers, and can use them for good or for evil. In stories of magic, the hero, who is usually at the beginning of the story unwise and powerless, must learn to absorb the powers of the sorceress. Similarly, the patient can be, at the beginning of an analysis, quite unwise and powerless. During the analysis, the analyst explores how the patient has created a psychic universe, and then confers onto the patient the power of being its master.

Scientists are only at an early stage of developing a science of the mind, enabling us to be able to tap into the innate power of our mental capacities. Researchers and clinicians have techniques that can improve memory and enhance creativity. But it is clear that in waking consciousness, we use only a fraction of our cognitive brain capability. Dreams, and other states of consciousness, sometimes lead us into the untapped reserves. I remember once dreaming a symphony; I composed an entire symphony while asleep (though in a life-time of playing the piano, in waking life I have only composed a small and uninspired melodic ditty). My genius symphony was completely gone the moment I opened my eyes. I have dreamed *haute couture* fashion designs (though I have never spent more than eighty-nine dollars on a dress) and lyrical poems (I hate even reading poetry in waking consciousness, much less creating it).

Some famous people have had better luck than I in remembering the gifts from their unconscious and, as a result, have created great and enduring works of art. William Blake reported on how he "wrote" his poem *Milton,* suggesting that he (the "he" that he identified with as being) did not write it at all: "I have written this poem from immediate dictation twelve or sometimes twenty lines at a time without premeditation and even against my will." Goethe, similarly, claimed to have written some of his work with no input from his conscious thought, bringing to mind the woo-woo (and often discredited) processes of automatic writing or the Ouija board, wherein one holds the pen and it moves on its own, creating letters, words and sentences. Paul McCartney dreamed the melody of his song *Yesterday*. Einstein said that his entire career was an extended meditation on a dream he had had as a teenager. He dreamed that he was riding a sledge down a steep, snowy slope, picking up speed, approaching the speed of light. Then all the colours blended into one. Thus began Einstein's dynamic, life-long preoccupation with what happens at the speed of light.

The science of the soul

Psychoanalysis is different from all other forms of psychotherapy. Most treatments of the psyche support the *ego* (the self that we live from, the self we experience as "me"). Psychoanalysis *expands* the ego. Support builds upward; expansion goes outward, which then allows steadier building upward. You get more support if you build a ten-storey building that has a ground floor support area of 10,000 square feet than a twenty-storey building that has only 5000 square feet supporting it. You've got the same square footage in both buildings, but a strong wind might topple the taller building. So too with the ego. It is supported by the drives, impulses, feelings and desires—by all the stuff that we're always trying to squash down, the stuff that we generally think of as "crazy" or irrational. Unless we give freedom of flight to all the materials constituting the foundational support, the ego built on top will be weak and fragile.

The unconscious not only connects us to deep regions within our mind, but it also connects us to our soul. Freud had deep respect not only for storytelling, but for the spiritual notion of "soul" as well. Freud made no secret of his disdain for religion and religious doctrine, interpreting them as unnecessary and immature crutches that men sometimes need, and comparing religion to neurosis, psychosis, and infantilism: the "universal obsessional neurosis of humanity." Nevertheless Freud did not relinquish his self-identification as a spiritual Jew that led him to conceptualise psychoanalysis as a treatment for the soul. As David Bakan argues in *Sigmund Freud and the Jewish Mystical Tradition*, there is ample evidence that Freud did maintain a deep sense of spirituality related to the precepts of Jewish mysticism, and it is probable that his sense of spirituality as a Jew led him to conceptualise psychoanalysis as a treatment for the soul. In outlining his vision for the future of psychoanalysis, Freud said: "I want to entrust (psychoanalysis) to a profession that doesn't yet exist, a profession of secular ministers of souls . . ." And later, he said: "Psychoanalysis is a part of psychology which is dedicated to the science of the soul," and he continued by stating that his life's work had been devoted to understanding as fully as possible "the world of man's soul."

Freud's conceptualisation of his discipline as soul-work is evidenced by his choice of the very term of the endeavour: "*psychoanalyse.*" When he decided on this rather complicated word to describe his new technique, he thought carefully about the meaning of the term, the hidden meanings as well as the overt ones, for his science was a study of hidden meanings. Freud had a dichotomy in mind when he combined the two Greek root words *psyche* and *analysis*. He knew that the words contrasted strongly with one another. *Analysis* connotes reason and logic. It suggests a kind of mindfulness, a scientific taking-apart in order to see and understand component parts. The definition of the word *psyche* from the original ancient Greek, on the other hand, is "soul." It suggests just the opposite:

it refers to a kind of etherealness, a softer essence with the connotations of beauty, fragility, and insubstantiality that connect with the soul. There is the suggestion inherent in the word *psyche* that great respect, care, and consideration should be rendered in this technique.

Psychoanalysis, then, is a fusion: it is a study and an experience. It is both eminently rational/scientific and completely irrational/spiritual. It is heavy, weighty, and grounded, as well as light, airy, and spacious.

Also, there was an earlier meaning to the root word *psyche*, and this earlier meaning gave Freud's new science added depth. As well as meaning soul, *psyche* also meant "butterfly." The butterfly is an archetypical symbol of the transcendent soul, transformation and mystical rebirth. The soul is a liberated being. It flies. It is not bound by earthly restraints, not by the weight of the body or by gravity. Psychoanalysis, the understanding of the soul, leads us to the freedom of flight.

Yet butterflies, as every school-age child knows, begin as ugly, wormy larvae, and then transmute into hairy caterpillars. One would never predict that a thing of such beauty could emerge from a thing of such ugliness. When Freud chose the term "psychoanalysis," he was sensitive not only to the meanings of the root word *psyche* as "soul" and as "butterfly," but he would have had in mind, as well, the transformative connotation of the word. Beyond infancy, after the point at which we can begin to disconnect from our selves, soul flight is still possible. But in order to be released from our own weightiness, in order to be free as a butterfly, to see the world from an overview, we must first make the journey inward, to our own underground. We must pupate.

How psyche became mind

Most contemporary analysts (and patients) are not aware that psychoanalysis was a treatment that was originally designed to return people to their souls. When Freud's work was imported into this country and taken hold of by the medical profession, the translation of his words changed the meanings not only of his words, but of his thoughts as well. Wherever Freud used the word *psyche*, referring to soul, it was translated into "mind." (The German word for mind is "*geistig*" and bears no relation to the word "*psyche*" that Freud chose.) Bettelheim concludes in *Freud and Man's Soul* that because of the decisions made in relation to the translation of specific words and concepts from German to English, rather than instilling a deep feeling for what is most human in all of us, the translations attempt to lure the reader into developing a strictly scientific attitude toward men and his actions. What Freud had clearly intended as a spiritual quest became, instead, a medical methodology, and psychoanalysis lost its connection to its original concept of searching for one's soul.

One of my first psychoanalytic teachers confessed that the main change in her since her successful (she claims) analysis was that she took up knitting. If you have a theory that addresses the "mind," then becoming able to take up knitting doesn't sound very impressive. But if the theory posits that it is the soul, too, that is touched in this process, then freeing your fingers to knit, or to play Chopsticks at a party because the spirit moves you to be silly (as one of my patients, a concert pianist who had spent his life being serious, reported that he had done recently), or freeing your voice to begin singing lessons after a lifetime of believing that you were incapable of carrying a tune (as I did at the age of forty-five)—these are all sea changes. These are mind-changes, but they are brain-changes as well. We now have documented evidence, from research conducted by Jeffrey Schwartz wherein he took PET scans of brains of individuals both before and after psychotherapy, that the "talking cure" changes and normalises brain activity. When you make these changes on the levels of the mind, the psyche, and the brain, you have created a different world that the soul is able to inhabit. The soul longs for that kind of freedom. The soul can thrive only in that kind of freedom.

The soul's fondest desire

It is easy to understand how the early twentieth century physicians made the mistake of inserting "mind" instead of "soul" as the object of study in psychoanalysis. In our modern world, most of us have been raised to value mind, to diminish the importance of feelings, and to doubt altogether the concept of a soul that is organic and living within us. As a result of these dismissive views of the various aspects of self, mind and body are split off from soul and the self becomes divided within itself. The soul becomes separated from the rest of the self.

When I observe in my work that my patients' souls are out of sync, or are separated from the rest of who they are, I think of a visual metaphor, a series of concentric circles of ever increasing sizes, each lying on top of the others, each representing a different aspect of self-being. These various selves normally develop with conflicts and contradictions, yet with an essential integration, into the complex personalities that give definition to a whole self. However, when my patients experience a kind of psychic disequilibrium, the concentric circles of their various selves no longer lie on top of one another. Rather, they have become askew. The innermost concentric circle, representing the innermost self, or the soul, no longer supports all the rest of the various selves that should have developed outward from that centre. There is no convergence of meaning between the centre and the rest.

Revisiting our emotional past, as we do in psychoanalysis and other forms of psychotherapy, gets us to approximate more closely the early state of soul-living, the baby-soul that all infants personify. Our strides as adults to return to our baby-soul state are incremental, sometimes infinitesimally small. But it helps to know, at least, that that is the goal. Psychoanalysis, and the exploration of self that it represents, is soul medicine.

As adults we can approximate the freedom of children. In our dreams, and in the waking equivalent of dreams, fantasy, we are most free. In our dreams and our fantasies we can feel anything at all—love, hate, rage, compassion, hurt, revenge, empathy. But there is no danger from the darker impulses. In our dream and fantasy lives, we can burn houses and hurl rocks at our enemies and balloons and stuffed teddy bears at our friends. In the dream-world, mothers who feel imprisoned by their commitments to their children can break free and live, for a little while, without awareness of the demands of motherhood. We can perform all of these acts in our minds, but no destruction has been wrought. When we are situated in our unconscious, we are not bound by reason, sanity, concern, altruism, rationality, or justification. In our dreams and fantasies, our thoughts and feelings, like our souls, fly.

Freud found that we can free ourselves from the chokehold that the past may exert on us. As we are enabled to face the ways in which we warehouse and store events and emotions of our past, we come to feel freer: unburdened, unleashed. This freedom from the past enables us to live more fully in the present, and this progression propels us into the future. Our soul is then able to remember its original purpose and thus find its wholeness. It remembers that its fondest desire is to take flight, a skill of which we are all capable in infancy. As we each struggle with the crucial and continuous milestone of separation, and then master our own personal separation issues, we return once again to our original, natural ability to let our psyches be whole and our souls be free. We are unbounded by the earthly, self-imposed restraints of guilt, rage, sorrow, and pain. We are able to lift off into flight, to reach the heavens of our whole and complete selves.

17

The World of Words

As Molly and I proceed with our separation, as Molly begins in earnest her process of individuation into being her own person, we struggle with our desire to return back to the heavenly symbiosis that we have forsaken. Daily, she and I are conflicted by our wish to return to our symbiosis and our opposing need to continue our march toward separation. Frequently, our mutual needs for togetherness and separation are at odds with each another. When she wants to sit in my lap, I need to see a patient. Then, when I am ready to play with her, she is happily ensconced in drawing and doesn't want to be disturbed. Molly grapples mightily with the stunning realisation that she and I are separate and that, in fact, I am not always at her beck and call. She is destined, as we all are, to experience over and over again the painful feeling that there are times when her desires for another person will not be met, that there is not always an instant route to the person she needs, wants, and loves most of all. This is Molly's plight as my child and it is, as well, my plight as her mother: her sometime inaccessibility to me is just as painful to me as my unavailability is to her.

Little rehearsals of separation

I observe Molly's need to be invisible to me, her games of hiding in which she wants me to be aware of where she is without my actually seeing her. Conversely, she asks me to look at her, to admire her, and to just notice her. She dances for me and preens in front of me as though I am her mirror. I witness her little preparations for separation—her "Mom, go away" while she is busily putting all twelve of her dollies to sleep or placing one of them on the potty. These little acts of separation are rehearsals, her planning for the time when she will want to be even more distant, when my interest in her may feel intrusive or overbearing.

Already, I see harbingers of this conflict between us. I observe that, at times, the only way she can separate from me is to say, "Mom, go away," as an order, as though she were a Commandant rather than a young child making a request. Or, when she gives her first impromptu singing recital for my friends Sheila and Sol, she insists that I turn my head and not look. It is as though she is angry that I am there, offended that I exist when she has not called me into existence. When we go to our Music and Movement class, all the other moms are singing and holding their children in delightful togetherness. Because I started Molly early in this class, she is an old-timer at it, and she has outgrown her need for mom/tot togetherness here. She tells me emphatically—even aggressively—that I am not to sing, and then she proceeds to sing and dance with everyone else, having a grand old time, while I watch passively. I do this, I allow myself to become passive because I know that she is moving through an important stage of separation. She is saying to me that at this moment there is not enough space in the universe for us to coexist on equal levels. She can sing and I cannot. In fact, she will sing only if I do not. She needs to tap dance on my heart, and she needs for me to survive the savage trouncing.

Of course, Molly's need to control her universe extends beyond our relationship. It extends to everything that she encounters. We find a ladybug in our kitchen, and she wants to capture it—to give it a home so that she can see it all the time. We play with the ladybug a bit, and then it flies away, Molly chasing after her, yelling "Come back." Then the next day, we are off to stay at our friend's house in Connecticut. Our friend has multiple sclerosis and she has made the downstairs of her house wheelchair-friendly. But she hasn't been able to get upstairs in a year. We carry our bags up to our bedroom on the second floor, and Molly beholds a vision of ecstasy: 200 ladybugs strewn around the floor under the window. The fact that they are all dead—have probably been dead, accumulating and lying there undisturbed, for months—doesn't faze Molly. She gathers them all together, and creates a makeshift home for them—a little shoebox that she finds. She insists even on bringing them in the car, back home the next day. When I ask her why she wants all these dead ladybugs, she tells me that she actually prefers the dead ones to the live ones: "They can't fly away and leave me."

The sole mother trying to sort out the conflict

The fear of being left is the conflict that Molly has caught so ferociously. This is the feeling that my mother and I struggled with most assiduously. My mother passed on her fear of being without me, and now, I think to myself for a moment, it looks like I have passed on the same fear to Molly. But I know better. I know that her fear, as was mine and as was my mother's, is instinctive. It exists in all of us, no matter what our specific emotional histories are.

Molly has started pre-school and, although she is almost frighteningly precocious in her language development and her cognitive skills (she is routinely thought to be a year and a half older than she is), she still struggles mightily in her ability to separate from me. She cries when I try to leave her in pre-school, beseeching me to stay.

Two weeks into the school year, I am one of only two mothers still sitting in the classroom. The other children seem to have separated effortlessly from their mothers. They are happily playing with each other, while Molly's chief concern is identifying how far from her I have moved. I wonder if finding a way to keep objects with her—dead ladybugs or an alive mother—is Molly's way of working through the original abandonment she felt when the familiarity of her first mother's heartbeat, voice, and rhythm of breathing suddenly disappeared from the small universe Molly had known.

I have to fight for my right to stay with Molly in school. Her teacher tells me that I need to leave the classroom. She says this with great insistence, pressuring me to submit to her higher wisdom and greater experience.

The other mother still in the room, like me, wants to stay with her child until she can leave without her child crying. We have become compatriots in this fight against administrative harshness.

Then we observe a sobering event. Harry has been the biggest crybaby in the whole class. He has cried for the entire class period—two and a half hours—every single day. His nanny is upstairs, knowing the whole time that Harry's only desire in life at those moments is to be reunited with his nanny. Yet she explains to us that he must learn to separate, that he *will* learn to separate, and she remains firm in her decision to leave him in the classroom, crying, for as long as it takes. Harry's crying is so unending, his demands for his nanny so unyielding that it is impossible to relate to him, to have sympathy for him. The teachers even have started to ignore his pleas.

Quite suddenly, one day Harry stops crying. He begins to look around him. He learns the names of the other children. He starts playing with them. He actually begins to appear quite happy.

I cannot quite give up my smugness on this issue. I look for signs that, in spite of Harry's newfound happiness, it is an adjustment—that there is a trade-off. I look for signs that there is some underlying sadness or depression—something, anything—that will confirm for me that he never should have been subjected to such unyieldingness. I can't find any signs. He really seems truly content to be at school. It appears to be a perfectly adequate adjustment without negative consequences.

Harry is now more integrated into the class than either Molly or the other child whose mother is still in the classroom. Molly has moments of distraction when the teacher tries particularly hard to engage her. But mostly, Molly is still sullen and withdrawn, terrified that I am going to leave her, always watchful for any movement I may make to clandestinely slip away from her. The other child cries continuously as her mother tries to cooperate with the request of the teacher to leave the room. Finally, after struggling with indecision about whether to leave her child crying or to chuck the school, the other mother decides to chuck the school, thus leaving me alone, the sole mother still trying to sort out this painful conflict.

Every issue I bring up about Molly with my own analyst, including what to do about leaving her in school, leads us to the same road. All roads lead to my inability to separate from Molly, and thus Molly's inability to separate from me. My analyst tells me that in giving her too much symbiosis, I am not aiding her in developing an independent mind. I ballast my argument by referring to native tribes in remote lands who carry their children on their backs at all times—when they're working in the fields, when they're resting, when they're eating. She asks me how many of those native tribes have produced children who are clever, bright, ambitious, and—here is the key, the real point of her inquiry—individuated. She is in favor of individuation. Perhaps she is right. Perhaps I am rearing a child who will grow up to be too dependent and always need someone else to care for her and to respond to her need for rescue by rescuing her instead of imparting to her the confidence that she can do it on her own. Or, perhaps I am right. Perhaps I am giving Molly a sense of security about someone's being there when she feels afraid in new circumstances. Instead of not knowing where she is in this new world to which she has not yet fully acclimated, she will have internalised my comforting presence. Maybe that will enable her to confront all new places in her life—when I am not around so much—with better resiliency than she would have otherwise.

But all this speculation about who Molly will be, who I am forging her to be through my decisions about how to handle our separation, is beside the point. The point is that my analyst falls squarely on the side of individuation as soon as possible and I fall squarely on the side of symbiosis as long as possible. And further, the point is not really about whether I am still in school with her. The point is that I cannot do it any differently than the way I am doing it. My own fears and pains over separation and abandonment have been so intense that I cannot bear to allow this child to experience the same pain.

After three weeks, the school administration and I have gotten to the point of butting heads. They have ordered me to leave the classroom, and to allow Molly to cry. I tell them that if they make me leave, I will take Molly with me. And then, just at the point when it seems that there is no alternative but to pull Molly out of the school, Molly tells me that I can leave. "Mom, you can go home now." I walk home from her school that day in tears, moved and exhilarated beyond words that my daughter and I have accomplished this feat of separation together, she from me, and I from her.

Trying, senselessly, to stop the tide of separation

The relationship between mother and child is an ever-evolving dialogue. It is the basic dialogue of human love, beginning with the unconditional love of their state of oneness and then maturing into separation. The mother of infancy holds in abeyance her own world, the world that is separate from her infant, the world that has yet no relevance to the infant. And then she, too, must aid her child in that long progression from the utter self-involvement of infantile narcissism, to the world outside, to otherness. All later loves are a striving to reconcile the longing for the lost bliss of oneness with our equally intense longing for separateness and individuality.

It is primarily through language that this journey takes place. When we are fused, when there is only symbiotic oneness, only one "us" and no separation in this "us-ness," there is no need for words. At first the language is all coos and goos, the language of pre-words. Words, however, travel from a "me" to a "you." Then the sounds become words and the words become attached to meaning. The mother gives voice to her own thoughts and feelings in order to enable her child to understand and give complex expression to the his or her own thoughts and feelings.

It is because of language, more than any other cognitive or emotional development, that I begin to see how frighteningly (and wonderfully) separate Molly is becoming from me. As she begins to develop a life of her own, away from me at times, she has a host of experiences that I am not privy to. Now that she is safely ensconced in pre-school, she comes home using words that I have not taught her, exhibiting mannerisms that are not mere imitations of me.

Molly has entered a new stage in her language development. She has developed the ability to understand symbols: words standing for something else. A word is bounced to Molly from someone else much in the same way that a ball was bounced to her when she was younger. But, while previously the meaning of the word was given to her, now, having entered this phase, she can herself create meaning.

This new world brings children to places previously unimagined, places that cannot be reached without words as the springboard. When words can be strung together, the child can go further back in the past, further ahead in the future, and to new places with another person accompanying him through dialogue and conversation. This capacity for dialogue provides the child with a method of togetherness that rivals even the intensity of the early symbiosis.

And, here in this new world of words as symbols, Molly suddenly seems different from the child I used to know, so separate from me. I wonder who this child is. I try to keep my astonishment to myself but, in the end, I cannot. It is too much of an overpowering experience for me. I ask her if she is still my Molly (shades of my mother asking me if I would ever grow too old for "lovin'). Even as I ask, I know I shouldn't because the answer is in front of me. She is not still my Molly—not the "my Molly" that I am referring to—not the "my Molly" that belonged to me, the "my Molly" whom I held to my chest when I wanted to be close and put down when I wanted to be separate. This is a different Molly—one who makes the rules about our relationship just as much as I do. This is not Molly who belongs to me any longer. She belongs now more to herself than to me.

Yet, I ask. Molly assures me that she is still my Molly. Well, of course. Molly wouldn't know that she has changed. I am still her Mommy, so to her, of course, she is still my Molly. I ask her to tell me that she is still my Molly in some futile, mystical hope that I can stop this child's growth and that we will stay frozen in this time of togetherness. My wish to stop this tide of separation feels like my trying to hold onto a slippery rubber ball—equally senseless, doomed to frustration and failure.

As I observe Molly's increasing mastery of language, I see that language is, in fact, the sine qua non of separation. It is the without-which-there-is-none of emotional growth. Language is what enables the self to have a solid foundation, and it is what allows us to digest feelings throughout the psyche. The ability to use words as expressions of selfhood integrates body, mind, and soul. The spoken word can bring us together, but it is also what separates us. Words define an "I" and a "you." With language, we give ourselves a rich medley of expression of our various feeling and thought processes. Language both grounds us in our bodies, holding us back by its very limitations, and frees us, as our words take flight in their airbourne journey to the ears of another.

The crossroad of deceit

Language is amazing because it helps us to get more effectively what we want. "No Mommy, not the chocolate cookie, the vanilla one." It enables us to communicate what we feel and think—"Mommy, I hate you," "Mommy, I love you."

I know that what I need to do with Molly to keep her as close to her soul as she was before language, is to help her to use words that are true and honest. Molly's first complete sentence came through sobs as her nanny was carrying her away from me: "I want Mommy." A few months later, she blessed me with her second complete sentence as I was handing her a bottle: "I don't want that." (Hooray for Molly's glorious first articulated "no," it being one of the most defining marks of her individuation.) And, now, as a toddler in pre-school, the rule of "no-ness" still exists for her. The teacher hands her some materials. She walks away. The teacher follows her, asking if she wants to colour. She sits down in the middle of the room, refusing to be budged, and then announces clearly and emphatically: "I will do it if I want, and not do it if I don't want."

Molly has always known what she feels, what she wants, and doesn't want. She operates, still, from desire and from the centre of her being. When she spies a cookie and I won't let her have it, she knows that her rage is from her frustrated desire, and she shows it. At two years old, she is able to whine or complain to tell me what she feels. And then those primitive sounds become sophisticated articulation.

Molly is demonstrating why analysts say character is formed in early childhood. Even young children already have a well-defined sense of self. They have predilections and aversions. They're friendly or shy. Molly's first sentence-creations—a progression from mere imitation and comprehension of single-word meanings—reflect the mature ability to string inner thoughts together. The first two sentences she articulated expressed respectively: desire—the frustration of unsatisfied longing; and then separation—erection of her own psychic boundary through rejection.

Language also allows us to deceive. Once you have language, you can think and feel one thing and say another: language is what gets con-men millions of unfairly extracted dollars; it's what gets married men to seduce unsuspecting women into being their mistresses for years based on false, promised hope; it's what gets adolescents to convince their all-too-willing-to-believe mothers that they're not doing drugs. Language may represent the best of us, the thing that separates us from the animals, but it is also the thing that allows us to be utterly false.

Here, too, in the world of words, as with all other stages of her development, Molly and I exist at a crossroad. Here, too, I have the power to either centre her, or subvert her from her one true path of becoming herself. Depending on how I attempt to influence her, Molly will continue to express her feelings, through her words, or she will begin to hide. I could, for instance, give her the idea that feelings, and the words that express them, are unacceptable. Or, I could give her the idea that there is no use in having desire because she'll never get what she wants. I could give her the idea that she's only a child and her feelings and desires are not important, not worthy of being taken seriously, or that she doesn't really know what she wants. Or that desire is bad because it's not thinking about the other person. There are a thousand other ways that I might subvert her. Then she would start to drift from her soul. She would begin to hide herself from me, and then from herself. Words would become vehicles of deceit rather than of truth. And then, at some future date, she would need to re-learn the truthful use of words that accompanies soul-living, that I, her mother, took away from her.

PART III
MY SELF

18

Who I was Meant to Be

Remembering the past (my mother) gives me a vision of and a desire for the future (my daughter), and, snuggled between the two, I find who I am in the present (my self).

An evolutionary leap into the eternal questions

Adopted children almost invariably wonder about their birth parents. And children who were not adopted often wonder if they were. None of us is immune to these important questions of our true origins, and we grapple with the vexing questions: who am I? who am I meant to be? Like others, I spent time in my early years wondering, as did so many of the heroes of fairy tales, about my true identity: am I a princess or a pauper?

As soon as this question of self-identity emerged many thousands of years ago, simultaneous to our ancestors' brains becoming larger with more sophisticated connections within, humans took an evolutionary leap. We separated ourselves from all other animals that remain incapable of self-reflection. We have been asking, ever since, the eternal questions having to do with our beginnings and endings, and our identities.

We have, endlessly, sought out the meaning of our existence, both collectively as a species, and of our own individual lives.

When I come to know who I am most deeply, I know that, above all other fragments of the self that I call "me," I am a woman. This, of all things about myself, is what I have always felt both most sure about and secure in. My mother gave me a love for the female body—first, hers for its mothering capacity: I remember, as a child, loving my mother's breasts. I am sure that when I was even younger, as an infant (before conscious memory), I must have snuggled against those welcoming, full breasts and allowed myself to feel embraced by them. And later, the experience of my own, individuated body became a source of pleasure for me: initially for the joy of movement, which later became translated into my passion for athletics. Like my mother, I devoted myself to sports at an early age. Then, for its attractiveness to men, and the accompanying ability to experience sexual pleasure. I remember gloriously celebrating the growth of my own breasts when I was thirteen, proudly showing off my new, feminine shape when I got my first bra. When I began menstruating, my mother congratulated me, imparting to me the feeling that I had been selected as a member of a distinguished, elite club: the club of womanhood.

Living, moving, exponentially growing vitality

The bond that I had, still have, with my mother, even though she has been long dead, and now have with my daughter, who personifies living, moving, exponentially growing vitality, transcends all other emotional ties. Being a woman, a daughter, and a mother, being this woman that I am, of and with those two other females, is the largest identity I have. Before I am a person who is loved by a man, before I am a person who gives love to a man, before I am a Jew, a southerner, a liberal

Democrat, a dog-lover, I am a woman. When I wake up every morning, this is the fact that I know with more surety than anything else. My man-of-the-moment may or may not love me, and I may or may not love him—it depends on how one defines love. My Jewishness has always been there, important more as background, though, than religion. I lost my southern accent decades ago when I moved away from New Orleans to go to college, and it only comes back when I am either back home, surrounded by the familiar cadence of the drawl, or when I am in the thralls of deep feeling. I care about politics because liberal democracy addresses the care of the whole populace, including the disadvantaged and disenfranchised, and I believe that democracy is itself an outgrowth of the kind of freedom of mind that my chosen profession of psychoanalysis requires—even demands. But the truth is, other than for Presidential elections, I barely get myself to the voting booths, and, like many Americans, I am more interested and know more about the sexual exploitations of politicians than about their positions on any issues of consequence. I loved my poodle, Oscar, for eighteen years as though he were my beloved one and only child. And there are certainly times when I feel closer to dogs and their innocent, yappy lovingness than I do to other humans. But even with all this closeness, dogs—even men—don't comfort me in my despair. Women do.

Home away from home

My mother chose her analyst specifically because she was a woman and my mother had never felt loved by a woman (and thus sought to have the experience). I chose my analyst specifically because she was a woman and I had had the experience of being loved by a woman (and thus sought to repeat the experience).

The first time I saw my analyst, she told me that she would help me to get married and have a child. At the time, I was so entrenched in my declaration of independence from my mother that, until my analyst made that promise to me, I hadn't even known that I wanted to repeat my mother's life—to get married and have children. I had lived, up until then, with the express purpose of *not* repeating my mother's life. I was thirty, an age when many women already have made the decision to settle into a lifelong relationship—with partners, with children. My mother had already had all three of her children by that age.

Much has been written about the first dream that a new patient brings into analysis. Frequently analysts find that we can look back after a lengthy analysis, and we see that everything that followed was essentially contained in the first dream. It is as though the unconscious were programming itself, readying itself to be revealed (much as the fetus readies itself to be born, perhaps beginning an analysis should be considered to be the third birth). I cooperated with my analyst by having my first analytic dream:

> *I am knocking on the door of my analyst's office. Then I notice that there is a sign on the door announcing THIS DOOR HAS NO HOLE. I am undeterred by the sign and walk in. I am waiting for someone to appear, but instead of a person coming in, a big growling dog walks in. I want to jump onto a piece of furniture to escape this dog, but I see that there is no furniture in the room tall enough for me to get away from him. The dog begins taking the pounce position. I realise that the only way to make sure this dog doesn't get to me is to scream so loudly that its ears begin to point up and forward. At first my scream is a bit timid; and I am more frightened*

*than I have ever been in my life. I scream louder than I
thought possible. I scream so loudly and so deeply that
I come to feel an incredible emotional release. I feel freer
than I have ever felt in my life. The dog cowers over to
the corner and then I see why she has been so aggressive.
She has a litter of seven puppies that she is protecting.
She is a mama bitch. I go over to her and she lets me
pet her and we are friends at last.*

Dream interpretation can be arrived at through the free
association method that defines the psychoanalytic method:
saying what comes to your mind. Some of this may be distant
memories; some may be events from the day; some may be
hoped-for wishes or dreaded anticipations. Understanding
the symbolic nature of the dream language is essential to
understanding the meaning a dream holds to the overall
character of the person as well as to the particular conflict
that is being worked through at that moment in psychological
time. Thus, I begin the process of dream interpretation. I free-
associate—I let my mind wander and follow its course to the
images of the dream.

Since I am at my analyst's front door in the dream, the
dream is giving me a message about my search for emotional
growth. The image of a door with no hole conjures up the idea
that there is no way out: there is no place for a doorknob that
would allow for free access in and out. Also, some doors have
glass portals that let in light. But this door has no glass. Once
this door is closed, there will be no penetration of light. The
note in the dream is warning me that the journey through
my analyst's door is for keeps; there is no turning back. The
insistence that once I'm in, I'm not going to be leaving, feels
oddly reassuring to me rather than frightening, controlling
or suffocating.

The dog image is particularly resonant for me as it returns me back to my earliest memory of childhood: fear. When I was four years old, a large dog started chasing me, and I was terrified of his aggressive nipping at my legs. In my dream, I see that once I am inside, on the other side of that door, I am going to be forced to confront my terror.

The play on the words "hole" and "whole" tells me that my psychic integration into maturity is the concern of the dream. The *double entendre* of the word suggests that my sexual maturation is intimately involved in all other aspects of my growth process. The ferocious dog turns out to be a protective mom: it suggests that the progression of my psychic maturity is related to my sexuality and to motherhood, and that these are both related to the resolution of my fears and anxieties; and finally, the dream tells me that coming to experience my aggression is essential. Sexuality/motherhood/aggression: all tied together.

My defensive, self-protective, and aggressive scream, and the freedom I find from the release it gives me, is the antidote to my terror. I understand that the move into conscious awareness will not come from the outside, but rather through the internal transformation from fear to the emotional freedom of feeling my aggression. And, threading through this process, or perhaps as a result of this process, I will be enabled to embrace my self as a mother.

Time travel

During that first session with my analyst, so many years ago, her promise to me that she was going to help me get married and become a mother punctured through the defensive nature of my wishes for a family—my Tarzan chest-beating stance of independence. I cried when I left that first session, exhilarated at the news of my imminent wedding and the birth of my child.

(I was unperturbed that we didn't yet know the identity of the groom—and further, that there was no prospect in sight.)

From that first session on, long before Molly's arrival, I spent hours trudging weekly to my analyst's nondescript Manhattan brownstone on East 13th Street. I did this in exploration of my history, mentally retracing my steps, returning in psychic time to my past. This process continued all through my training as a psychoanalyst. This time-travel, this retrieval of lost memories, even of lost selves—the stuff of psychoanalysis—has been a daunting task.

One of my patients told me about finding a dead groundhog in her bed at her country home. There was no one in the house and somehow the groundhog had crawled inside. He must have spent some time while in her house looking outside, not quite knowing how he became separated from his home, not knowing how to find his way back. And then, maybe he just gave up his struggle to go back home (or at least this is how I would like to think about it), found a soft place to lie down his anxious, weary bones, and peacefully died. This is how I used to feel: that I was in a world that was away from my real home. And in this home-away-from-home, I would look around, like that groundhog must have done, as though from the inside-out, and I wouldn't know how to find my way back.

I think this is what first pulled me into analysis—my having left home, and not knowing how to find my way back. I would try intermittently. After I moved to New York, I would fantasise about going back home for good—being again in the same town as my mother. I would leave a trail of stones, or bread crumbs, like Hansel and Gretel, showing me the path back. I fell in love with a man in New Orleans during one trip down there, and imagined I would go back home and marry him. That didn't work out. (He didn't want to

marry me—didn't even want to date me after a few months.)
I thought about abandoning New York to share a house with
Cynthia, and raising children together with her. (One week
of vacationing together convinced us we could never live
together: she smokes, I don't; she drinks, I don't; she eats meat,
I don't; she screams when she's angry, I don't.) Ultimately,
I guess the birds ate the breadcrumbs, as in the Hansel and
Gretel fairy tale, and I couldn't find the path back to New
Orleans, back to my one true home.

All the myriad Janes

In psychoanalysis (as well as in fairy tales), the examination
of one's misery—no matter the current nature or cause of
the misery—usually leads back to mother. Before Molly, my
misery was always about men—one failed relationship after
another. But my analysis somehow always led me back to
my mother. Because my mother is my origin, she is my past.
And, because her mothering has helped to shape me as I am,
she is my present. And because her mothering has shaped the
way I myself mother my daughter, she is, in Molly, my future.

For such a long time, home had meant for me the house
I grew up in. This was true even after I had long left that
home and moved to New York. Home, and its ineluctable
entanglement with my relationship with my mother, was
where I returned to in states of pride and the desire for
closeness. But it was also where I retreated for comfort in
states of fear and pain. It was the landscape of my struggle
to find my independence, the establishment of my true self.

I have talked in my analysis about all the time I spent
putting distance between my family and myself, between New
Orleans and myself, and, most of all, between my mother and
myself. In spite of our closeness throughout my childhood
and adolescence, a pivotal event in my early twenties led me

down paths that felt far away from her. For that next decade, I fled from the relationship with my mother, feeling that I could have no independent "I" as long as she and I were living in the same city.

The reason for my interest in my past is that it has been a struggle for me to find my connection to it. This is not because I doubt that I, as I was, ever existed. It's just that I sometimes have trouble finding the connections among all the myriad Janes.

Each Jane feels entirely different. I can't find a connection between the Jane of New Orleans, the pleasant, unassuming Jewish Jane that I was raised to be, and the Jane of New York, the fierce, fiery ecumenical Jane who is going to send Molly to a school that does indeed celebrate Hanukkah (and Christmas), but "most of all celebrates the changing of the seasons." It doesn't feel as though there has been a linear connection, leading from all the past Janes to the Jane of today; rather it seems that new personalities, new lives, have just been plopped down into my body. And this new Jane, this Mother-Jane, has been a long time in coming—longer than it takes for most women. This new Mother-Jane takes some settling into.

Until my mother died, I had spent most of my adult years believing that family life, and my own family of origin—apart from my mother—had little relevance to me. I left New Orleans as soon as I could get out, attempting to leave behind all vestiges of that Jane. My sister, on the other hand, came back immediately after college. My brother never left at all. I always felt there were just too many differences between me and them—they were soft, fluffy southerners and over the years of being away I had become more urban, more northern, more distant from the Jane I was raised to be. Everyone in my family was all fixedly married (even my brother had a pre-legalised gay "marriage"), while I went through men like water being poured down a drain. My sister was busily propagating, and my brother was busily paying orthodontic bills for the nephews of his partner. First cousin Carol, my inseparable best-friend growing up, too, was married; and even her younger sister Phyllis (how did baby-Phyllis grow into this role before I did?) had embraced the role of wife and mother. I, on the other hand, was busy trying to kill off the fruits of my fertility through an illegal abortion. I simply felt too exotic, too different, too wild—most of all, too filled with emotion for my hometown, my sister, my nieces, my aunts and uncles, and for my cousins who populated the town. I felt, in fact, too much like my mother who, too, never quite felt accepted, never homogenous in the culture in which she found herself.

After I moved to New York, going home became a disquieting experience for me. No matter how long I had been away, no matter how firmly entrenched I felt in the new Jane of today, when I would return home, suddenly and unexpectedly old Janes would start vying for which Jane was going to present herself. I would become quiet and shy (as I had been in the not-Bashful days) instead of opinionated and verbose (as I have become). I would favour staying close to home instead of going out for new adventures. New York, and my growth that had accompanied my years of living there, would feel as though they had never existed. It was the same conflict I had acted out years earlier when I hid in my mother's closet: wanting to be found by my mother (seen for who I am); wanting to hide and be invisible, not found (unseen, maybe even uncreated).

And now that my mother is dead, there is the "Jane" she never knew. I have read that the human body changes all of its cells every seven years. We are all, in effect, reconstituted soup. I see, from observing the various permutations of my life and the fluctuating changes of my emotional construction, that the psyche, too, is continuously reborn. Since my mother's death, my body cells have had two full revolutions. I can't even imagine how many rebirths my psyche has undergone. Would my mother even recognise the person I am today, the self I have become, were she to come down from her other-worldly perch?

Sometimes it is in my dreams that I remember best who I was when she was still alive. I wake up filled with long-lost feelings. For years, decades even, I lived almost entirely from my feelings. I loved voraciously and joyfully, as well as despairingly and dejectedly. I attached myself with grand ardour to girlfriends and to boyfriends. I still dream about the protagonists of my past life. They walk through my dream-world as though in a procession. And in these nostalgic dreams about love-found and love-lost, I reconnect to the immensely feeling-Jane that I was.

I was carefree back then. I broke rules; I challenged authority; I moved with ease and impulsively from activities, from relationships, even from cities. Now, I live much more from my very ordered mind. I live from decisions, schedules, and accomplishments. My life is utterly structured. Even my daily jog is by the clock, a half-hour—no matter (like the postman) rain, sun, snow, or sleet. The other day, I accidentally left my watch at home when I went running. At first I felt disoriented, not knowing how long I had been out. The next day I ventured out decisively without the watch. This was a great adventure for me in my now fully organised life. How freeing that was, that small act of defiance against myself, against whom I had become, returning back to the girl I had been.

My mother knew a different person from the woman I have become. My mother knew a sweet, southern-bred girl who never dared to disagree. She never knew the hard-edged

New Yorker I now am, the woman who can stand up, fearlessly, to aggression, irony, and sarcasm. She knew a daughter, but she never knew her daughter as a mother. As a mother, I live now by the precepts of being a mother: I make rules now instead of breaking them.

My own emotional work for all these past years has been to fuse all these separate Janes, to make them one, to make one Jane whole and complete and to give this one Jane a true home. This has not been easy work. It never is. But, it is the necessary work for all those who aspire to psychic wholeness.

The past often contains painful truths, many of which we have tried assiduously to forget. The work of self-discovery is akin to archaeology. It is an archaeological dig into the soil of the psyche. It is hard labor, tedious, time-consuming and delicate. But at the end, we are able to reconstruct the lost civilisations of our minds. Our own lost memories, like ancient civilisations, are buried under the heavy sands of forgetting, sometimes deliberate memory loss, sometimes protective. Our memories are like the civilisations of fragmented personalities lying on top of the original construction. Yet, the old self, the original self, lies underneath, waiting to be excavated. The past is put together piece by piece. Of course, primary in this work of digging up the past is the first relationship we had—the relationship with our mothers.

19

In Search of History

From the time of my mother's death, returning home has meant going to my sister's house. With Molly's growing at the same pace as I am losing memory of my mother, with my sister, brother, and me all circling around the age of fifty, I draw closer to the family I came from, the family I have left.

Unexpected pleasures

I am, for the first time in my life, interested in the things of my childhood, the aspects of life that I took for granted: family, bar-mitzvahs and other things Jewish as well as things New Orleans. Now I crave those family gatherings that I spent so many years avoiding. I want to be invited to every event that brings us all together—anniversaries, surprise birthday parties, Passover Seders. I take an unexpected pleasure in picking the pecans and crab apples from the trees that fill so many New Orleans backyards. As I wander through the streets of New Orleans, I try to remember the names of all the bushes and trees that my mother taught me: the bright-red hibiscus and the fluffy hydrangea flowers that she tended to in our own garden; the fruiting fig and avocado trees (that we grew up calling "alligator pear") growing in our backyard—all of which I never paid attention to when she was alive.

But, even more important than my own attachment to my past, is my desire to create a memory bank in Molly. Even though my mother is dead, it is because of Molly that I still return home to New Orleans as often as I can. I want her to know this family even though she is too young to understand the meaning of family. My sister is the one other female link—besides myself—to Molly's grandmother. It is we two—my sister and I—who will give Molly the stories of her grandmother that will form the early memory representations of her placement in this family.

Yet, with my sister's recent diagnosis of a cancer parallel to that which felled my mother, it feels like a race against time for Molly to become acquainted with my sister. I am in a hurry to be able to enjoy this family that I have re-entered, returned to.

My sister's imminent death feels too horribly familiar—too much a repeat of the time of my mother's dying days. It feels like what I imagine claustrophobics feel when they are trapped inside an elevator that has stopped moving: walls closing in, ceiling getting lower, options for freedom and movement being sealed off. With my mother alive, home had an expansive with unlimited-possibilities feel to it. The day she died was the last day I spent in that house, home of my memories, home of my childhood and adolescence. Every night since, when I have been in New Orleans, I have slept at my sister's house, and home began to feel a little smaller. I have had to move home base from a house of memories to a home that holds no memories for me. And yet, there is still comfort here in this new home with no memories. There is still a place to come back to.

And now, after these many years of making my sister's home my new home base, of having created a new memory bank for this house, I am losing this home, too. When my sister dies, I fear there will be no more home base for me.

Since my mother's death, it is my sister who has held the position of family matriarch. It is my sister to whom my brother and I invariably turn to remind us of the definition of family. It is she who organises the family Passover Seder and reminds my brother and me of the date of our parents' *yartzeit*—the yearly anniversary of a death. It is she who gives the announcement of family weddings and news of family illnesses. Also, I think of my sister as the repository of memory—conscious memory—as well as genetic memory. She, not I, and not my brother, only she of the three children of Meyer Goldberg and Madeleine Malvina Levy Goldberg, has passed on their genetic material, their immortality. I am past childbearing years. My gay brother is uninterested in propagation. My sister's daughters, Kim and Lisa, are all that's left of the Levy/Goldberg soup of genes.

I am reminded, in a plethora of ways, that my sister, not I, is this family's biological link between the past and the future. As a psychoanalyst, and as an adoptive mother, I like to believe that the weight of the legacy that we parents give to our children falls heavily on the side of nurture, not nature. I want to believe that the enriched environment Molly is being raised in from having a mother who has spent most of her adult life studying feelings, becoming sensitive to emotional communication, doing inner work in preparation for becoming a mother, building up a financial reserve that will buy for Molly an education in a fine private school—French lessons from the age of nine months, tap, ballet, piano, and whatever else meets her fancy—that all that will be a more important influence than the particular way she tilts her head, or squints her eyes, mannerisms that she might have inherited from her biological mother. I would like to think that all this that I will give her should and, indeed, *will* carry more weight than what she has received from the woman whose genes she shares. I want this slope toward nurture because I want to feel that I am the most important connection Molly has. This is what I want Molly to know ten, twenty years hence should she and her biological mother search each other out, or possibly even (improbably) coincidentally appear on the same block at the same time, and have the startling experience of discovering themselves looking into a magical mirror, "finding (them)selves within" each other.

Before my patient Marnie had children, she would talk in her sessions about not knowing a single person who was biologically related to her. It was, for her, an awful, painful feeling of aloneness. When she gave birth to her first child, her daughter, Emma, for the first time in her life, she saw her feet on another human being. She cried and cried at the joy of having her first child, but most of all she cried at the recognition of her feet.

It is my sister, not I, who has passed on the feet of our mother, the feet that are I-know-not-how-many-generations old. We, of the Madeleine Malvina line of ancestry, are petite women. My sister is all of four feet eleven inches. Small height means small feet. My brother used to tease me, asking me if it was hard to keep my balance with feet so small. I have my mother's feet. My sister has my mother's feet. My sister's daughters have my mother's feet. Molly, I suppose, has her bio-mom's feet.

Yet, Molly's feet are the most beautiful feet that I have ever seen. I go to sleep rubbing her feet. I kiss her feet, play with her feet. I have taught her the beginnings of language by reciting to her the names of all the parts of her body. There are a surprising number of body parts in and around the feet. But I know that the older Molly gets, the less those feet will look like Madeleine Malvina feet. So when my sister dies, which I expect to happen much sooner than I can get myself prepared for, there will, sadly, be one less set of Madeleine Malvina feet on this planet—one less link to my mother.

It is now because of my commitment to give Molly a strong sense of family that I feel I need to re-find these lost connections. It is, I think, the only way to give her a sense of the history of this family that preceded her—this family whose feet will look so different from her own. The day will come when she will become painfully aware of this difference. I want this awareness, when it comes, to be as comfortable as possible. I hope to ease the pain of knowledge that her very first experience in life was of rejection. I hope this pain will be eased by having her feel solidly placed in this new family of hers that she has, by accident rather than biology, inherited—that the pleasure of my hello will outweigh the pain of that first good-bye.

A family without memory

One night, during a visit to my sister's house, my sister, brother-in-law, nieces, and I are all talking about sleep, as we are trying to get Molly to go to sleep. We're in the living room together—my sister and her husband cosy on one couch, my nieces on the other couch. I am on the floor with Molly, lying next to her. I have thrown an afghan over her small body, creating for her a makeshift bed on the floor between the couches. I feel too attached to this family-life/family-scene to separate from them to take Molly upstairs to the bedroom.

We are all silently aware that our times together will end soon, and our conversation takes on a kind of nostalgic poignancy. My sister reminisces about her nightly prayer with our mother. She says the prayer had three verses, each one ending with the *Shema*, the central, ancient Jewish prayer that announced its departure from paganism and proclaims God to be One. ("Hear O Israel, the Lord our God, the Lord is One.") I am stunned to realise that I didn't even remember, until my sister says this, that my nightly prayer, too, was the Shema. All I had remembered was my little epilogue. It started with "God bless my family, the big family, and all my friends." But during my growing-up years, guilt, and a burgeoning morality that was probably the forerunner of my college radicalism that morphed into Jewish liberalism, got mixed up with this simple little prayer, and it became ultimately: "God bless my family, the big family, all my friends, the families of all my friends, all the people who will become my friends but aren't yet, all the people who aren't my friends, all my enemies, all the enemies of my friends . . ." It got quite long. But the important thing is: I had forgotten that it all started each night with the Shema. With my sister dead, who is going to remember things like the fact that my long bedtime routine with my mother, each night, started with the Shema?

With my sister dying, with the prospect of only my brother left to remember with me (whose memory seems worse even than my own), I am afraid that I will feel too alone, part of a family without memory.

I decide that I want to confront the house that I grew up in. With my own childhood memories sporadic, with my desire to give Molly a rich sense of the history of her new family, I stand now ready to search for these old memories. For the years that I have been returning to New Orleans after my mother's death, staying with my sister, the house that I was raised in loomed over me. Every time I walked in or out of my sister's house, I would gaze longingly and nostalgically at the house next door—the house I grew up in.

My sister tells me that the owners who we sold the house to have completely renovated the house. I don't think I can bear to see the changes they have made. I am afraid I will feel a little territorial about it, resenting that they have, perhaps, given my bedroom a new floor, hung drapes that are so different from my plantation-style shutters (a style-statement now replicated in my New York bedroom). I am afraid that a new image will superimpose itself upon my old memories, and, in losing visual memory, I might lose my already fragile connection to my past. The decision to finally go back to my old home is made only through force and will.

I stalk the house for a few days, waiting for someone to be entering or leaving at an *oh-what-a-coincidence* moment, just the same time as I am coming or going from my sister's house. Today, a young woman—she is the daughter, a teenager when they bought the house, now grown up but not yet married, not yet out of the house—is leaving, and I saunter up.

She and her mother are actually thrilled to show me the house, thrilled to meet me. We go through every little detail, every change in paint color. We end the tour in my bedroom, and these nice two women remind me, not knowing that this had been my bedroom, that this was the room where the stained glass window had been. My stained glass window that is in my New York apartment now—the first possession that I had brought with me to New York, my small act of unity, in hope of fusing my two homes, my old one that I was leaving (with my mother), and my new one that I was creating (without my mother).

Wanting to be like her

Throughout my younger years, I never stopped reaffirming to my mother that I was not too old for "lovin.'" This little mantra that we said to each other was reassurance that we were still just as close, not separate. The reaffirmation was important to us both.

When I was eight, my mother served as the inspiration for my learning the piano. I would sneak under the baby grand, and hear, and feel, too, the resonance of the music as she played. I wanted to play like her; I wanted to "be" like her. She returned the favour of ardent listening after I started my lessons, devotedly eavesdropping on my practising every day after school. This went from when I was seven, all the way to when I was sixteen, entering contests and winning, and performing solo recitals of Beethoven, Mozart and Haydn at the concert hall of Tulane University. Although she couldn't tell one classical composer from another (and I soon enough learned that her own playing was woefully bad), she never stopped encouraging me, calling out to me from the kitchen where she might have been preparing dinner, praising me for my "musicality," or my "expressiveness" as she called it.

I remember a time when she was so unlike herself. She came home as a blonde, and we three children insisted that she march right back to the beauty salon and make them restore her back to "herself." She complied, as though understanding that her transformation seemed to us as though this person was another mother, a mother we did not recognise. That very afternoon, we had our mother back.

And, even when I was an adult, my mother understood my concerns that I am sure most people would have thought were irrational, even ludicrous. We were in California on a trip to see my mother's nutritionist for her cancer treatment, and I had brought Oscar with me. I was a bit nutty about this dog. He was in the habit of sitting on my lap while I was working, tending to my patients. Every night, he and I slept together, imparting to me a feeling of safety as he watched over the somnolent me. Everywhere I went, Oscar went. My mother and I, that day, had left him in the hotel room, and forty-five minutes into our car trip, I couldn't let go of the idea that the maid at the hotel was going to open the door and Oscar would run out, never to be seen again. I voiced my concern, and, beyond that, I didn't have to ask. She just said, ever so matter-of-factly, reading my mind as though it were the most natural thing in the world to suggest: "Well, we'll just have to go back and get Oscar." Never mind that the turn-around cost us an extra two hours of travel time. To my mother, my feelings, my comfort, and my well-being were all-important.

The mermaid we called our mother

I remember, too, my family's love for water and our many ventures around water. Water was a constant in our life. Given that New Orleans is a city surrounded by water, situated as it is in the crescent of the mighty Mississippi River, and enclosed to the north by the large Pontchartrain Lake, it is not surprising that we, as many other New Orleanians, centred our recreational activities around water. My mother was a champion swimmer when she was a teenager; after she became a mother, she gave children's swimming lessons at the public pool at Audubon Park. As children, Lee, David, and I would accompany her to the pool, and when my sister and I became teenagers, we, too, became swimming teachers. As well, the house that we built and moved into when I was still young backed up to a drainage canal, part of the extensive levee system that defines much of New Orleans geography, and it was this levee that was our gallop-track for riding our horse Crackers—all the way from Old Metairie to the lake. We had a dock on the canal where we parked our water-bike that we rode every weekend: a bicycle body mounted on pontoons, with the pedals leading to a riverboat paddle in the back of the contraption. Eventually, we built our own swimming pool and we shifted our water passions to swimming in our back yard. But it was the noble lake that was our water-home, more than the canal, more than the swimming pools. There were countless summer evenings spent sitting at the lake's edge, watching the undulating waves caress the steps that constituted the seawall adjacent to scenic Lakeshore Drive. As a teenager, once I learned to drive, I and my friends spent many-a-Saturday evening parked at the Point, presumably "watching the submarine races" (a New Orleans catch-phrase for making-out in the back seat of a car).

Most Sundays, the whole family would pile into the car and ride out to the lake to take my father's Chris-Craft out for an afternoon cruise. My father would sit at the helm, guiding the boat into the centre of the lake. Then, as we were safely far away from the shoreline, Lee, David, and I would alternately take turns sitting in his lap, steering the boat, giving us a joyful experience of grown-up power—operating a vehicle of massive proportions. I remember, too, our jumping off the boat—splashing around in the water with glee, waving at my water-resistant dad who remained at the helm. And then we children would chase each other in the water, confident in our aquatic abilities because, after all, the mermaid we called our mother had been our swimming teacher.

No longer telling the truth

Even with the sense of togetherness that I shared with my mother, there were times when I fought fiercely for my separateness—fought against her wishes for me that were markedly different from my own. As separation became my overriding desire, as I began pushing my mother away, as all children must do in order to become their own person, she never stopped asking me the question about my getting too old for lovin'. I no longer told her the truth about that. But even as I was already too old to unambivalently enjoy our hugs and kisses, even when I began to enjoy hugs and kisses from boyfriends, replacements for hers, I kept reassuring her, kept going through the motions of affection. I know, though, that she felt the difference. I think her sensing that I was moving beyond her is why she couldn't let go of the question. As my world broadened, our dreaded separations loomed ever larger in her mind. Later, her question became more of a fear of hers. Ultimately, I think, it became a terror.

I came to know that about her—her fears of my leaving her. I understood her fear—not because she ever told me, not because she tried to hold too tightly to me. After all, she sent me to sleep-away camp for two months when I was eight years old. I was the youngest camper, and while our separation was excruciating to me, she never indicated any of her own discomfort with it. Her fear of the looming distance between us wasn't about physical separation. She even claimed to enjoy her summers without her children when we were all at camp. (I never quite believed her though, and, even now, I remain convinced that she was lying. Perhaps it would have been, would be now still, too painful for me to imagine that my mother enjoyed her existence without me.) Rather, her fear was far deeper than the mere physical distance between us. It had more to do with a fear of losing me, not being able to find me—ever—not merely missing me. It was more like a fear of utter abandonment.

Suffering her dying in silence

Leaving my old house, I return to my sister's home and to the present. I know that our conversation about my visit to our old house will never go much below the surface. We will talk about the kind of decorating the present owners have done, or structural changes, that kind of thing. But we will not talk about how it felt to be in there. What my sister and I have never talked about is feelings. These topics—topics of the heart—are just not part of our repertoire. We have never grown comfortable hanging out in the world of the language of feelings. Even her imminent death lacks the strength to break this mold that we have created for our relationship. We suffer her dying in silence between us.

This is so different from the way it was with my mother. The thing my mother did so exquisitely well, better than anything else she did, was to live in the world of feelings. She gave me this. She talked with me always and endlessly about her feelings, and was always interested in hearing about my own. With me, she was utterly emotionally open, incapable of guile or coyness or distance. It is the most important legacy my mother left me, and the most important legacy that I can give and want to give to Molly—that there is, or should be, or can be, an interest in the internal worlds of people.

Finding a home within one's own self

With my sister's death looming, I know that my next emotional adventure will be to carve out a space for a home base in my heart instead of its residing in a geographical location. I realise that I can't keep depending on my sister as the keeper of family history. I have to begin to allow the past and present to coexist, but deep within my own self.

And, finally, Marnie, too, comes to feel at home in her own self. Like myself, like my mother, she has lived in the world of fear of loss for so long that she and I have come close to abandoning all hope. She has been stuck for some time in the same place in her analysis, saying the same words, feeling the same feelings, tortured by the same conflicts. She remains ambivalent. She wants to stay; she wants to leave. Her life is fine and she doesn't need me; she is desperate for my love and acceptance, and cannot feel whole without them. It is the same dilemma she has been struggling with since she began treatment with me.

But, now, finally, she has a breakthrough. The issue is about my taking a vacation—leaving her, abandoning her. She finally finds expression of her deepest, most hidden self. It has taken quite a long time and great effort, but she is, at long last, at the point of no return. She knows now that she cannot leave therapy in spite of extreme feelings that are impelling her to flee. She is in the midst of having truly intense emotions, but she knows that her work, the commitment she must make to herself, is to stay with me, to stay with her self, and to give voice to these feelings. She expresses her rage at me for going away. She is both rational and irrational. She knows that I have a right to take a vacation, but she is no longer devastated by my departure. She is just angry. She is able to articulate, finally, the idea that she has been fighting all these years—that she wishes I belonged to her; she wants me to have no life other than to care for her. She wants me to be like Sleeping Beauty, asleep until she awakens me. Marnie is giving herself over to that earliest period of life when symbiosis between mother and child is the definition of life. She tells me these wishes without any need for them to be true. Merely acknowledging them and feeling comfortable with them is sufficient.

And then the rage spills out into her feelings about the rejecting mother. She writes her third and final letter to Freida, the woman who gave her up for adoption, and she is no longer kind, nor whimpering. She is outraged at this woman's failure to have even the basic human decency to acknowledge, in words, face to face, that she cannot continue the relationship. This silent, unresponsive woman does not have the decency to tell her daughter to go away. She just disappears on her.

Marnie has reached the point where she can just let her feelings be. She has stopped judging them and trying to butcher them to death.

> *Dear Jane,*
> *For the first time in a great while I left the session feeling hopeful and with the same amount of energy I arrived with, if not more. I did not feel drained, broken, or crushed. I feel somewhat energized. Now I believe our relationship has possibilities. It can become a source of pleasure for me. When you said that you have been more of a mother to me than Freida ever could be, it didn't have the same sting as it would have in the past. It was not an altogether unbearable thought. It did bring tears to my eyes. You know those basic laws of decency—like you don't sleep with your siblings or your parents, you don't fall in love with someone else's spouse. I have been feeling that loving a mother other than my own was like breaking one of those laws.*

Marnie has come to accept what was formerly unacceptable. She has explored the closets of her psyche, the places that were previously dark and forbidding, and has made them into open spaces with light. She reports to me a dream:

> *There were rats in the basement. When I discovered them, they were asleep and somehow I got them into a box with low sides. I covered them all with a blanket because I wanted them to sleep while I figured out how to get rid of them. I called an exterminator and I told him not to wake them up when he looked at them. I didn't want to kill them in the basement because I wasn't sure if I could get them all once they started to run.*

And then she says about the dream:

> *I haven't had a rat dream in a long time. In the past*
> *I think the rats represented my fears, and they were*
> *terrifying. Now I think the dream is about self-awareness.*
> *I feel freer these days. Now that I am sharing my deepest*
> *feelings with you, I feel less burdened. But I know there*
> *are still hidden places, and I guess I'm still a little fearful*
> *of waking up the rats again.*

Marnie knows that hidden spaces still exist. But she can now make a conscious choice to explore them, or to leave them dark. It is her choice. It is within her power.

20

Sex as an Act of Betrayal

When I was seven or so the favourite thing I did with my mother was to stand on the dining room table and shake out my long blonde hair, which I was forever insisting on growing, and which she was forever insisting on cutting (she had this crazy idea that long hair would make me look unkempt, and people would think she was a bad mother). My mother would obediently play the game with me and utter the refrain, "Rapunzel, Rapunzel, let down your golden hair so that I might climb your golden stairs." I loved feeling my hair swinging from side to side down the back of my neck. I loved that my mother allowed herself to be ruled by me. I was the boss, the leader; she devotedly followed my instructions. I loved the sense of power that I had over her. And I loved the sensuousness of the fantasy that my mother could climb up my hair; only together could we solve the dilemma of how she was going to reach me and rescue me as I was imprisoned on the table.

Mother is the first lover

I think this was the first game of overt sexuality that I played. My mother was, of course, enacting the role of both the sorceress and the prince. As such, she was both my mother and my lover in the game. And, as the story goes, Rapunzel couldn't always tell the difference between the two. The prince gains his first access to Rapunzel by tricking her into thinking that he is really the sorceress.

That was, of course, Freud's point about sexuality: there is little difference between the first mother of symbiosis and the lover. The mother is, in actuality, the first lover. The mother/infant relationship is tinged with sexuality. The mother wants it this way, and so does the child; it is pleasurable to both—at least, at first. (Was it necessary, evolutionarily-wise, for the organ that is so exquisitely sensitive to sensual touch by the woman's partner to be the same organ that her infant needs for nourishment? It is perhaps in this interlocking of functions of the woman's breast that Freud's point can be more simply, and less controversially, understood.)

As the tale goes, Rapunzel spent her early years with the sorceress contentedly. But when Rapunzel reaches the age of twelve—the age when sexual maturity commences—the sorceress decides to isolate her in a tower where no one except the sorceress herself can reach her. The sorceress has thus prevented any possibility of Rapunzel being able to leave her. Rapunzel has no means of interacting with other people about whom she might transfer her affection. Yet, Rapunzel accepts her fate without question or complaint. After all, what children want most is to be loved and held by their mothers. Selfish love from the mother feels better—is better—than no love.

The prince, however, proves to be clever. He tricks Rapunzel into letting down her golden locks so that he, rather than the sorceress, can climb up her tresses to the tower. The tale tells us symbolically that in spite of the sorceress's attempt to keep Rapunzel all for herself, Rapunzel does adequately make the transfer of relationship from her mother to her lover: age-appropriate interest in her own sexuality and in a suitor.

Rapunzel has now lived most of her life with her adoptive mother. She has come to know the good and the bad in her adoptive mother, as all children come to know these things about their mothers. Now that Rapunzel has met her prince, she understands that the sorceress has not allowed her to meet anyone, that she cannot bring herself to share Rapunzel. At first, it seems that Rapunzel is willing to protect her adopted mother from the searing pain of separation, and she determines to hide the prince.

Eventually, however, Rapunzel makes what Freud called a "slip." There is, for all of us, a conflict between wanting something to be known and wanting it to be hidden. The conscious mind wants it hidden, but the unconscious mind insists on revealing it. The conflict results in the truth just "slipping out" without conscious forethought or control. It's a secret that is demanding to be told. Rapunzel lets the truth slip out, her secret, when she asks the unwary sorceress why she is so much heavier to pull up than the young son of the king. Rapunzel lets out the truth "slip out" because she unconsciously wants the sorceress (her mother) to know that she has emerged into her sexuality. Not only does she want her to know, she wants to be accepted for it.

Rapunzel wants, in fact, what every growing daughter wants from her mother. Every emerging girl/woman wants to keep her actual sexual activities to herself, but she wants her mother to know that this is who she has become. She wants her mother's blessing to move into the developmental stage of womanhood where she will become both like her mother as well as in competition with her mother.

The trauma of coming to know your child is a sexual being

Parents are often traumatised by the knowledge that their child wants to have sex. This knowledge is particularly traumatic when it pertains to a girl-child, who is often seen symbolically as the embodiment of innocence.

The awareness of the sexuality of the child is painful to the mother because it is a blatant manifestation of how separate they have become. In my work with pregnant women, I find that there is one sentiment that recurs repetitively: pregnant women almost always express the fear that they will become like their own mothers. On a conscious level, they pledge that they will not repeat, as mothers themselves, all the mistakes that their own mothers made with them. But this fear reflects, on a deeper level, a wish as well as a fear. Every woman who allows herself a pregnancy has, already, unconsciously, become her mother. The act of pregnancy could not occur unless the woman allowed herself this unconscious identification with the sexual mother. And, in this identification, in allowing herself to repeat the role of pregnant woman that her own mother once embodied, the girl-child replaces her mother. Pregnancy is a necessary act of separation from the mother so that symbiosis with the unborn child can occur.

The daughter's sense of completeness, her symbiosis with her unborn child and the concomitant loss of longing for her mother, is often experienced by her mother as a betrayal of their previous relationship. The daughter will now be one with another rather than returning to the union with her mother. The mother may feel that she is being cast off, soon to be replaced by a competitor. The mother may not know how to redefine her role and may be left feeling abandoned and rejected. I believe it is this sense of abandonment and betrayal that fuels the rage mothers can feel toward their unexpectedly pregnant daughters.

One of my patients, Karen, has had three children. Each pregnancy has brought the same dilemma: she cannot tell her mother. All three times, she has asked her husband to deliver the happy news. She says to me with a combination of mirth and questioning in her voice: "Of course my mother knows that I am having sex." I ask responsively (also with a tinge of mirth): "Karen, are you sure she knows?" Karen's pregnancies, as the outward manifestation of her sexuality, are sources of embarrassment to her in this regressed place of her relationship with her mother. Karen is Hispanic, and she exemplifies something about their culture and the use of language: the Hispanic word for pregnant is *embarazada*. Even as a mother of three, Karen, like many women in relation to their mothers, is embarrassed by her sexuality, and still has an unconscious need to hide her sexuality from her mother.

Mothers often have trouble accepting their daughters' growth into sexuality, too, because of the looming loss of their own sexuality. The most frequent complaint I hear in my practice from married couples is that there has been a decrease in sexual interest in each other. The complaint comes from couples who, in the past, enjoyed frequent and pleasurable sex, and from couples whose relationship is positive in many other respects. Thus, envy is aroused in the mother, who is not having much sex, in relation to her daughter, who seems to be having a surfeit of sex.

In studying the relationship between motherhood and sexuality, Charles Darwin found that motherliness and pregnancy are universally regarded as deficits to sexual attractiveness, even in cultures where fertility is highly valued. Every woman runs the risk of losing her husband's interest when she becomes a mother. Within every husband are residues of the incest taboo with respect to his own mother. Often the wife stepping into the mother role will awaken these old conflicts in him. It is estimated that ten per cent of men—the majority of them previously faithful—cheat on their partners during pregnancy.

Daughters sometimes intuitively understand these subterranean issues that their mothers struggle with. Like Rapunzel came to understand, daughters can know that when they become sexual, their mothers may feel betrayed. This feeling of betrayal can come about when the mother wants an exclusive love. In this case, the love from another will feel like a deprivation as well as a betrayal to the mother. Or, the feeling of betrayal can come, as it often does, when the child has acted contrary to the morality of the mother. Winnicott talks about the need to rebel as necessary for emotional growth. He calls this the need to kill off the other in order to love them. Often the rebellion comes in the form of sexuality.

The mother's response is often the same as was the sorceress's: when Rapunzel makes her "slip," the sorceress responds by cutting off Rapunzel's long tresses, cutting off the prince's avenue to Rapunzel, and, in doing so, attempts to destroy Rapunzel's very sexuality. Mothers of sexual girls/women often forbid their daughters from seeing the boy/man who is arousing her sexuality.

But even with so vile an act having been committed against her, Rapunzel still knows that the sorceress loves her. And although selfish love, as the sorceress exhibited, is wrong and always loses out (at least in fairy tales), children can understand that if they are the recipients of an exclusive love, then the love is a selfish love. In his retelling of this fairy tale, Bruno Bettelheim interprets: "To love so selfishly and foolishly is wrong, but not evil." Having acted foolishly and selfishly, the sorceress loses her beloved daughter—but since she acted from too much love for Rapunzel and not out of wickedness, no harm befalls her.

An odd battleground of conflict

As with the sorceress and Rapunzel, it was sex that put the first strain on my relationship with my mother. I was a teenager, bursting with adolescent sexuality, bold in my indulgences. On the face of it, this battleground of conflict would seem a bit odd for my mother. There was never a time that my mother didn't talk about sex with great enthusiasm for its pleasures. In our household, sex was not, as it is in so many households, a forbidden topic. I assumed that, because of the way my mother extolled the virtues of good sex, while my father may have been less than loquacious and personable with her outside of their bed, it was clear that once they got between the sheets, he understood my mother's desires as well as has any Romeo to any Juliet.

And, there was her humour, too about sex, and her quick-on-the-draw use of it. With glee, she reported the dialogue of a phone call she received:

> Ring (phone is ringing).
>
> My mother: *Hello*
>
> Caller: (deep breathing)
>
> My mother: *Oh, my God. Are you having a heart attack?* (knowing full-well that she is now the recipient of an obscene phone call)
>
> Caller: *No lady. I am not having a heart attack. I want to suck your pussy.*
>
> My mother: *Ohhh. You want the vet. No, this isn't the vet. You have the wrong number.*

Caller: *Lady. I do not want the vet. I want to screw you.*

My mother: *OHHH. I'm sorry. I misunderstood. Now I get it. You think you called the hardware store. No. We definitely don't have any screws here. Or any other hardware stuff. As I said, you have the wrong number.*

Caller (with ever more exasperation): *Lady, I do not want the hardware store. I want to stick my cock up your box. I want to fuck you. You get that, lady.*

My mother: *I know just how you feel. There're lots of times when I feel people are giving me a cock-and-bull story too. I agree you don't seem to have very good luck. Have you discussed the situation with your wife?*

Caller: *What's the matter with you lady? You hard of hearing or somtin'?*

My mother: *Listen, I gotta' go now, but I'm sorry you've had so much trouble hearing me. You know I think you better go have your hearing checked out by a doctor.*

Yet, in spite of her openness about sex, in spite of her humour about sex, it was because of my mother's attitude about <u>my</u> having sex that I first learned to lie. My mother's complexity was that her heart and her head were in conflict with one another as often as they were together. Her heart knew, truly, as she had always told me, that when sex was loving and caring, it was an exquisite expression of feelings. Her head, however, encapsulated her into being a woman limited by her times, who believed that sexuality was permissible only within the context of marriage. But that might have been just subterfuge. The real pain may have been the fact that she was no longer a main object of interest to me.

Like other young women (including Rapunzel), I wanted to hide my emerging sexuality from my mother. It became the one thing in our relationship that I hid from her, the one point of dishonesty between us, my "secret."

She had made her objection to my sexuality clear enough to me when I was in high school. I was sixteen and in love. Wolf was a senior and had given me his senior ring that I proudly displayed on a chain around my neck. I had my first car, a bug-eyed, powder blue Sprite which my Daddy had bought for me and which I tooled around town in. Wolf had, coincidentally, the same car in white. After school we would go back to his house, our caravan of Sprites cruising through the local streets, and we would spend the afternoon making-out. These afternoons were my first, innocent pre-sexual explorations.

One day, I was driving my little Sprite during my lunch hour to the local Burger King. The top was down and the car was piled with my girlfriends: I was in the driver's seat, one person sat on top of the gear shift, another in the passenger seat, and a fourth more or less on top of all of us. My mother happened to be on the same street in her car, and that night I got the first (and last) lecture of my life. She accused me of speeding (which I wasn't). Rather, it was, I am sure, the aura I was projecting that she objected to—the devil-may-care kind of attitude, the hair-blowing-in-the-wind metaphor that suggested about me a freedom, an unleashing that went with my sexual interests and explorations.

All criticism of me stopped when Wolf dumped me a few months later for another girl. It was the most painful time of my sixteen-year-old life. I went to my mother in my pain and she comforted me as only a mother—my mother—could do.

Through my teenage love episodes, first with Wolf in high school, and then in college, I learned my lessons about love and sex—the lessons that would stay with me throughout my early adulthood. They were the lessons my mother taught me, neither through instruction nor didacticism, nor through her trying to rein me in, but rather through the woman she was, the comfort that she herself had as a sexual woman. I learned that sex and affection and sensuality with a man were wonderful, incomparable pleasures for a woman, as my mother always told me that they were between her and my father. I learned to give myself over to the feeling of being in love with a man, just as my mother explained she had done when she met my father. I learned that my sexual life was not something that my mother wanted to know about, that my emerging into a sexual woman who sought satisfaction of my sexual urges was an uncomfortable, if not intolerable, idea to my mother. Most of all, through our closeness, I learned that men could inflict untold pain and that women were the only real safe haven when the seas of men got rough, and that in states of pain, it was a woman to whom I could turn, a woman who was the ultimate comfort.

21

When Men Matter

I n my practice, I have had mothers of daughters of all ages tell me their own stories that sound and feel like my own anxieties—the dreams of disaster befallen to me and Molly when she first came to me, the sense of fear and foreboding I have whenever I leave her in a place other than the "safe" place of home, with the safety net of me as Mother underneath. Mothers of young children, of teenagers, and of married adults tell me stories of fear of the loss of their child. Many use the specific word "loss" to describe their fears: "I feel like I am losing her"—as though the child were on life-support and fading precipitously. I've listened to mothers describe their feelings, as though it were grief and mourning, when their child first went off to pre-school. I've seen mothers fall into serious depressions when their child goes to college; I've seen cancer diagnoses made following a depression from bereavement at a child leaving home, as though the departure was too much for the body as well as for the psyche.

Demeter's Dilemma

One of my mother/patients, Demetria, has come in specifically to talk about her teenage daughter, Priscilla, who is fourteen and exhibiting behaviour that Demetria feels is inappropriate for her age. Priscilla is fighting her mother on the establishment of weekend curfews, wearing clothes that Demetria feels are too "revealing," spending too much time alone with her boyfriend. Too, after finding a "hickey" on Priscilla's neck one morning, Demetria suspects that her daughter has begun having sex. Every time Demetria tries talking to Priscilla about her lifestyle, Priscilla becomes hostile and argumentative, telling her mother to stop being intrusive and annoying. Demetria longs to see her "real" daughter again, instead of having to confront daily the teenage stranger who only looks like her daughter.

In one of our sessions, Demetria makes reference to the Greek origin of her name: she was named after the mythological Demeter, goddess of fertility and earth. Demetria is well-schooled in the tragedy of Demeter's life and feels like she is now re-living the destiny of the goddess herself—losing her daughter due to forces over which she feels powerless to help her daughter to resist. In hopes of some spiritual enlightenment, or reassurance, or better clarity on her situation, Demetria and I decide to look at the ancient story of Demeter and her maiden daughter, Persephone.

> *At the beginning of time, mother Demeter and her daughter Persephone were always together. The world existed as an eternal one: there was no hunger on earth and no separation of seasons, just never ending good crops thanks to the generosity of Demeter, who was the goddess of earth. Demeter caused brilliant flowers to bloom from her soft earth and strong trees to rise to the heavens—*

all for Persephone's amusement. Demeter called down rain from the sky to cool the earth on hot days so that Persephone could joyfully frolic in the grassy meadows. Demeter whispered to the air until it sent soft breezes to linger over Persephone's delicate face and lulled her to sleep. Persephone lived in peace and tranquility during this time, both with her mother and, too, communing with the symbolic representation of her mother—Mother Earth.

However, Hades, on one of his trips to earth, and wearing a helmet that conferred on him the power of invisibility, caught a glimpse of the lovely girl. He became instantly smitten by her considerable beauty and charm. After approaching Demeter to ask for her daughter's hand in marriage and being turned away, Hades decided, to the misfortune of both mother and daughter, to abduct the girl.

So far, the story bears resemblance to the Rapunzel tale: contented symbiosis between mother and daughter. And next, the intrusion of the male, disrupting the bliss of the mother/daughter connection. But, then the stories part:

His chariot emerged ferociously from a chasm in the earth, and he took Persephone to his underworld kingdom, forcing her into a loveless marriage with him.

Persephone has not gone willingly to her lover. She is captured, and raped. Hades is no prince. Both mothers, the sorceress and Demeter, are bereft at their loss.

Demeter was inconsolable over the loss of her daughter. She fell into a deep depression, and abandoned her divine functions, refusing to nurture earth. All the world

*became parched and arid, and humanity's cries were
strident because there were no verdant plants to eat, no
protective shade from the strong trees, no sweet rustling
of the leaves in gentle breezes, no color from the once
brilliantly vivid flowers.*

And the real-life mother of Priscilla feels the same as her namesake: Demetria has come to feel depressed, hopeless and helpless at the loss of the daughter she knew. She expresses how she feels even in the clothes she wears. When Priscilla was young, mother and daughter dressed alike, in mother/daughter clone dresses, bright colors, lighting up the room. Now Demetria has lost all interest in how she looks; she wears dark clothes and has a perpetually gloomy expression. She describes that she feels as lifeless as the earth itself after Persephone's abduction. To Demetria, the world has transformed itself from a place of colour and activity and excitement to a place that seems grey, cold, still, and uninviting.

Demetria and I talk about when her daughter was first born, their time of symbiosis, and how it was the happiest, most contented time of her life. And we talk about the various milestones of separation. We do this in an attempt to understand at what point the paths of mother and daughter had so diverged that only anger and dissatisfaction exists between them now. She explains that she and Priscilla had had an unusually close mother/daughter bond, which she attributed to the facts that Priscilla was an only child, had come late in Demetria's life, and that Priscilla's father had abandoned both of them immediately after Priscilla's birth. Demetria explains that during Priscilla's childhood, she held onto their closeness fiercely and protectively, not wanting to "risk losing the one person who had come to mean the most" to her. In talking about the turn that their relationship has taken, from harmony to acrimony, Demetria keeps returning to the idea that she feels her daughter is being "taken advantage of" and "unduly influenced." Demetria blames the boyfriend, blames the school, blames the entire culture. She cries at the loss of her daughter's innocence and their closeness (much as the goddess Demeter herself had done). The only solution Demetria can think of is to try to prevent her daughter from seeing the boyfriend. But she knows that attempting such a step would not only further antagonise her daughter, it would be useless and ineffectual as well.

The Demeter Mother

We learn from the Demeter myth that the Demeter woman is, like Demetria, an earthy, feeling type of woman. She is highly emotional and looks at the events of her life in such a way that their emotional centre is revealed. At her best, the Demeter-Mother has a more positive mothering capacity than other mythological types of women. Her gift for nurturance means that she excels at being emotionally responsive to others. She has a warm personality and expresses love easily. She nurtures, she is acceptant, and she has the ability to endure despite great pain and suffering. It is her nature to give of herself and her motivation for her generosity is love. Her involvement in eternal cycles gives her the capacity and strength to cope with even death (Hades). She is strongly empathetic. Since she is sympathetic, she can frequently be a comfort to those around her. She is an excellent nurse, whether caring for her own child early in life, babysitting her grandchild later in life, or tending the wounded or distraught professionally. She often finds a career in the helping professions, perhaps as a counsellor or psychotherapist. And, of course, either a man or woman can express the Demetrian qualities.

Demeter is Persephone in her renascent form. Modern women experience this force in the continuity of generations.

The matrilineal line extends back to one's grandmother and mother, and forward in one's daughters. It isn't the same for sons; they are distinctly other, as our fathers are. There is an essential blood-bond between female members of a family who share the mystery of the generation of life from their own substance: a woman's essential self is reborn in her daughter.

The dark side of the Demeter-Mother

As well as symbiosis going awry from the emotional environment providing too few opportunities for attachment, the opposite can occur. The mother may not be able to let go of the symbiotic relationship, as happened with Demetria and Priscilla. This is the dark side of the Demeter-Mother. The ease with which the Demeter-Mother loves and is able to attach can convert to pathology. We remember that in Demeter's grief, she ravages the earth with drought; she withholds the life-giving waters and kills most of earth's plant life, opening the bare earth to erosion. She is willing to allow all of mankind to die. She suffers greatly; and, out of grief, or perhaps out of a wish for revenge too, she makes others suffer with her. Thus, she becomes her shadow-self, a goddess of death and destruction rather than of life and fecundity.

Within these distorted mother/child dynamics, a mature and whole personality may fail to develop as the child moves into adulthood. There may be no overt signs of this truncated development; there may be a personality that seems quite normal and wonderful, a personality that functions "as if" it were whole and complete. The person may not even sense that there exists within only a half-aliveness, disconnected as the individual is from an essential aspect of the authentic self. Sometimes there is a vague sense of emptiness; there is a search for "meaning" because, for these people, being half-alive—half-whole as they are—is not sufficient. Or sometimes there is an event that propels the person into recognition of a sense of incompleteness. It may be the death of a loved one and an inability to move on with life. It may be a spouse leaving and a rage that can't be quenched. It may be a simple, everyday task that can't be completed.

Father the intruder

The presence of the father constitutes what Freud called "The Family Romance," an idealised version of the child's longing for the happy, vanished days when his father seemed to him the noblest and strongest of men and his mother the dearest and loveliest of women. But, more often, the father is experienced, at least initially after a child's birth, resentfully and negatively.

In the Demeter myth, Hades is the ultimate culprit. He has kidnapped Persephone to be his wife. But abducting Persephone for his own purposes, without her consent, is not his only offence: he has also interrupted the symbiotic bliss between mother and daughter.

Many mothers come to feel that their husbands are either irrelevant to the mother/infant dyad, or, worse, an outright interference. With my own Molly, I catch myself inflating my importance as the parent to her. I find myself thinking, and operating at times, as though I am the *only* parent. I want to make the decision about which school Molly goes to. I want to determine what foods she eats, who her play-dates are with, which extra-curricular activities she participates in. And, for most of these decisions, Gregg does defer to me, and there is no conflict between us.

In my mind, I allow Gregg's influence on Molly to fade into insignificance. Of course, this is not the case—is never the case in the endeavour of raising children. Research shows that in families where there are two parents, the children function better intellectually, academically, emotionally, and even physically, in terms of their overall health. From observing how Gregg and Molly play together, I see how different fathers can be from mothers. I see how Gregg brings something to the relationship that I, as the mother, do not, cannot bring. Gregg (and most fathers with their children) plays with Molly differently to the way I do: he is more physical; my play with her is softer. He (as most fathers) communicates differently with her to the way I do: he is more action-oriented; I am more emotional. He (as most fathers) thinks differently with her: their discussions have more of a sense of classification, organisation and categorisation; mine are more freewheeling, free-associative, less planned. And he (as most fathers) comes to her from a different angle: he is more prone to wanting to control her; I am more prone to wanting to understand her.

In spite of Gregg's general compliance with me as Molly's mother, there are times when he insists on asserting his rights as Molly's father. When he has opinions, he is forceful and emphatic in them. There are issues about how to raise Molly on which Gregg and I do not agree. And, at times, we have genuine and profound disagreements about the way to respond to her. For instance, Molly's joy in the use of her voice means that at any moment she may let out a yell that is almost glass shattering in its intensity. It actually hurts my ears. Gregg tells her with some irritation to stop making so much noise. I just cover my ears. I do this because this is how my mother raised me: she gave me absolute freedom of expression. This difference between Gregg and me permeates practically every aspect of who we are individually and how we intersect in our relationship. As I see it, he wants the world to change to accommodate him. I accommodate myself to the world.

As the first male to the infant, fathers are often the forgotten victims of family life. Experiments on infants' interest in fathers' voices reveal an almost shocking indifference. They show no greater interest in their fathers' voice than in those of total strangers. Yet the father has a special role to play in the lessening of the symbiosis between mother and child. It is the father's task to change the relationship of dependency between mother and child. The father must help cut the psychological umbilical cord between them. It is he who divides the mother/child dyad and converts it into the triangular relationship that constitutes the continuation of family life. It is his job to make the child understand that the symbiotic time with the mother has ended; he re-claims the mother as his own and as his wife.

Without the interference of the father, children are hampered in the development of their own sense of self. In the child's eyes, the father embodies law, structure, strength and the outside world, while the mother symbolises communion, merging, and the home. Most importantly, to both mother and child, the father is the protector of the children. It is only when the child has internalised both paternal law as well as maternal nurturance that (s)he can come to have an autonomous ego, that (s)he can experience her/himself as an independent agent, and that (s)he will become capable of confronting the outside world. The father's act of interference, then, frees the child to have relationships with people other than the mother. The father is, after the mother, the first real "other," and as such becomes a prototype for future relationships.

Contemporary research shows the benefits to children of having a father who is actively engaged with them. Children whose fathers are involved in their upbringing are less likely to become violent, have higher IQs, have better impulse control and have better social adaptations.

Interactions between fathers and infants, like those between mothers and infants, follow a pattern that transcends class and culture. Each mother has a distinctive way of holding her child. She will do it nine out of ten times. Each father, in contrast, picks up his baby in ten different ways. Mothers play with children in distinctive ways; mothers use toys. Fathers, in contrast, use themselves; they will use their bodies as rocking horses, monkey bars, runaway trains. Fathers do not mother. They father. Fathering is different to mothering. And the two are better together than either one alone.

It is a thankless job, however, to have to break into the symbiotic union between mother and infant. In the care of a newborn, the father's role seems insignificant in comparison with the mother's. His intrusion is not necessarily welcome; both mother and child can experience his desire to come between then as unwanted, threatening to break up their symbiotic bliss. Fathers of newborns often feel abandoned, neglected, and unimportant.

When mothers don't want to recognise their own children

As Persephone's first lover, Hades understood something profound about the relationship between daughters and mothers. As Persephone begins to make her exit from the underworld, Hades entreats her to eat the seeds of a pomegranate in order "to bring colour to her cheeks so that her mother would recognise her." Hades understands that when children are exposed to stimuli other than their safe symbiotic encounters with their mothers, they become transformed, and their mothers don't seem to be able to recognise them, sometimes don't even want to recognise them.

This is the sentiment Demetria expresses—that an entity other than her daughter has taken up residence in her body. Demetria does not want to attribute the change in her daughter as originating from within her own self—that her daughter is not a hapless victim of "undue influence"—but rather is actively constructing the life that she wants. And, while Priscilla's journey into sexuality and into separation from her mother, like the journey of Persephone to the underworld, is fraught with uncertainty and foreboding, it is nevertheless an essential one for all daughters. Persephone, as a young maiden, needed to travel to the underworld in order to become transformed into the mature and sexual Persephone, where she became Queen of the Underworld. And too, the journey of Priscilla from the young girl Demetria recognised as her daughter to the sexual woman she has become, is inevitable and necessary.

The mythic meaning of Hades is not as simplistic as that he is "bad" or "evil" (as we are wont to think of the owner of the place we call "hell"). Hades personifies wisdom, too, in being able to see what others can't see. Hades was a place as well as a god. Most entered Hades involuntarily (like Persephone), and the experience of going into the darkness of the underworld was always shocking, disruptive, and frightening. Symbolically, Hades refers to a place within us, a psychic place. And, as a place within our own being, the notion refers to the depths of the soul, an interior place and a sacred place as well, the deepest layers of the psyche where memories and feelings, images, patterns, and instincts lie buried. This is the part of us that remains invisible to our own self (as Hades was rendered invisible due to his special helmet).

This aspect of the psyche is the "shadow" side of us, as Jung referred to it. Therein resides all the material of our inner lives that are too painful, too shameful, too unacceptable for us to consciously acknowledge. Left out of conscious life, this aspect of self can dwell only with a hidden malevolency in the underworld.

Persephone, then, represents the budlike quality of the naive, virginal psyche before its encounter with and transformation in the underworld of the unconscious. Each of us is the archetypal virgin bride when we are torn from our union with what is familiar and forced into congress with what is alien and repugnant to our consciousness.

The Demeter/Persephone myth ends with Persephone dividing her time between her mother and her lover:

> *When Persephone and her mother were re-united, Demeter sang to the earth, air, water, and fire spirits with such a beautiful voice that they awakened from their slumber and began to dance. Precious life clearly -- and ambitiously -- was evincing its return. As earth twirled happily once again, it left brilliant flowers and trees in its wake. Air learned again the steps that allowed it to quietly breeze through the forests. Water tapped its feet on Persephone's eyelashes. Fire undulated before Persephone and she felt the warmth of its passion.*

> *In the six months of spring and summer, when Persephone is above ground with her mother, the air is warm, the sun shines brightly, the days are beautiful and the crops are ripe with life. In the six months of fall and winter, when Persephone returns underground, the air becomes cold, the days are short and the earth is less endowed with goodness.*

In using the myth to think about her emotional pain, Demetria is able to come to an understanding that, as in the myth when Persephone ate the seeds of the pomegranate and sealed her fate to move forever between mother and lover, so too will Demetria's daughter never again be the child that she had been, never again totally protected and insulated from the encroachment of the outside world. Demetria and

I talk about the universal struggle of mothers to let go of their children, and the efforts of all mothers to keep pace with the on-going developmental separation progressions of their children. We talk about the natural instinctual drive for mothers to guard their children from being seduced out of childhood, from being "captivated" by another, and spirited away from her domain.

For Demetria to come to a point of acceptance of her daughter's actions, she needs to understand that it is Priscilla herself who is making the decision to separate from her mother in order to carve out her own path in life. Perhaps Priscilla even has to displease her mother in order to effect that separation. Demetria has to come to accept that the young girl who had walked out in the morning had come back in the evening as a woman. And, indeed, she does come to understand that Priscilla will always have another life to live in another world, sometimes away from her mother, always away from their previous protected world of only togetherness.

When all that remains is spring

How can any of us, like Persephone, enter into the realm of Hades and eventually find escape? We can do it with the knowledge that we must return to that dark place from time to time, and that the memory of our struggle will stay with us, like a scar on our soul. In Zen there is the saying: "Spring comes and the grass grows all by itself." The statement shows us the wisdom of letting go of all attempts to maintain control and hide from our pain. To let go of control is to enter into creation in the act of becoming; it is to enter into spring. When there is no clinging or condemning, when there is no desire for control or evasion, then all that remains is spring.

At its core, the Demeter/Persephone myth expresses the mystery of mothers and daughters: it is a union of sames. Paradoxically, we women are mature female and child in one being. We always remain our mother's child, no matter how old we are.

Women experience themselves as the biological and spiritual source of life. When Demeter finds her daughter again, the reunion of mother and daughter begins the process of annulling the suffering and violence of the "marriage of death" that Persephone suffered, and restores the unity of mother and daughter on a new, more mature level. The fundamental difference is that a male has now encroached on the female world. Persephone has been initiated into male aggression and sexuality.

There is yet another dimension to the Demeter/Persephone myth. Hekate, the crone, completes the image of the life cycle of women: maidenhood, motherhood, and old woman. The Hekate part of us can watch the soul's struggle with the dark forces, and she can make her observations impassively, without drama, without intensity of emotional involvement. Hekate is that part of woman's consciousness that is at home in the dark. She dwells in caves and has the power of foreseeing the future. In her wisdom of age, she knows the necessity of the abduction and its purposeful value. She provides us with an objective viewpoint on our own and sees it as an integral part of the cycle of life and death. Her perspective is from that of the final stage. And all of her comfort in the darkness of shadows, her interest in understanding the world of death as well as life, and her ability to look forward as well as back in time: all this is, too, what the psychoanalyst is and does. As Marion Woodman explains the pertinence of the Demeter myth to modern life: "Where the woman is caught in unconscious identification with the mother...she has to be raped out of that identification before she can find her own individuality."

The interpenetration of worlds

The intrusion of the underworld into quotidian life can come at any time. And, when the unconscious forces its way out of its hidden realm, it comes to us with unbridled force; it feels like a chariot emerging from a chasm in the earth that has unexpectedly opened up, grabbing us, threatening to pull us down, away from safety, into the darkness of the inner recesses of uncertainty and fear. When we are invaded by the dark power of the unconscious, we come face to face with the inevitability of our powerlessness, our griefs, perhaps even our own demise, and we recoil in anguish, resisting the abduction, thrashing and fighting our own darker natures. The Underground can be a conflict or a situation; it can be a Demon Lover, in the form of a person or an addiction. It always takes us utterly by surprise and we don't quite understand what has happened. We may find ourselves in a place within our own psyche that is frightening in its unfamiliarity. Or we may find ourselves in a place that is frightening precisely because of its familiarity; it can be a psychic home that we have always inhabited in a kind of eerie twilight state. This is how being confronted with our own unconscious feels.

In *The Immense Journey*, Loren Eiseley talks about an encounter he had with a crow one morning when it was particularly foggy: the worst fog in years; Eiseley describes that he couldn't see his hands outstretched in front of him. He was suddenly confronted with the bird rushing over his head, cawing frantically in an outcry of hideous terror. Eiseley understood that the encounter happened because the fog had created a misperception for the crow—a shift in borders of worlds. He surmised that the crow assumed the usual—that he was flying high, and then, in encountering a man—a man seemingly walking on air—the crow was disoriented and terrified. The land-world of man had interpenetrated into the air-world of bird. And, this is, I think, as good a description as any of what it feels like to be suddenly confronted with our unconscious: the interpenetration of two worlds: the heaven-world of Demeter and the underworld of Hades; the two intersecting worlds of conscious and unconscious.

Each of us is at risk for being dragged from the surface of the earth—our "day-world"—to below—the underworld—the world of night and darkness, where confusion lives. We feel cold and numb, or lifeless, and would like to flee in an attempt to try to recapture days when our disposition was sunny and warm, but we cannot; we are powerless to escape. This underworld is below the threshold of consciousness; it is where things are not seen; it represents what remains invisible. In the world of psychological and mythological symbolism, surviving the winter of the soul means coming through a dark and alienated time of ambiguity, perhaps a time of deep depression, almost always a fallow time of hopelessness. The winter of the soul is a dark descent into the hidden aspects of self. Hades is the shadow side of us—not an absence, but a hidden presence— even an invisible fullness: Hades represents the unconscious. Hades is the god of destruction and death; but he also connotes sleep and unknowingness—the place where dreams originate. Dreams tell us what we don't know and what we don't want to know. Dreams reveal to each of us our own personal underworld. Jung said that "...by entering into the figure of Demeter we realize the universal principle of life, which is to be pursued, raped, to fail to understand, to rage and grieve, but then to get everything back and be born again."

Frolicking in the springtime of my soul

Demetria reports that she has had a healing dream. In her dream, her daughter has returned home from a trip, and suddenly the weather has turned to spring. It is as though the whole earth has burst forth in colour and life as an expression of Demetria's joy. Her dream ended as the myth of Demeter ends, mother and daughter re-united. As Demeter came to accept Persephone's entrance into the world of male sexuality and aggression, so too is Demetria now able to accept this about Priscilla.

And, from my work with Demetria, and from re-visiting the myth of Demeter, I now know why I have had nightmares about my separation from Molly. I travel to my underworld at night in my sleep to visit my fears and griefs precisely so I can laugh and sing joyously during the day. "Spring" is not only a season, but also a state of mind. I visit the underworld at night in the winter of my soul when all things are dark so that I can dance and frolic with my daughter in the bright light of the sun that represents the springtime of my soul.

22

Murder as Metaphor

I am taking a nature walk with Molly. Now that she is a little older and walking, this is something she and I especially like to do together. It is summer, my favourite time of the year because I can walk out of my house and within about fifty steps, be swimming in my lake. The area around our home is buzzing with the song of the cicadas—alas, this has been the year of this particular breed of cicadas. These singing insects come only every seventeen years to live long enough to make their strange ethereal music before they drop their eggs from a tree. The eggs then hatch into larvae and the larvae burrow deep into the ground and live off the roots of the trees until they re-emerge after their long rest.

So, as we are walking through the woods, we come across a cicada in the last waning period of its life. It allows us to pick it up by its wings, to place it on a tree and then take it off. It sits in our hands, walks on our arms. We spend twenty minutes with this cicada. Molly even names it, King Bug, and then she decides she wants to take it home with her. We set it in Molly's oversized blue carriage, and it sits perched in the empty seat like it is the king that she has named it, and then we start to walk home. Suddenly Molly reaches for it, takes it out of the carriage, puts it on the ground, and proceeds to stomp on it.

For just a little while, Molly seemed to love this little cicada. For that moment, Molly embraced love and life and togetherness. Then she had had enough of it; she was ready to be done with it. In that moment of stomping, she embraced hate and death and separation. In her acts of love and then of murder, she embodied some basic principles about love and aggression, attachment and separation: you don't have one without the other. And they are usually directed to the same object; you don't necessarily love one person and hate another; you hate most of all the ones you love most of all. You don't want to leave someone unless you also want to be close; the people you most ardently want distance from are the same people you want to possess.

The fact that we have these two conflicting desires—that, on our deepest level, we are divided—means that we are perpetually at war with ourselves. On the level of our psyches, we have the capacity to both *think* and *feel*. On the level of biology, our bodies are essentially two sides that meet in the middle: we have two eyes, ears, arms, and legs. We even have two brains, two halves that make up a complete brain, with one part capable of logic, reason, and language, and the other capable of reacting instinctively, playfully, and creatively. With all this duality, it should be no surprise that we are as uncomfortable, as discontent with ourselves and with one another as we are. It is no wonder that our aggression—and its concomitant urges toward death, destruction, and annihilation—wins out as often as it does.

Licking and biting

The child's world is animistic—filled with the images of all things being alive. And though we adults try to convince the child that living and dead are different, or that objects in the natural world do not talk—the child "knows" otherwise; some part of the child's psyche remains untouched by adult knowledge and rationality.

I see in how Molly relates to the world around her that her own interior world is populated with living spirits (her stuffed cat talks to her; the pencil that fell off the kitchen counter "jumped" of its own volition). And she knows, already, that the world around her is not entirely benign. She knows there can be danger.

Molly has a favourite question that she has been asking for several months. She asks it about every creature, dead or alive: does it lick, or does it bite? She knows that it has to be one or the other. She knows, in her childish, three-year-old way that every living being wants to either love (and live) or kill (or die). As both a psychoanalyst and as her mother, I see it as a developmental milestone for Molly to understand that all living creatures have urges to both live and die, to love and kill. And later, when Molly comes to understand an even more complex concept—that a biter can also lick and that a licker can also bite—she will manifest an understanding that represents a feat of cognitive maturation from millions of years of evolutionary progress of the human mind.

Molly's conceptual understanding sums up the most core idea that Freud struggled with as he was formulating his theory of psychoanalysis: in his struggle, he developed his theory of two drives. He called Molly's notion of licking (and loving) *Eros* and Molly's notion of biting (and killing) *Thanatos*.

In positing that two drives are behind all human activity— behaviour, feelings, perceptions, desires, ambitions—Freud leads us to the understanding that these drives are, in fact, comprehensive explanations of the human spirit. Eros, also referred to as the sex drive, represents life, love, fusion, and survival, as well as sex. Thanatos encompasses all that separates us from one another, all that is destructive and that which leads us back to our past, including our earliest origins, "the return to inorganic matter:" death. These drives or energies, however, are not opposites. Rather, in the emotionally healthy person, they work both conflictually and in tandem with one another. We live and die simultaneously. We only die while we are living, and we only live while we are dying. We are always doing both. They are also not choices. They exist in each of us, given to us as our human legacy, manifesting themselves in both overt, obvious ways as well as in subtle, hidden ways.

Freud thought of these drives as energies. In describing them, I suspect that he must have had something in mind like the energy of children. Drives, like children, represent raw, unfiltered, not yet socialised energies.

What Molly seems to grasp instinctively, as do all children, is that we want to be close to each other and, simultaneously yet conversely, we want to be apart from each other. We want to fuse and we want to separate; we want union and we want to be alone. It's the dilemma that Schopenhauer presented in his tale of the porcupines: on a chilly day, porcupines have the choice of standing apart from one another and being cold, or huddling close to each other for warmth, and being uncomfortably poked with the quills of their fellow porcupines. It is in the complex permutations of these conflicting desires and needs that our living together, living in relationships as the social animals that we are, is made interesting as well as confusing and painful.

The "if onlys" are just ways of not being with what is

When I am imagining being alone, being away from those I love the most, my unconscious is on the subject of murder. I am living psychically in the realm of Thanatos. Within the unconscious, symbol and reality become fused, and all mental life is reduced to its lowest level. Conversely, in the ego, we make fine gradations of differentiation. Separation can look like: "I want her to leave;" or "she wants to leave;" or, "I want to be alone for a moment;" or, "I want to be without her for the rest of my life." The ego has a sense of time and placement that gives all thoughts and feelings that flow through it a context and a limit. But, within the depths of the unconscious, these distinctions disappear. There are just the two energies coexisting in their purest form: togetherness and separation; love and indifference; life and death.

There are times, for instance, when I would like nothing more than for Gregg to disappear so that I may inhabit our home without him in it. Or, I imagine my next vacation without him, taking a reprieve from the machinations of our daily life together. Or, there are those times when Molly's demands have pushed me beyond my tolerable limit and there is no babysitter in sight. Rather than screaming at her until she submits to leaving me alone, I strap her into her car seat with hopes that the rolling motion of the car will mercifully lull her to sleep. These are murderous thoughts and feelings from my unconscious toward my lover and my child that I commit regularly. They are wishes and desires about the temporary obliteration of the other person. They arise out of a need to be away, to be separate, and separated from them. Of course, I do not say to myself (or, God forbid, to anyone else) that I want these people dead at these moments. I say to myself that I just want them to be a little different from the way they are. Or, I want them to go away, if only for a little while. I want Gregg to be less abrasive, more gentle and caring toward me: "Hey Gregg, can't you think before you speak? Can't you use some modicum of discipline in what you say and how you say it to me?" I want Molly to be less childishly narcissistic: "Come on Mol, have a heart. Be good to your over-aged Mom. Be a good girl who can put my needs before your immediate, ever-changing entirely appropriate-for-a-child impulses. Be a good girl and take care of yourself for a while and leave me to my own pleasures."

But here is the ghastly truth about the unconscious: wanting someone to be different is the same as wanting them to not be there; and they are both equivalent to wanting the person dead, if only symbolically and if only for that moment. It's saying: "You'd be just fine, if only..." But, of course, that brings us to the infinite list of "*if onlys.*" *If only* Molly were acting like a mature ten-year-old instead of the three-year-old she is, our trip to Toys "R" Us would be going swimmingly; or *if only* Molly was thankfully asleep so that I could, at last, get to the murder mystery I'm in the middle of. But if I really could change it all by brandishing a magic wand, then I would have missed out on a lot of Molly's early conflicts and psychic struggles—frustrating, angry, and miserable as they can be at the moments she is enmeshed in them.

The *if onlys* never stop at just one. The *if onlys* are a thousand contingencies that aren't true. They're hope against hope that the time Molly and I have together could be easier, or that I could have more time to myself, be without her. All of the *if onlys* are just ways of not being with what is. They're ways of killing what is. They're ways of killing, without the actual act: metaphorical murders.

When Molly decided that she had had enough of that little cicada, she could have engaged in a metaphorical murder. She didn't have to kill the unfortunate creature. She could have just *separated*—gone on home, leaving him to die a natural death that he was on the verge of doing anyway. But she is only a child and she is still close to her impulses—both loving and destructive—in an unfiltered, unadulterated way.

The most murderous creatures around

It may be a race for who is the most murderous: men, women, or children.

The earliest known picture depicts men killing one another. Men win the contest, and the statistics show it's not even a close contest.

While it is true that men murder much more often than women, when a woman causes the death of another, that person is most likely to be her own newborn baby. It happens a lot: it has happened throughout history and it still happens, even today. British law has an interesting and unique understanding of mother-murder. It allows leniency for the concept of survival of the fittest, when the definition of "fittest" is interpretive and when a new mother is the one who makes the interpretation. The Infanticide Act of 1922, and then its revision in 1938, deemed the act of a mother deliberately killing her newborn child as a felony with punishment applied as being the same as that for <u>manslaughter</u> (as opposed to murder). For a year and a day after childbirth, a British woman may not be judged criminally liable for killing her child. As the case-law reads: this defence applies to cases where "at the time of the act or omission the balance of her mind was disturbed by reason of her not having fully recovered from the effect of giving birth to the child or by reason of the effect of lactation consequent upon the birth of the child." Call it however they want; they know that women can be a little "crazy" after giving birth, and some might say that this "crazy" is related to trauma and to symbiosis.

We have studies showing that the female monkey, deprived of parents at birth, is unable to show any maternal affection to her own offspring. From apes to Pleistocene-era foragers, females have been influenced by a host of factors that affect their decision on whether or not to have children and whether or not to nurture them. We consider the availability of food and shelter, the presence or absence of a father, and even our community stature—and the costs of all these things—in deciding whether to first "invest" in a full-term pregnancy, and then, after the fact, whether to actually show up for the job after the baby is born.

There is as much torture in having an infant as there is bliss. The cry of an angry infant is so loud and so filled with hateful rage that it is equivalent to having an unmuffled sixteen-wheeler truck running through the home. Infants want to be fed when they are hungry, they want to be changed when they are wet, they want to be warmed when they are cold—and the mother's needs be damned. The four distinct infants' cries are all dis-stress signals, and, as such, they each promote in the mother parallel physical stress signals: a quickened heartbeat, pounding in the head, and rapid, shallow breathing.

Excessive crying is the trigger that sparks eighty percent of the reported child abuse cases for children who are under one year of age. It is only in the fact that infants are small, uncoordinated and ineffective in carrying out most behaviours that they are not equally destructive with their murderous, narcissistic impulses, urges and needs.

Mostly, we mothers forgive our infants, knowing that it is the expression of their survival mechanism to tell us, in the only way they have available to them, that their bodies/psyches are in need. But forgiveness does not always happen. Children bind their mothers to home. Working mothers rush home to spend their precious little time with their children. Women who previously worked long hours at the office, or who travelled prior to motherhood, can feel too guilty, or they miss their child too much, to continue this lifestyle. They willingly suspend their ascent up corporate ladders to spend more time at home. But the sacrifice is not always without a price. Even a trip to the supermarket with a child can exhaust the mother as she struggles to meet the needs of the infant and the home. I observe that the supermarket is a regular stopping ground for emotional child abuse. It is a place where I never fail to see mothers screaming at, threatening, or even hitting their children.

J.B. Watson, founder of the school of psychology of behaviourism, studied how mother and child influence each other negatively. He sought to find the stimulus that caused the first provocation of anger in the mother. He identified restraint of movement as the main instigating factor.

Mothers need to have the freedom to move away from their crying, demanding children. They need an escape hatch. Often this escape is found by insisting Baby go to sleep. Hence, the generations of mothers who have bundled up their screaming children in the middle of the night, strapped them in the car or the carriage, and rocked them into silence. It is, of course, just this dichotomy of love and hate that is the theme of our most famous lullaby:

> *Rock-a-bye-baby on the tree top,*
> *When the wind blows the cradle will rock.*
> *When the bough breaks the cradle will fall,*
> *And down will come baby, cradle and all.*

It is no accident that this lullaby is, as are many nursery rhymes and fairy tales, a death threat wrapped in a melodic refrain. In fact, it contains reference to the only two stimuli that J.B. Watson asserts are innately feared by infants: a loud noise and loss of support. Most nursery rhymes and fairy tales are attempts to aid both mother and child in tolerating the intensely negative feelings that are stimulated by their relationship. The lilting melodies and charming language are good protective covers for the destructive wish the mother harbours toward her infant.

And older children, too, are not exempt from their own murderous inclinations. In observing British children during World War II, psychoanalysts were at first concerned that exposure to the atrocities of war conditions would horrify and repel the children. Yet they discovered that, to the contrary, rather than repelling the violence that surrounded them, the children embraced acts of violence with glee, joyfully playing on bombed sites, throwing bricks from crumbled walls at one another. Anna Freud, psychoanalyst and Sigmund's daughter, concluded that children need to be safeguarded against the horrors of war, not because the horrors and atrocities are so strange to them, but rather because we want them, at this decisive stage of development, to overcome and estrange themselves from the primitive and atrocious wishes of their infantile nature.

A necessary psychic murder

The mother who is self-aware knows her own aggressive feelings, a legacy from her own infancy, a fact of her basic nature. And mothers, too, know that their own dearly cherished children, at times, embody aggressive wishes for others. Mothers recognise that they themselves are often the most fierce targets of their child's aggression. But they also know that their beloved child is often, more than anyone else, a target for their own brutal rage. There is no particular order to which comes first—child wanting to obliterate mother, or mother wanting to decimate child—since it is in the nature of both.

Throughout each of the stages of emotional growth, maturation involves an aggressive act of separation from the mother, a necessary psychic murder. The issues that surround separation—the desire to progress, to discover the world and be adventuresome, even to risk danger for the sake of this urge; and the conflicting desire to regress, to return back to Mother, back to safety—these two dichotomies are successfully resolved only when aggressive energies are allowed into conscious awareness. As psychoanalyst Hans Loewald has said in describing the child's point of view, "The assumption of responsibility for one's own life and its conduct is, in psychic reality, tantamount to the murder of parents." And there is no new life that can be made successfully until this primary separation/murder is mastered.

If, as Molly's mother, I have not helped my daughter by the time she is an adult to channel her raw aggression and to temper it with love, she will have great difficulty in her life. If I don't help her curb the expression of her aggression in non-destructive ways, she may become too expressive in her aggression to be well liked by her peers. She may become too pushy or bossy. She may be mean. Or, conversely, if I do too much to quell her aggression (for instance, after my horror at witnessing such a heinous act of murdering her "pet" cicada), she will learn from me that any expression of aggression is bad, and she may then find a way of turning this energy against herself. She may, then, grow up with too little self-esteem like my mother. Or she may live from a sense of desperate longing that feels frantic, and not quite understand the feelings, like my patient Linda. Or she may be depressed, feeling nothing at all but emptiness, like my patient Marnie when she first came into treatment. Or she may repress her natural rage, and not know that she has it until it comes out in one great big surprising explosion, like Marnie's mother. Molly may, like myself, have anxiety dreams about her most cherished loved ones disappearing and dying.

One of the secrets of good mothering is, therefore, for the mother to make the commitment to take her child's raw energy of wanting to kill her and to turn this into something wonderful, into a splendid act of metaphorical murder: successful separation. And every mother must make the commitment to take her own raw energy of wanting to kill her child and to turn this into something wonderful, into another splendid act of metaphorical murder: successful separation. It may well be that these murderous feelings are inherent in the mother/child relationship precisely for the reason of effecting separation. Perhaps we would not be enabled to place the appropriate boundaries between ourselves and our loved ones without these feelings of wanting to murder.

Splitting asunder what was once together

It is around the issue of separation that our murderous feelings can come most prominently into play. Separation between mother and child cannot be affected without conflict, without pain, and without some modicum of hate and aggression. Perhaps it is inevitable that splitting asunder what was once together will hurt. This process of separation can never have complete simultaneity to it. One person will often want more closeness or more distance than the other. And thus anger, frustration, disappointment—these are the inevitable aftermath of the heavenly symbiosis that has to be taken apart.

It is metaphorical murders that occur in most families: rage not dealt with; hate expressed destructively; guilt and an overarching sense of responsibility that is acted out through self-sacrifice. These metaphorical murders may consist of acts that are as overt as being told hateful things about yourself or telling someone else hateful things. Or, they may be as subtle as getting the message that someone you love wants you to be different from how you are: maybe less sensitive, or more sensitive; maybe less angry, less shy, more outgoing, less outgoing; more disciplined about food, more appreciative about the food that is fed to you.

It is these metaphorical murders in family life that lead children to grow into adults who continue to feel, as they did when they were children, unhappy, insecure, fearful (sometimes of others, sometimes of themselves). And it is these feelings that lead these people into the office of a psychotherapist. These metaphorical murder victims and perpetrators seek help because either they have felt killed in some deeply damaging way by someone who is important to them, or they feel horrified at their own murderous desires toward someone whom they love.

It is the mother who almost always has been the original recipient of these rages/murderous feelings. It is in the first years, during the time of symbiotic closeness with the mother and the first stirrings of separation, that the basic structure of the personality begins its path toward mature development. It is this early period of growth when anger and rage are felt most purely, raw and unfiltered. It is largely the mother's response to the murderous rage of the infant that will determine whether murder remains as metaphor or becomes transmuted into actual acts of destruction.

The psychoanalytic method allows the patient to return to this original murderous rage in a safe and contained way. Even more, all this murderous rage can come to be experienced with the analyst as its object. But, for the "well-trained" patient, this experience will remain on the level of feeling. Actual acts of behaviour expressing these feelings (as well as acting out all other feelings) are prohibited in the analytic sessions. The therapy is (unlike many post-Freudian therapies) a treatment of no-action.

During the course of the therapy, the analyst comes emotionally and psychically to embody the mother. The patient experiences the analyst as though she were the mother—not just the good mother who loves and gratifies, but the bad mother, who is capable herself of hating. This new mother, however, can contain now the hatred of the child/patient in a way that may not have happened with the original mother. Metaphorical murder not only leads patients to the office of a psychoanalyst, but the office of the psychoanalyst is a place where metaphorical murder is re-experienced by the patient, observed and analysed by the analyst and, then, resolved and released by the patient.

Most of us—not just my patients, and not just me and Molly—live with a plethora of metaphorical murders. Metaphorical murder demonstrates its effect in a host of ways, from our wanting to strike out to injure, to killing off a part of our own selves in order to not know the murderousness that lies below our hurt and pain.

The long-lost, now-found mother

Marnie has felt for her whole life deeply killed off—a metaphorical murder—by both mothers—the woman who birthed her and then the one who adopted her. In Marnie's decision to contact her first mother, we develop the hope that the wounds of that initial rejection-injury will be healed. We begin to hope that her story will have a happy ending.

When Marnie first contacts the woman, this long-lost/ now-found mother responds to her by saying, tearfully and movingly, "I have thought about you every day of my life.

When I look at pictures of my other two children, I always know that there is one missing." I cry when Marnie tells me this, and I think that maybe Marnie is right, maybe this mother will fill in the hole in Marnie's psyche that I have been unable to fill; maybe Marnie will, at last, find a resting place for a few moments. Maybe Marnie once did have a mother who relaxed into their togetherness, if only for a brief moment. Maybe she could have that mother again. Marnie's spirits do seem to pick up quite a bit during these contacts with her mother.

But such was not to be the case for long. After a few phone calls and letters, exchanging news of lives missed, exchanging photos, just as they were poised to meet, the woman disappears. She refuses to return Marnie's calls, and ceases responding to her letters. This is a mother whose emotional stance today is just as it was thirty years ago: abandonment and rejection. Marnie writes, begging her to please just say that she can't handle the contact, or that she is too ashamed to tell her other children—something, anything, to assuage Marnie's feeling that the problem is not just that she herself is disgusting, hateful, unworthy of love, not deserving of even a note explaining the reasons for her need to disappear from Marnie's life once again. Marnie's first letter to her after the rejection is sweet, undemanding—a mere request. In the next letter, she pleads.

Marnie and I struggle with the bloody aftermath of her having found this woman who, so different from my mother, and unlike the mother I have been to Molly, was never a mother at all to her. Marnie has entered a profound depression—much worse than the kind of low-level chronic ache she felt before she found this woman (it is hard, under the circumstances, for either Marnie or myself to now refer to this woman, Freida, as Marnie's mother). This is an acute pain—a red-hot inflammation, rather than a dull never-ending throb. It seems that I am not helpful in guiding Marnie through this pain. Or, it seems, I am even worse than unhelpful: the sessions re-evoke the sense of loss that, at times in the past, she had been able to successfully retreat away from. But there is no more distraction. Before her sessions, she comes in feeling eagerness and hungry anticipation, looking forward to seeing me and talking to me. She longs for some comfort from her pain, that she hopes being with me will bring her. She can maintain this hopeful posture until she crosses, approximately, the Queensboro Bridge. Sometimes she gets as far as when she parks her car. On rare occasions, she makes it to my front door in good spirit. Then her depression begins to set in again, and by the time she reaches the analytic couch, she is as close to catatonia as a functional neurotic can get—unable to speak, lying on the couch in a confused stupor, not knowing what she feels nor why she feels it. She often leaves the sessions with a headache, wondering when her misery will end and what will make it go away. She is convinced, after these sessions, that she means nothing to me, that she needs to find a way to make me mean nothing to her, and that our sessions are torture with no purpose. Yet, she doesn't end our relationship.

The letters are abundant. Twice a week I get letters from her, truly heart-wrenching, soulful letters that describe in exquisite detail every nuance of feeling she has had, both during those mute, unrelaxed sessions and, as well, since the last time that she saw me. Her letters are breathless to me, so moving, so reflective, and so articulate of her inner processes.

> *Dear Jane:*
> *You were so right about how Freida's rejecting me makes me feel—did I tell you that or was it an educated guess? This may sound dramatic but I do believe this is killing me. I know I can't be a complete nothing, there has to be something to me, but what little there is—is being chipped*

*away. I remember this feeling. I know how people can
reach the point of not wanting to live—I'm not at that
place, and I don't know if I will ever reach it again, but
I can see it. It is there for me to see, not so very far away
from where I am. I look at my girls and I promise I will
<u>never</u> leave them—and I know Charles and I will be
together forever—these are the only people on this earth
I can be sure about. I wish I could be sure about you. I
always think about you and I want to talk to you and
be near you. These are my first thoughts. If I really think
about it, I always come to the conclusion that you really
wouldn't be interested. I know I'm not good enough for
you—you're just too nice to tell me. You once asked if I
felt humiliated because Freida rejected me. The answer
is yes, but I am too humiliated even by the humiliation
to even want to admit it. Also, I am deeply hurt by her
rejection. The most humiliating part about all this is
that I still have to hunt around for all the facts about
the beginning of my life; the one person who knows the
whole story refuses to speak. How can she do this to me?
And I know what she is doing is fucking up my thoughts
and my relationship with you. Today when I saw you, I
just wanted to leave. I want so much to be near you, but
I feel like you are going to kill me too—as if my loving
you will lead to my destruction. I believe that when I was
in her womb, Freida probably wanted to kill me. This is
so hard for me to know. But I do know it now.*

*I wasn't sure at the time, but I believe it was the birth of
my girls when I began thinking about finding my mother.
It was after Charles almost died (Charles was, at the
time, shot in the line of duty at a bank robbery) that I
began searching. I think my love for the girls and my*

connection to you was what really triggered this need to find what I think, what I thought was my lost connection with my mother. Now I can see that she and I never lost each other. No one stole me from Freida. She ran away from me. And let's face it, if my own mother can't love me, how can I expect you to? I can't write any more.
—*Marnie*

PS
When I was leaving your building today, I heard the construction men downstairs say that your building is seventeen years old. That means I've known you for over seventeen years, and I can't even look you in the eyes. I hope this is going to get better. I'm really tired.

It is clear that Marnie, in analytic terms, is now reliving the very early rejection from her mother when her mother gave her up for adoption. This is clear to both of us. Some would say that this act of knowing is what is helpful, that it should be helpful. It isn't.

What Marnie can't say to me and can't feel when she is with me is that the painful, unvarnished truth is that her long, arduous search for her biological mother has been simply a diversion from her analysis and from attending to her relationship with me. It's been a way of running away from her true devotion, her true love affair with me. What she can't say is that I am the only mother who has ever mattered to her. She can't say it because she is humiliated to feel it and she wishes that it weren't true. She wishes that she did not have the psychic construction to care as much about a relative stranger, a person whom she sees for a mere fifty minutes a week and to whom she has to pay money to see. This feeling of caring so much seems perverse to her, and she feels herself to be perverse, really "sick" as she puts it, to be this person. She fights being this person every time she sees me, and her internal fight gives her headaches, depression, and catatonia in my presence.

Yet I know that there will be no real resolution, no place of peacefulness that she can come to until she is able to own who I have become to her. She can run away from the analysis, and from me, as often as she wants, but for the sake of her healing, she can no longer run away from the contents of her own psyche. None of us can.

The motherhood paradox

Mussolini said: "War is to man what maternity is to woman." It is true, as he implied, that men are wont to express their aggression in noble (and not so noble) world causes. But his statement means more, I think, than he intended. Not only are both war and motherhood inevitable consequences of the respective natures of men and women, but also, mothering is often very like war. As often as not, children and their mothers battle each other for love, for possessions, and for nothing at all.

Some mothers allow their aggressive urges to supersede their wisdom, and cross that all-too-fragile line that separates feelings from action. A battering mother often has a distorted view of parent/child roles. She characteristically experiences herself as the child and sees the child as a hostile, persecuting adult. She speaks of her child as though the child had an adult's capacity for deliberate, purposeful and organised behaviour. A mother I interviewed for a court case who had victimised her young daughter said: "She provokes me into a rage. She won't stop her neediness, and her screams and cries make me look like I am an inadequate mother."

The recognition of childhood as a distinct and wholly different life phase has been the norm only for the past one hundred years. Bettelheim has interpreted the historical lack of understanding of childhood as an indication of cultural immaturity. Similarly, a mother who perceives her child as a miniature adult, with the expectation of adult behavior, harkens back to that earlier period of history. Mothers who themselves were never babied properly are still, as mothers themselves, in need of babying. The quality of parenting in one generation depends upon the kind of parenting that the earlier generation gave. As William Wordsworth wrote: "The child is the father of the man."

The caveat (and paradox) of motherhood is in the discrepancy between the extraordinary lengths to which we will go in our care for our offspring, and our inability to escape the sometime feelings of resentment and rage toward them. Mothers may have difficulty accepting that the way they think they *should* love their children is different from the way they *do* love them.

The heart of motherhood

We might ask: what does it mean to be born with a sophisticated emotional apparatus that makes us capable of caring for others, yet simultaneously to have the sex drive of a primate, and the urge for fighting, aggression and destructiveness that we share with all other mammals? Freud struggled with this question throughout his life, and much of the framework of psychoanalysis constitutes his answers to this dilemma of our contradictory humanness. We humans have urges that arise from the unconscious—quite beyond our conscious will and desire—and we struggle to master them: the urge to return to that from which we have come (our inexorable movement toward death—the death drive, or Thanatos); the urge to love and have sex (our unrelenting physical attraction to another— the sex drive, or Eros); the urge to have sex even when we are young (one of Freud's seminal discoveries—childhood sexuality); the urge to have sex when we are children with the parent of the opposite sex (Freud's most controversial discovery—the Oedipus complex); and, finally, the urge to kill the parent of the same sex who stands in the way of our access to the parent of the opposite sex (Freud's most hated discovery—the aggressive drive, postulated as under the death drive, fused with the Oedipal conflict).

It was all these questions and issues that Freud struggled with in his last, terminally pessimistic work, *Civilization and Its Discontents*: how do we embody our humanness when there is so much animal still in us?

When the burgeoning and rudimentary psyche of the infant begins to entertain the idea that somebody outside of himself exists, an essential step in the development of the personality has been taken. Once an "other" is recognised, impulses, sensations, feelings and ideas become more complicated. Feelings of aloneness are aroused with accompanying feelings of fear and rage, and these states are directed toward the apparent cause of the separateness: the mother herself. The mother who is able to contain her own aggression is able, then, to aid her child in learning the containment of his aggression. And, it is precisely these feelings of aggression toward the separate mother that become a guiding light for the continuing development of the infant.

True, our capacity to mother our children is affected by our own early mothering experience. But those mothers whose mothering was damaging need not pass on a legacy of destructive mothering. Love in childhood is important. Without it, one is much more likely to be emotionally damaged. But, it is *not all*. If childhood, and the quality of mothering we received in it, were the only criteria for our later capacity for loving and productive relationships, no mother would ever be able to improve upon her own mothering. And while there is strong inclination to repeat the past, to visit the sins of our fathers and mothers upon our children, some of us learn to do better. Such is one of the tasks of motherhood: to dispel the dark shadows that remain embedded in the heart of motherhood, and to counterbalance them with the light of mother love and wisdom. Our innate capacities are only our first lessons in who we are. Next, our childhood exposures help to shape us. But, finally, and by no means least important, our capacity for growth—into the unique, creative "I" that develops independent of our reflexive and learned responses—gives us promise, not only for our individual selves and lives, but for all of mankind.

23

A Grotesque Frankensteinian-Combo

There is a line between metaphorical murder and actual murder, but the line may be thinner than we like to think. Being a psychoanalyst is similar to being a homicide detective who tracks down the murdered and the murderer—the aspects of self that have been killed off and those that want to kill. The themes of life and survival (sometimes against all odds) and murder and destruction (sometimes for no good reason) are common to both endeavours. Ordinary, run-of-the-mill ghetto crime, street-killings, random killings and such are of interest to a sociologist. But intimate murder—murder where Eros and Thanatos have become fused in some grotesque-Frankensteinian combo—this is the stuff of psychoanalysis.

A psychopath is a person who has moved into a death-land of indifference and utter non-feeling. But a killer who kills with feeling will choose as his victim whomever he loves the most. These murders of passion happen when the love and death drives meet, and then in that sudden moment of passion the death drive—Thanatos in all its glory—takes over, and, in its ascendancy, erases all memory of eros.

Our cultural fascination with murder arises not out of some perverse, other-than-human part of our selves, but rather from a deep, often unacknowledged awareness of our own murderous inclinations. Most if not all of us find ourselves with an inexplicable (shameful to ourselves) attraction to killers. We share a collective, cultural fascination with wife-murderers, child-murderers, mother-and-father-murderers. Yet, even as we attempt to distance ourselves from our own fascination, as we profess to recoil in horror at the acts themselves, we devour more and more material: on the deed, on the people—both alive (killer) and dead (victim)—on anything that we hope will shed understanding light on these events of violence so far away from the ordinary quotidian life that most of us live.

Murderers embody life lived on the edge, and beyond. Murderers entice us, even seduce us, with the fact of their having crossed a line in actuality that we only dream about. I have read that Jeffrey MacDonald, in prison for the murder of his wife and two small children, has a large fan club and gets marriage proposals from women all the time. It is just this fascination—with eros and with thanatos and with how the two can, at times, intersect at destructive angles—that led to my interest in Donna Kayson. I think, too, it was my own brush with violence, my almost-murder that occurred during my last year in college, that brings me, now, years after the event, to Donna Kayson.

I read about Donna in the *New York Times*. It was a small article, hidden away in the back of the Times, page 39 or so, describing a lawsuit that an inmate had won against the correctional system. She, Donna, had had a cold, developed an ear infection, and asked to see a doctor. The doctor arrived finally about three days later, but not before Donna had lost partial hearing in her ear. For her travails, she was awarded a quarter of a million dollars. At the end of the article, there was mention, as though an afterthought, that this woman, the lucky recipient of all this cash, was a former Harvard University Graduate School of Business honours student and that she was in prison for the murder of her mother.

After reading the article, on an impulse, I write to Donna. I write to her because I want to know what it takes, what odd mechanism is at work in the mind of a bright, relatively affluent Jewish (I presume from her name) girl from Long Island. What I want to know is how a girl with roughly the same background as myself, privileged in both money and opportunity, can bring herself to kill her own mother. Such a heinous act seems, on the face of it, inconceivable to me.

Donna writes back and invites me to visit her. The prospect of coming to know this woman thrills me like no prospective patient ever has. I want to know Donna Kayson, mother-murderer, because I imagine that my coming to understand her is going to reveal to me some previously unknown key about life, something wild and untamable that is no part of my now wholly ordinary and subdued life. Perhaps some part of me that I have renounced and am now ready to reclaim. Perhaps in coming to understand Donna, and through understanding her egregious act of destruction, I am going to come to know better how murderous rage, the need to be separate, and love and togetherness, can co-exist in the same space.

I am in the car, proceeding toward Bedford Correctional Facility in Katonah, New York, Donna's home for the last nine years. As my thoughts travel to this yet unmet woman who is absorbing all my attention, I become aware of how unimportant, at that moment, everyone else has become to me. This woman who has killed her own mother, this woman whom I have not even met, has a larger presence to me than anyone else in my life.

My thoughts travel to Gregg who has graciously offered to drive me to the prison. As I sit next to him, I feel his maleness and I become aware of the psychic distance I have to travel to feel a kinship with him. I see the differences between us—differences that are, of course, responsible in large part for the attraction, but differences that have made me feel the separation between us, not only anatomically, but emotionally, cognitively, intellectually—different in so many of the ways that define me as who I am. Men want to do. I want to feel. Men want to advise. I want to empathise. They want adventure. I want safety. They say that the difference in brain material between apes and humans is about one percent. Surely ninety-nine point nine percent of that one percent has to be the difference between men and women.

The unfortunate truth about the man/woman thing for me is that this man with whom I share minute details of my life, this man with whom I share my bed and my body every night of the week—even with all this closeness and intimacy—must compete unsuccessfully to be as important, to create a bond as tight as the girl/girl thing is for me. And, in the end, it's a losing battle for him.

This shared lineage of womanhood feels to me like a bond that cannot be broken, no matter the sins we each have committed. The fact that Donna is a woman puts her into a whole different class of being for me. This is a commonality that transcends all others. Women have always been there, are always there, will always be there. About this, there is no conflict, no ambivalence, no uncertainty. For no other reason than that she is a woman, Donna Kayson interests me and invites my compassion. We girls, we mothers and daughters, we are sweethearts and we are villains. We are decent and we are cruel. We can be as different from one another as day from night, but that common bond of like-vaginas and breasts, and soft skin and dewy emotions, links us together, unseparate.

The only history will exist inside my head

I am led into a large, sparsely furnished room. I have had to give up my pen and paper as well as my tape recorder: no note taking and no recording. With no written or recorded documents possible, the only history of this meeting will exist inside my head. I wonder about the meaning of being unable to create a written record of history. The danger seems to be that it allows for the possibility that history, and the lessons learned from it, can be forgotten.

There are at least fifty tables in this room, and only ten or so people occupying them. We ten are congregated in far regions of the room, assuring that nobody is able to get too close to anybody else. I choose a table next to the window, as close to sunlight and outside as I can get.

In seeing some of the prisoners, it is easy to distinguish between the inmates and the visitors. The inmates' faces are more alive; their eyes sparkle with greater intensity. These women have spirit. One inmate sits with her newborn infant in her arms. The child is dressed for Valentine's Day, a week away, all frilly and lacey, red and white. She is as proud of her child as any mother could be. Another sits with her ten year old on her lap, the two of them clearly never getting enough physical contact to sustain them between visits.

It seems almost like a family night-out for lower-income families. There are no men and this impersonal drab room takes on the feeling of a living room of a large, extended and chaotic family, a matriarchal family. There is a female camaraderie here: women caring for women and women caring for children; women doing what they have always done since the beginning of time.

Overseeing it all, monitoring every movement, every minute aspect of behaviour is a large woman who apparently revels in her task of vigilance. I observe her as she keeps her attentive watch over us. There appears to be little logic in this woman's edicts, but we are all on her turf, subject to her whims. After I have been waiting for about ten minutes, she suddenly decides that I am at the wrong table, and insists that I switch to a table in the middle of the room. I think for an instant with pride that, though she can control my behaviour, there is still freedom in this place—that no one can reach inside my head and control my thoughts and feelings. And then, I realise I am wrong. Her "correction" of me—and her successful directorship of me—has left me feeling humiliated. I am not angry that I have been forced, illogically, to switch tables, but shamed that I have "made an error" and been "publicly chastised" for it. I know that my feeling of shame is entirely a creation of this woman's S and M-mistress-like attitude toward all of us unfortunate enough to have to be in this room. I am wrong about my internal freedom because my thoughts and feelings have, in fact, been masterfully manipulated, all without my knowing, and this is after a mere twenty minutes in this place.

Beginning with my relationship with my mother, who wanted to know all my thoughts and feelings, and continuing through my analytic training, I have been well schooled in concept of freedom of thought. The principle is the foundation on which our country was created. I have dedicated myself to a profession whose *raison d'etre* is absolute internal freedom of thoughts and feelings. Writer Jonathon Lear has written about the political (as well as the psychological) implications of psychoanalysis, pointing out the lengths that Freud went to in order to avoid a treatment involving suggestion. A primary importance of psychoanalysis, then, is that it was the first therapy that set freedom as its goal. It doesn't promise happiness; it doesn't even define happiness; it doesn't dispense worldly success, or improvement in self-esteem; it doesn't offer a redemption of a get-out-of-jail free pass (though there have been those who have used arguments for all of those). But because of its emphasis on freedom, Lear concludes that "psychoanalysis is crucial for a truly democratic culture to thrive."

I instruct my patients on this freedom by saying: "tell me everything," or "tell me whatever comes into your mind," or "tell me what you want me to know." This principle is as dear to me as anything in my life. And yet, in a mere few minutes, within the confines of this airless, dreary, claustrophobic room in which I find myself while waiting for Donna Kayson, I have been successfully reduced to feeling constricted, constrained, unfree.

Then I see Donna enter the room. I know it is she by her age and that she is white. I don't know factually how old she is, but the woman walking toward me could be anywhere from 25 to 40. She seems ageless in a way, caught in a time warp. She walks with a bit of a shuffle, a walk without much conviction. She is slightly overweight, clearly a victim of too little exercise, without particularly caring. She is dressed in pants and a blouse that look at least ten years old, and this, too, seems to be a point of indifference to her.

It takes Donna a moment of negotiating with our Mistress to identify where I am. Her smile is quite faint, a weary, tired greeting. What is most noticeable about her appearance is her eyes. They're fuzzy, drugged. She has the eyes of a zombie— empty. I realise that she is on psychotropic drugs.

We are tentative with each other at first, staying far away from any discussion of the reason she is in prison. It's like a first date—feeling each other out to see how far trust can go.

She has a lot to say about the prison system, confesses even that she would like to write a book about it. She has many complaints: the college equivalency programme was terminated for the female prisoners, but not for the males at another facility; the health care is abominable; the guards are unreasonable and arbitrary.

Donna describes to me the prison population. Jean Harris, in prison for killing her lover Herman Tarnower (the once famous, so-called "grapefruit diet doctor"), is her floor-mate. The women are awaiting the arrival of Amy Fisher, notorious for firing a shotgun in the face of her lover's wife's face. Most of the women here are black and have been incarcerated for murder. Many of them killed men who had been physically abusing them.

The effect of the drug seems to fade away as Donna begins to talk. She is clearly an ideas person. She reads voraciously. She talks easily and spontaneously about her thoughts on what she has read. They are ideas that reflect thoughtful psychic integration. She says that she figured that she hadn't done something right with her life to end up where she was. So she decided to read about other people to find out how they did it more successfully than she did. She reads biographies, and has great gratitude to the Inter-Library Loan system. Reading George Washington was a revelation. She started with the twelve volumes of his own writings, then settled into the kind of Cliff's Notes that suits only someone who has all day to read, a reduction to a 400 page biography. She explains that it became clear to her, just from the sheer volume of his notes, why the man was so successful. He wrote down everything. Everything about everyone he met; everything about his thoughts and ideas. Everything. She thought it was a "marvelous" idea. "Things become clearer when they're written down." And there's no worry about amnesia, clearly a pivotal concern of hers given the absence of memory for the significant events of her life.

George Lukas is another favorite. Donna has taken some sociology classes at Bedford Hills. Her eyes begin to sparkle when she asks me if I know that Lukas studied sociology. She explains, as teacher (her) to student (me) that he just wanted to figure out how he could change society, and that was why he studied sociology. But he concluded that films were a much more effective means. She sees him as a man on a mission, a quest. Not a mere filmmaker.

Mothers and daughters co-existing in the same space

In coming to learn about the details of Donna's life preceding the murder, I think about the points of contact—and the points of divergences—between her life and my own. Our backgrounds are remarkably similar. We are both Jewish. We were both raised in predominantly Jewish, upper-middle class communities (I, in a southern city; she, on Long Island). We both went to quality colleges and graduate schools (my B.A. is from Washington University and my Ph.D. is from City University of New York; her B.A. is from Hofstra University and her M.B.A. is from Harvard University). We both have siblings (I have two, she has three). We both left home to study. While each of us was living away from home, we each experienced a traumatic event; we both moved back home after the trauma to live with our mothers, presumably to find some sense of safety. For both of us, our return home ended not with a feeling of safety, as we had hoped for, but rather with the feeling that our mothers and we could not co-exist in the same space.

And, too, our mothers both died in the same year. Independently, over a thousand miles apart, Donna Kayson and I both spent the spring of 1983 watching our mothers die. My mother was dying a slow, painful death, surrounded by her loving children. Donna's mother died a sudden, violent death at the hands of her own child.

Donna and I share, too, that we have both had a significant event that was defined by violence. We should be sitting on opposite sides of the fence with this: she, the perpetrator of a violent crime some ten years earlier; I, the victim of one some ten years earlier. Yet, for some odd reason, I feel drawn to this woman rather than repelled. I, the victim of a brutal, random assault that almost killed me, feel compelled to know this woman, perpetrator of murder. Areas of sameness, in spite of the one obvious difference between us—she is in prison and I am not. Donna and I started our lives so seemingly close together, and now we have moved, seemingly, so far apart.

And, finally, we share something about our mothers. I come to understand that the most problematic theme of my life has been, as well, the most problematic theme of Donna's life: the issue of separation from our mothers. My mother covered me with a cloak of closeness, while I struggled with my own conflicting desire to be more separate. On the other hand, Donna's mother seemed to need more distance in their relationship than Donna had the ability to withstand.

We both moved away from home. She moved to California to begin her career as a computer consultant. Donna remembers California nostalgically. It was the last time that she felt normal, able to be on her own. And then something went wrong. Perhaps it was, as she now believes, chemicals in her body gone haywire. Perhaps it was an emotional time-bomb from old, unresolved issues that chose their moment finally. Perhaps it was too much aloneness, too frighteningly far away from home. Donna had what she refers to as a nervous breakdown and ended up in a psychiatric hospital. Afterwards, she went home to Long Island, to Mother, hoping to recover (as I moved to New Orleans, after my trauma, with the same hope).

But Donna Kayson did not have the kind of mother I had. She did not have a mother who searched her out, fought for closeness even as she might have needed to pull away, as mine did. Donna's mother did not provide her daughter with a sense of easy access, nor did she give her the feeling of being unequivocally, unquestionably loved, as mine did. I believe that Donna Kayson lived without the assurance of care and interest that was so utterly constant in my own life.

Donna Kayson professes to have loved her mother, even referring to loving her mother now in the present, as though her mother were still alive, still able to be the happy recipient of Donna's love. Donna tells me, as well, that she had a normal childhood, a happy childhood. This is difficult for me to believe. This woman cannot make a move without permission. She has to be fetched for her meetings with me, and taken back to her room under guard. She has to borrow a quarter from me to buy herself a cup of coffee. This loss of freedom, she is asking me to believe, has arisen from a healthy, happy childhood.

A revision of history

I believe in alternate worlds—that somewhere, somehow, everything that didn't happen in this world is happening out there in some other place. Creating alternate worlds is a way of revising history. Dreams are little peeks into these alternate worlds. In dreams we can make anything happen. We can change the past.

In one of these alternate worlds, I suppose it is possible that Donna's mother is still alive, and that Donna loves her, and she loves Donna. I have the impression that Donna lives in an alternate world in order to make this world that she finds herself in more tolerable. I think maybe Donna has made her dreamy, drugged world the world in which she lives.

Donna's memory of having a happy childhood has to be a revision of history. This revision cannot be accomplished without consequences. In many science fiction books and movies, the cardinal rule is that the past can't be changed without concomitantly changing the present. Donna's consequence in her revision of history is that she changed the present by paying the price in repression. When I ask her if the prison has provided her access to psychotherapy, she explains that she has talked with a violent crime counsellor, but that the sessions cause flashbacks that are upsetting to her. She and the counsellor have agreed to stay away from material that upsets her, and rather, to stay on neutral topics. Donna won't allow herself to process the horror of her past deed because it makes the present too horrific.

It is clear to me that it is not just incarceration that has been Donna's punishment for her crime, for her inability to figure out how to handle her rage at her mother in some way other than firing a shotgun into her back. Her punishment is, too, that a part of her own self has been killed off. The psychotropic drugs that the medical department of the prison supplies her with keep her far distant from her emotions. She is grateful for the distance from her feeling self that the drugs have given her. Donna sees feelings as her enemy, and she has gladly, through drug therapy, dispensed with them altogether. Feelings, emotions— that which gives colour to the world—are no longer a part of the self that is allowed to live. The drugs have killed any true self of hers that is lying in wait, wanting to be reclaimed, excavated. She has eliminated a chance to confront the demons in the theatre of her mind. Rather, she is like a walking corpse, a soulless zombie.

Sometimes there is almost a feeling in Donna. On occasion, her feelings, like her intellect, are able to bleed through the haze of the psychotropic drugs. She explains that her father had Parkinson's, and that as a result her family lived frugally. They never had a stereo. The first time she heard stereo music was when she was in prison. She got a Walkman, and had a love affair with stereo. It is easy to imagine. She is an internal sort of person. It is easy to imagine her walking the halls of prison oblivious to all but the exhilarating sounds of stereo next to her ear, shutting out the bitterness and drabness of where she is.

But her love affair with stereo was short-lived. She explains that she had her Walkman only six months before she developed an ear infection and lost total hearing in one ear. She blames the prison—the lawsuit I have read about. When she talks about this, her eyes well up with tears, the one tearful moment in this meeting, a breaking through of thrown-away-feeling when she explains with lucid vividness what it feels like to hear in only one ear, to have lost stereoscopic listening. But I think perhaps the mourning of her loss of hearing is a metaphor, a screen against a much more painful loss. I think perhaps the deeper loss is that of her emotional self, the disruption from her soul.

I believe that Donna had a surfeit of feeling before her act of murder and before the drugs that now render her zombie-like. I believe that she did love her mother, as she professes. But I think that, in spite of that love, Donna could not abide the hate and rage that had come between them. I imagine that there had been plenty of times when, before the actual murder, Donna and her mother must have felt murderous toward one another, little mini-murders, metaphorical murders—the kind that happen between loved ones as part of daily life.

According to newspaper reports, friends of Donna's mother described the time shortly before the murder as being a particularly happy period for her mother. She had begun seriously dating a man. Her friends have described her during this time as being the happiest they had ever seen her since the death of her husband five years earlier. But apparently Donna's mother's circle of inclusion for her new life did not extend unconditionally to Donna. The last significant communication Donna's mother made to Donna was that she was planning to remarry and that Donna would have to move out of the house.

Donna's murder of her mother was a crime of passion. Not pre-meditated, and not your ordinary kind of murder passion between lovers, by a betrayed sweetheart. This was a passion that went back to the original source, the first object of our passions, a passion for Mother. This was a murder stimulated, I believe, by the fright and rage in Donna at too much looming separation.

Murder—whether metaphorical or real—is mostly about separation. You don't want to kill if you don't feel caught by the involvement. If it's a mere matter of walking away without a care, then anger, rage, and murderous thoughts don't come into the equation. But if you have the feeling that you can't get away, or that you don't want to get away, or that you don't want the other person to get away, then you may resort to murder – either murder in thought and feeling, or murder in deed. It's the fastest escape route known to man. But not the smartest.

Real killer in my blood

During the time of meeting Donna Kayson and coming to understand her life, I find out an important piece of information about my father's side of the family. Most of the surviving Goldbergs are my first cousins, roughly my age, children of the original five boys of Dora and Jacob. These original five boys were all born and raised in southern Georgia, Jimmy Carter peanut-country. Of those five boys, only one remains alive: Dave who is in a nursing home in Baton Rouge, mostly senile. Besides Dave, there is one widow who remains alive—Muriel, my cousin Michael's mother. If there is anything left to know about the Goldberg history, Muriel is the only one left to tell it.

All my southern Goldberg cousins have come up to New York for Michael's son's bar mitzvah. My cousin Jack is interested in some bit of historical discrepancy he has recently uncovered. He has a record—a tax roll from the state of Georgia. This 1920 document declares Dora, my father's mother, to be the head of the household of the farm. Jack is curious. Where, in 1920, is Jacob, Dora's husband, my father's father? Muriel's face begins to turn ashen, and, of course, everyone watching knows that some odd little tidbit of familial history that has been hidden under a rock for seventy years is about to be uncovered. Muriel insists that she cannot talk about it.

For the next two hours we Goldbergs are determinedly dogged about pursuing Muriel's link to the past. We give her no rest. We tell her she **must** tell us, and finally, she folds under the pressure and reveals the dark secret of the Goldbergs. Grandfather Jacob was a murderer.

This is a rumour that all of us have heard at one time or another over the years. There were all those unexplained moves that my father had told us about, from southern Georgia to northern Florida, back and forth over the state line, endlessly moving about (murder, it turns out, is a state offence), presumably staying ahead of those chasing after him.

Muriel admits that Jacob shot his wife's lover. Dora, who I knew only until I was five and who I remember as a buxom, heavyset woman with a thick old-world accent, suddenly gets infinitely more interesting as a woman to me. Apparently, long before I met her, Dora was an intensely sexual woman, a woman who, like my own mother, was willing to risk the judgement and wrath of the limited culture she lived in. And I am reminded of the teaching of my mentor, Hyman Spotnitz, who argued the real value of monogamy is that it prevents murder.

After hearing the confirmation that my grandfather was a killer, I understand that Jacob has passed down to me a legacy of fascination with death. After all, I have killer in my blood. Real killer. Donna Kayson kind of killer. Not the pale imitation of it that is metaphorical.

A different sort of mother

I think about all the times that I reached out to my mother—yelled out for her when we were at opposite sides of the house, asked her to listen to my newly practiced piano piece. Or, when I wasn't home, the times when I called her on the phone. She was always responsive; I always knew there was a mother willing to make herself available. I think Donna's experience must have been very different from my own. I think she must have tried on too many occasions to call out to her mother, beseeching her mother to listen. I think that she had the feeling that there was never anyone at home to receive her call.

I always knew that if my mother didn't respond to me, it was not because she was choosing to ignore me. It was because of some event that was beyond her control. I knew that day when I saw her car pulling away from me into the traffic, that her ignoring me was not deliberate.

I allow myself to have a different twist in my thinking, to subvert the truth for a moment. I begin to reorder the way I experienced my mother, to refashion it from a different angle. Suppose, instead of my not being able to reach my mother because of events beyond her control—suppose it is her own act of volition that has made it impossible for me to reach her. Suppose she has cared so little for my need, so meagerly for my hunger for her that she could willingly, out of desire, deny herself to me. My anguish, perhaps, would turn from the dull pain of hurt and emptiness to the hot intensity of rage. I imagine then I might become something like an overwrought animal, vicious, wrathful, and teeming with the power of blood-thirst. I believe that this inaccessible mother is the mother that Donna experienced herself as having. I believe that this wrathful animal is the child that Donna became. (And, probably, the husband that Jacob became.) With this small reordering of thought, I have rendered myself, now, even closer to understanding this mother-murderer.

But in spite of all of the "*if onlys*"—the metaphorical murders I commit—I am still living a life that consists of freedom. Donna crossed that line that maintains order, the line that separates deed from thought, action from fantasy, behaviour from desire. As Freud said, the man who first hurled a curse rather than a spear was the inventor of civilisation. Donna is in prison for one real murder, and I am not in prison for my thousands of metaphorical murders.

Our most ardent believers in resurrection

I know that the cure for the terrible sense of disconnection from one's original home that leads to the kind of disturbance that Donna Kayson suffered from involves a journey of time-travel through psyche and soul. It is a journey that takes us back to our earliest years, the years when soul-separation begins. This is a journey that can be made not just by those ripped violently from their first homes, as Marnie and Molly were, nor by those who are asked to leave their mothers' homes as adults, as Donna was. All of us have had the experience, in some ways, of being away from home, and, for many of us, this is a journey not without pain. We must endeavour to seek to illuminate the darkened places within our psyches that are, in a sense, the closets of our past—the places in which we can hide—from others we well as our own selves, and the storage-place of belongings for which one no longer has easily accessible room, but which one cannot live without.

Children need to know that when they want to move away from their mothers and when their mothers want to move away from them, this is not a forevermore kind of disappearing act. Children who are adopted often have a vulnerability in lacking confidence for an eventual re-appearance of an absent mother. For adopted children, the threat of eternal separation is in their biology, in their unconscious, never so far from awareness that it won't be activated under a perfect-storm series of unfortunate circumstances.

My own history was so different from Molly's, Marnie's, and Donna's. Throughout all the years after I moved away from New Orleans, my mother kept my bedroom as I had left it. My room waited for me, for my visits, even for a permanent return, should I have chosen to make that decision. Unlike Donna's experience, I knew that my mother's home would always remain my home as well. As Molly's mother, I want her to know, as I knew from my own mother, that if she moves away from me, I will be there when she wants to come back, and that she is always welcome to come back. Such knowledge is, most of all, what children need to be reassured of—that they can want to kill off the other person—metaphorical murder—but that they will not succeed. When Molly tells me to go away, or when she herself goes away, she is verbalising and enacting her momentary wish to kill me off. She wants to kill me, but she also wants me to remain alive for future reference. Children are our planet's most ardent believers in resurrection.

24

A Zombie without a Mother

We humans have been interested in our dreams, and their meaning, for thousands of years. We have ideas about the meaning of dreams recorded on clay as far back as 3000 BC. In the Greek and Roman eras, dreams were thought to be direct messages from either the dead or the gods. Our ancestors accepted that dreams foretold the future, and dreams were used in political as well as personal matters. Dream interpreters often accompanied military leaders into battle, and were considered valuable in developing battle strategies. In Egypt, priests served as the dream interpreters and were considered to be divinely gifted. The Chinese believe that that soul leaves the body during the dream state. Native American tribes see dreams as ways of communicating with one's ancestors, and directions for pointing one toward the true mission of one's life.

Freud's first major work was an exploration into his own dreams: *The Interpretation of Dreams*. It was through his analysis of his own dreams that he came to understand the notion that dreams represent the royal road to the unconscious. Dreams provide a window into the unconscious—the inner recesses of our psyche that remain unknowable—and, through dream interpretation, we are enabled to find resolution to the tensions between our drives that pull us in conflicting directions.

The secreting of secrets

One of the main components of infancy is the inability to speak. The very etymology of the word *infancy* is from *infans*, meaning, "not speaking," or without words. Because psychoanalysts theorise that many of the core personality attributes develop during early childhood, they are as interested during the course of the treatment in the gestures of pre-language as they are in words themselves. In the adult personality these pre-words, this pre-language, is expressed through communications from the unconscious. These are the words that are unable to be said. Freud observed that there were some words, representing thoughts and feelings that were so objectionable to people that they would rather be sick than to think and feel and say the unthinkable, the unfeelable, and the unmentionable.

It is the words unsaid— secrets—that sometimes become the origin of neurosis. The bulwark of the psychoanalytic theory of illness pivots around the concept of secrets. The words "secret" and "secrete" come from the same root: we are impelled to secrete our secrets, and yet sometimes, too, there is an opposing force that mandates that we not tell our secrets. But, of course, secrets are hard to keep. Freud posited: "He who has eyes to see and ears to hear will be able to convince himself that no mortal can keep a secret. If his lips are silent, he chatters with his fingertips. Betrayal oozes out of him at every pore."

Secrets are, too, the real mark of separation. Secrets exist only when there are two: the keeper of the secret and the one from whom the secret is kept. But when we hold too tightly onto our secrets, these hidden contents of the mind can make the person sick. We know that victims of rape and incest who choose to not talk about their trauma do less well than those who are willing to talk about their experience. Measurable decreases in the production of stress hormones were seen after the secret-holders finally shared their secrets by talking about their experiences. Sometimes holding onto a secret is more damaging than actually having that experience.

Secrets, then, are both the disease and the antidote to the disease: secreting the secrets to another can be the cure.

Often our secrets become not only hidden from others, but are concealed even from ourselves, tucked away in the caverns of our unconscious. The thoughts and feelings that have not yet found their way into words do, often, find their way out of the hidden dimension of the unconscious into the dream-life of the person. When dreams are remembered, what has formerly been unsayable and unknowable—the material of the dream—is brought into conscious awareness.

My mother is alive again

I have a dream that is more intense than the anxiety dreams I have already had about Molly. It is brutally frightening:

> *I am back home in New Orleans. I have given up my career as a psychoanalyst, abandoned my life in New York, and have returned to school. I am taking a history class with Mrs. Scarborough, my high school maths teacher. I am anxious about my grade, but when the grades are passed out, it turns out that I have gotten a good grade after all. I want to share the good news with my mother. I rush to a pay phone and try to call my mother. I can't get through. At first I think maybe I don't have the right amount of change. Then I think that the telephone*

company has, unbeknownst to me while I was living in New York, raised the amount of money for a phone call. I feel frustrated but not frightened because so far, I have imagined the problem to be stemming from my own mismanagement of the situation. I feel hopeful that I will find a solution to the problem and will be reunited with my mother.

Then, finally, the horror of the problem descends upon me. I realise that something unimaginable has happened at home that has taken my mother away from me. This event that has taken her away is not my fault, and it is not her fault. This is an event of cosmic proportions, with what feels like to me implications equivalent to that of a cosmic disaster. Then I realise that as a result of this disaster, my mother is not there, is never going to be there again for me. I feel utterly helpless and defeated. I feel a pain like no other pain—a pain that is quite inconsolable, a pain from my centre that will never be assuaged. I know that I will be living with this pain, living without the easy access to my mother that I had been used to, her constant availability to me as a source of comfort, love, attention. And I know that the loss of my mother will make me into a person without life, without energy, without a centre. I will be, forevermore, a zombie without my mother; I am destined to remain a half-human trapped between alternate worlds—the world of the living and the world of the dead.

And then I wake up. I am filled with dread and utter aloneness. The world has become a dark and uninviting place. The feeling of the dream—of my being helpless and defeated—is the feeling that I am left with when awake.

I recognise this feeling. It is one that resides in a place—deep inside me (in fact, it feels like the deepest, darkest space that I have lived from)—that I have come back to frequently in my life. It is, of course, the feeling I had when my mother died.

I realise, though, that it is only the surface meaning of this dream that is about my mother's death, about my loss of her. I realise that my mother's death was not the first time these feelings have enveloped me, as they have in this dream. Throughout my life, there were times when our separations would come to me with the force of gale winds, times when I needed to cling to her like the infant I once was, separations that felt like assaults to my sense of safety. The dream describes not just how I felt when my mother died, but also my emotional state whenever I felt too far away from her, whenever there was a separation between us that I couldn't bridge. The dream describes how I felt when I first went to sleep-away camp at the age of eight and cried myself to sleep every night for the first two weeks. It describes how I felt the first day I took the public bus to school, when I was seven, with my mother following after the bus in her car to make sure I did it right. On that bus, I became intensely aware of the distance between the bus and her car—her and me. I felt that invisible rubber band that separates mother and child as they explore their ever-broadening distance from one another, and I felt that our rubber band was being stretched too tautly that day. The dream describes the feelings I had the summer my mother took a two-week course out of town when I was twelve, and I went to the movies with my father. Until then, my mother was the parent, my father more superfluous, at least to my conscious mind. I was so unused to being alone with him that I felt insecure, frightened that he was not going to get me back home safely. I pretended to have a stomachache and made him leave the movie early. All I could think of was my need to get that dreaded walk back to the car over with—across huge Canal Street, the largest, widest, and busiest street in New Orleans.

All the painful separations in my life

I realise that my dream describes not just my separations from the symbiotic mother of my childhood. It describes, too, all painful separations in my life. It describes how I have felt after each of the relationships with men whom I have loved has ended. I have never taken these love relationships lightly. When they failed, I would feel that it was my destiny to be alone forever. I would have no confidence that I would ever again have meaningful love in my life. I would feel utterly desolate, hopelessly filled with anxieties about my future. I know now that these are not rational feelings, though at the time they felt more real than real. Indeed, in spite of the losses of my men, I have always loved again, and again. I have never gone too long in my life without a man to love. I understand that the pain of the loss of a man is, deep within the unconscious, a return to my first loss: the loss of my mother.

The dream describes the momentary feeling that has come over me when I have been on a trip alone and wake up in a strange room, not knowing for an instant where I am. At these times, my need for my mother, for an equilibrium to right my sense of aloneness, would be so intense that, coming from within the interiors of my mind, I could hear my mother's hallucinatory voice calling me.

And the dream describes how I, occasionally, experience myself as Mother to Molly. There are times when I am not with her, when she is at school or at a friend's house, and I am not, for a moment, distracted by the everyday events of my life. I am able to pause and I realise, with unerring precision, how much a part of me she has become, and how I feel only half-whole without her.

I understand that all these separations, all these pains and anxieties about separation—are really the only deep pains that I have felt in my life. Nothing else has mattered to me as much as being with the people I have loved—whether my mother, my man, my daughter. The experience of all of these unwanted separations has been the same, and they all have their origin in my relationship with my mother and the symbiosis we shared.

This force—I can only call it a force, as it overtakes me, actually grabs me—has, at these various times in my life, lasted an instant, sometimes hours (as it has with this dream). With men, it has always been longer; with one man, it took two years after he ended the relationship for my confidence about having a meaningful love in the future to return. And when this force of aloneness is present, when it becomes me (because that is how it feels—I am nothing except this feeling, I have become this feeling of solitary morbidity), I can do nothing to recover, nothing to pull myself away from this feeling that is defining all of who I am at these times. I can only wait.

This periodic feeling of aloneness has been my greatest pain and it has followed me throughout my life. Most of the time I am happy, busy, and distracted. But I am never very far from my memory of past pain and anticipation of future pain. I live with the awareness that it may surface in moments of stress or fatigue, and I know that it will always engulf me whenever I experience loss—a friend moving, a lover ending our relationship, a death.

We might ask: when is it that a child can first experience anxiety? I think the answer is when the child learns to love.

Learning what I need to know

It is through my dreams that I will come to learn what I need to know, what I have been unwilling to know. My dreams serve as my guide, and, through my understanding of them, I will come to understand more fully the history and nature of my relationship with my mother, and thus, the remnants of my unresolved issues with my mother that creep into my relationship with Molly.

In my dream, Molly doesn't exist yet. I am still my mother's daughter; my mother is not yet dead. I have returned to New Orleans to be with my mother. The concept of return has a special meaning in the unconscious. It is true that pleasure is a great motivator. We seek pleasure. We go to great lengths to find pleasure. But we have an even stronger urge, more powerful, more primitive, more elementary, than our striving for pleasure. At times, the experience of familiarity is so compelling that the search for it overrides every other desire, that it is beyond and replaces every other pleasure. Beyond the urge to seek pleasure lies the stronger force, the impulse to repeat the past, to return and thus to re-experience the past. We will create out of whole cloth what is familiar, even if the familiar is pain rather than pleasure. As the compulsion originates in the unconscious, it is tenacious, and can come to feel ungovernable. (It is why abused children marry abusive spouses; it is why unloved children marry unloving spouses.) When we are in the throes of this compulsion, there is, in fact, no separation between our selves and our pain. We are one with our conflict and one with the person from our past who represents (or even stimulates) our conflict.

Going home to New Orleans, and going home to my mother, has always been synonymous for me. For twenty years after I moved from New Orleans, I returned to see my mother every few months. I went home because I knew she wanted me there; I visited because I felt I should be with her; I spent vacations with her because I wanted to be with her; I returned to bring my latest man home to her (perhaps like a cat brings home a stray mouse that it has captured, a proud showing off of its noteworthy acquisition); I went back to swim in our pool and make carrot juice with her; I returned because she had cancer; I returned to keep her up-to-date with my life, to share with her not only my "good news" (as in the dream), but all news, because for my mother, in relation to me, *all news was good news*—she wanted to know everything; I returned for any number of reasons—good and bad, loving and selfish, serious and trivial—but I always returned.

The mother to whom the child returns is not the mother of symbiosis. There can be no return if there is no division. The mother of return is the mother of separation. I understand from my dream that my psyche is asking me to look at my separation from my mother.

In the dream, I have inexplicably given up my career. This is peculiar because, in my dream as well as in real life, I have become a successful analyst. Since I have been an analyst, I have always thoroughly enjoyed my work. This pleasure in work is quite different from my academic experience in high school, which I hated and wasn't particularly successful at. Why would I want to give up a wonderful career to re-experience an event that was unpleasant and not particularly gratifying? Yet, there I am in the classroom. I think the dream is suggesting that there is some failure, or lack of satisfaction, that has led me to the decision to give up being a psychoanalyst. The dream seems to be telling me that there is something about either my own analysis or my being a psychoanalyst (they're really the same since all analysts are required to be themselves in their own analysis) that remains unresolved for me. It seems that the dream is challenging me to think about myself—my relationship with my mother and, as well, about my work as an analyst—in some new way. The dream is telling me that I prefer being with my mother to being separate from her. My desire (need) to be with her is so strong that I am even willing to sacrifice what I have loved most in my life, my career, in order to be with her.

The class I am taking in my dream is history. I hated history. I never learned a thing about history in school. I was too busy in the present to have any interest in the past. But I reached a point in my life where I wanted to know more about my personal history. Coming to understand my history held the promise of assuaging my pain. It was the promise of alleviating pain through the understanding of my personal history that first led me into psychoanalysis.

Even though the class is a history class, it is being taught by my high school maths teacher. This is, at first blush, an odd twist that my unconscious has created. But in dreams there are no accidents, and I must make sense out of these seemingly disparate entities being brought together.

The words here—*history* and *maths*—feel resonant to me. I think that there may be some key to understanding this portion of the dream in studying the etymology of the words. Jung talked about the history of every word going back thousands of years, touching upon the historical fibre of our ancestry. He felt that tracing back the lineage, a family tree of a word, would lead us to the parentage of our psyche.

So in order to understand my personal history, and why, in the beginning of my dream, I am taking a history class from my maths teacher, I am led to the *Oxford Dictionary*. The root word for *history* means, "to know." History is the narrative of what we know about the past. The word *mathematics*, on the other hand, comes from the root word that means "to learn." It is the science dealing with forms and quantities and relationships between these entities. It involves the use of symbols: numbers become symbols. The two disciplines both contradict and complement each other. One deals with facts; the other with symbols. One is a story, a tale that is told, a weaving together of sometimes independent elements to make a comprehensible whole; the other is precise and logical. "To know" suggests that awareness is just there, that it is inherent, maybe intuitive. "To learn," however, is an active process, and it is a skill.

It occurs to me that the contradiction that I have created in my dream is the same contradiction that exists in having both a psyche/soul and a mind. And it is, too, the same dichotomy of sensibility that Freud was striving for in calling his discipline a fusion of *psyche* and *analysis*. We have, in effect, two brains; two hemispheres, two modes of functioning from our dual brains: one feelingful and intuitive (psyche/soul) and the other logical and rational (the mind). The dream invites me to create a fusing together of rationality and intuition, of logic and soul. It tells me that I need to integrate the two aspects of self that are represented by both symbols and facts. I need to bring the precision of logic to the ephemeral entity of my soul in order to achieve wholeness. If I simply allow myself to tell my story, the tale of my history and my relationships, then I will come "to learn" what I already "know." And, this "knowing" is also "hearing" (in the Heraclitus sense). Through saying, and listening, and hearing, the information, knowledge, wisdom, as well as pain that my unconscious has stored away, will become released for conscious awareness, and thus available for integration and wholeness.

A scar is deposited

I am struck, too, by the reference to Mrs. Scarborough. Again, I retreat to my *Oxford*. A scar is created when there is a wound. It is the defence that is built around a trauma. In defending against the pain or injury of the trauma/wound, a scar is deposited, laid down as a permanent reminder of the wound that was/still is.

In my dream, a scar is connected to a borough. A borough is a fortified enclosure. My dream is telling me that I have a wound, a hurt that I have fortified, built defences around. The unconscious intent in building defences in the psyche is to ward off feeling and conscious knowing.

In the dream, I can't quite figure out what has happened. At first, I think that it's just a momentary snag that I can't reach my mother. I think that something has changed while I have been away. I think that the problem is of my own making. It seems as though I am blaming myself for not being able to find my mother. Perhaps the problem is my having left New Orleans. If I hadn't moved away, I would still know how to use the phones there.

Then the dream begins to spin out of control. Actually, it becomes a nightmare at this point. I have the horrible realisation that this is not just a momentary snag. My mother is gone. And now that she is gone, her absence is an inconsolable pain and a terrifying fear from which I feel I will never recover. It is a contradiction: in reality, in my waking life, my days are filled with joy and accomplishments, my life is fulfilling. Yet, in my dream life, the fear and pain of the eternal separation from my mother resides in the centre of my being, deep within my unconscious; and in this place, this space inside me, I remain only half-human, half-alive.

I understand that my dream is telling me that there is a part of my history that I have walled off from feeling and consciousness, and that I must return to it. I must re-study my history in order to *learn* what I have not permitted myself to *know*. And the content of this psychic journey will have to do with a traumatic separation from my mother. The dream suggests that there is still unfinished work around this issue.

My dream is a gift from my unconscious that will lead me out of the state of unknowingness in which I have lived.

My dream says that, without my mother, I am not fully human, living in an underground place. Without my mother, I have no real life. I am trapped as a half-human, a shell of a human, a zombie, without a centre. As long as I stay attached to my mother, who now resides in the world of the dead, away from me forever, then only half of me will be in the world of the living. My dream is telling me that in order to be brought back to life, I must let go of my mother. I must be willing to live even though she remains dead.

The unimportant scar

I know from my dream that my anxiety about being a mother is related to my conflicts about separation—both in relation to my daughter and to my mother; one causing the other. I know that after Molly first came to me, my anxiety dreams about her near-death experiences were related to my dread and terror of her leaving me (as my mother dreaded my leaving her), and I know that I need to not transfer onto Molly, as a legacy, my own dreaded anticipation of separation from her (as my mother gave it to me as a legacy).

And so, I determine to follow the message, the gift from my unconscious that my dream has given me. I determine to let myself "learn" what I already "know," to uncover and resolve the issues that lie behind the trauma that gave me my scar.

It is not just psychic scars that I have suffered from—not just anxieties and fears relating to the loss of my mother or daughter. I have another scar. I see it every time I look into the mirror, every time I pull my hair back to brush it or tie it in a ponytail. It is on the side of my neck. This is the scar that I have tried to ignore, the scar that I have dismissed as unimportant, the scar that I have refused to talk about whenever anyone (including Molly) has asked me about it. I have walled off the meaning of this scar, defensively fortified myself against it.

I force myself to think about the event that was the major trauma of my adult life when I acquired my neck scar—a fateful night that marked the beginning of a decade of fear and pain, and created within myself a very large secret that I didn't want to talk about, and that changed utterly the relationship with my mother.

25

The Year my Sexuality went Public

I t was 1968, my senior year in college. Throughout my college years, I had settled into an identity away from my family, separate from my family. It was an energetic, heavily political time. I had become involved in the civil rights movement and I had a job at the state mental hospital working with adolescent schizophrenic girls. My professors were smart, thought deeply about things spiritual as well as political, and expected the same of their students. My own family seemed somewhat colourless in comparison. It was a time of exploration for my friends and myself. We read up on Eastern religions and dressed a little more outrageously than the generations that had preceded us. Together, we were extending the boundaries of acceptable behaviour; we smoked marijuana, took a few LSD trips. College students all over the country were just gearing up to do a serious protest of a war in a faraway place that no one had ever heard of. My parents didn't understand my involvement in activities that were likely to get me arrested, or injured, or both. The reason I chose these involvements was clear to me though: I was my mother's daughter. She didn't understand that her being an

Adlai Stevensonian from the early fifties would naturally give rise, in the late sixties, to a civil rights/socially conscious/Vietnam protestor.

Most of all, we felt guiltless about sex. We were all having sex. After having my relationship with my high school boyfriends observed through my mother's vigilant eye, I was enjoying my sexual freedom from big brother/mother.

I have thought of it as the year that my sexuality went public. It was the year that my mother and I couldn't continue with our mutual *folie à deux* deception about my sexuality— the impression I deliberately fostered for her—that I was not yet sexually active. This was the year I was raped.

Time stops moving for the almost-dead

It happened in March. That night, my boyfriend, Steve, and I had fought. Later that night, I was sound asleep in my bed when a strange man climbed into my apartment through a window and found his way to my bedroom. With virtue, innocence, and naivety being my main life's experience, here was a man telling me that he was going to kill me. Hearing threats of my imminent death was how I thought I was going to spend those last few unguarded, cheerless moments of my life, still connected to my soul, still a person who did not know that these kinds of events happened to anyone I knew. Until that moment, life had been ordinary. Love existed, and true hate/aggression/indifference had not.

The man was on top of me, and for an instant I thought that Steve had come back into my apartment after our fight. Then I realised that this was not love, this was not Steve. This was brutal, impersonal. Surprise was the first feeling, the disorientation of not quite being able to understand what was happening. I was only aware dimly of what the man was doing. I wanted to reach out to the lamp next to the bed so that there would be light, but I couldn't move under his weight. He was talking to me as though we were lovers, but his skin was rough and unfamiliar.

Then I started fighting. I wanted to get up, to move this weight off me, and to flee. I was thrashing, waving my arms, screaming—screaming as loud as I could, screaming for my life. I tasted blood in my mouth and had the first realisation that this was violence. Then, as I swallowed my own blood, I realised I was hurt. *This man had hurt me.* The fact was inescapable. *This man doesn't care if he hurts me.* Very suddenly, the world was a different place than I had ever known it, different to the place my mother had ever allowed me to be exposed to, and this man was a different sort of person to any I had ever met. I stopped fighting, stopped screaming, and acquiesced to the assault. Inside my head, however, I was screaming (to myself, with disbelief): *This man doesn't care if he hurts me.* More than the physical invasion, this is what startled and injured me: his utter indifference to my pain.

This soulless man didn't care how anyone had been kind to me in the past. He was indifferent to the fact that I was a child born and reared of love. It became clear, in fact, that he was indifferent to whether he ended up with a corpse or just a mangled, barely breathing body. I became instantly, utterly relaxed. Every muscle in my body went dead with passivity. The man could have performed a lobotomy on me and I wouldn't have flinched.

With this man whispering the sweet nothings of death threats into my ear, I knew that I was going to die, and die alone. There was no safety for me, no rescue, no omnipotent mother who had soothed all previous pains. A sweet sadness crept over me as I sunk into dying without my mother, without Steve, without anyone I loved. The night became all calmness, not at all an agitation. It was going to be a screamless death.

The man left me for dead.

I heard him rustling around in the apartment for what could have been ten minutes or two hours. Time stops moving for the dead, and I was getting increasingly close to dead as my blood was seeping out from a razor-blade-slashed vein in my neck.

And then I started screaming again. It was a different scream this time. There was no anger, no outrage. Only fear and distress and a plea for help. It was more like a loud, impotent whine, like a noisy truck stuck in a ditch trying unsuccessfully to climb out.

One of my roommates finally heard me. I told her not to come into the room, but to call the police. Then I told her to call Steve. I told her to forget about the police. To just call Steve. She asked for Steve's number, which, until then, had been brightly emblazoned in my brain, but now was nowhere to be found.

The police, the ambulance, and Steve all arrived at the same time. I was sprawled out on the bed, coated in blood, my favourite red silk pyjamas ripped, or sliced off me, and my sheets too bloody to cover myself with. The police seemed to not mind that I remained undressed, nor that I was, apparently, bleeding from my neck. They were standing around, rumbling around my bedroom, whispering, and I couldn't discern what they were saying, but it seemed as though they were searching for drugs. They wouldn't let Steve near me. There was no caring hand, no gentle voice to bring me back to the world of the living. The experience of lying nude in my own blood, uncovered, with three strange men leisurely going through my belongings sent me over the top. I started shaking, every part of my body no longer under my conscious volition. I couldn't stop shaking, but my voice had gone silent, as though my body was expressing the outrage that my voice no longer could.

Maybe the side-effect of a brain transplant is nausea

My mother flew up the next day.

The moment I knew her plane had landed and that she was on the earth, the same latitude and longitude as I, only minutes away from seeing me, I began throwing up. It was an odd mind/body sickness. My emotions were both too intense and not there enough; part of my mind had vacated my body, but the part that remained was hyper-vigilant, as though waiting for a helicopter rescue during a flood, standing on the only high ground for miles. Somehow all of what had happened to me had been acceptable up until then—until I felt my mother's imminent arrival. I think maybe I had a brain transplant with her at that point and, instead of experiencing all the ghastly events of the past twenty-four hours through my brain, which had coped, I was now in her brain, not coping too well at all. Maybe the side-effect of a brain transplant is nausea.

I was a child and yet a woman. I was a bruised, battered child who wanted nothing more than to forever bury my head in my mother's breast that had once been the safest place on earth. My voice had lost its womanly confidence and had become more like a childish whimper. Fear dominated the whole of my being. There was no anger, no outrage; only fear.

I didn't stop throwing up until she came to me, put her hand on my battered face and ravaged body, and I knew, from her sad eyes, that she knew what had happened to me—really knew, knew as though it had happened to both of us—without having been told, and that I would never have to describe the horrible, terrible, dreadful event to her, never have to utter to her unspeakable words of indescribable acts done to me.

Not easy days

Those next days at Steve's parents' house were not easy. The tension between my mother and Steve was palpable. Steve's agitation was growing into a crazed inability to sit quietly, and my mother's maternal concern had grown into a frenetic heroism. We all fell into a pit of unreality whose black, messy sides were covered with guilt. I felt guilty for walking around my apartment the night of the assault in my red pyjamas (as though I had called that man in, the way a matador beseeches his bull). Perhaps my mother felt guilty that she had let me go away to college, released from her vigilant eye; perhaps she felt guilty for failing in her assumption of the role of omnipotent mother. Steve's parents felt guilty that they couldn't give more and because they didn't have a clue how to help or what to say. Steve felt the guiltiest of all. Steve was convinced in his heart of hearts that he had committed the act of violence against me. He was not the man who actually held the razor to my throat. But he was the man whose anger at me that night had reached such proportions that he might have wished some heinous thing to happen to me. He confessed later, to his psychiatrist, that he *felt* guilty for the whole episode. Sometimes a wish is almost as good as a deed. Sometimes wishes feel so real that you can almost forget that they're not. In a kind of misty dream state that my mother and I would drift into, we weren't really sure about Steve at all. She never said it, but I believe that I never quite convinced my mother that I was certain it hadn't been Steve that night. And even with my *knowing* that it had not been Steve, there were times when my mind would play tricks on me, and I would start wondering, against all reason, against absolute certainty, whether or not it was possible that it had been.

Steve's guilt was basically all my mother could see in Steve. And she hated him for it. She blamed him because he was willing to absorb the blame. She had hated him instantly, hate at first sight, the moment she laid eyes on him at the airport. She couldn't or didn't want to see the love we shared. She saw only his guilt, looking, as she was, through the filter of her own guilt, as well as through the filter of her old wish that there never had been, never would be any men in my life.

Steve's guilt and my mother's wish to make Steve disappear kept them both busy with each other. Everyone, including myself, was too busy feeling guilty to ask what I needed, felt or wanted. The only other time that I had ever felt so utterly alone was the night of the rape.

On the third day after the rape, the hospital called. The doctor at the hospital where I had been brought that night had had the prescience to do a test to see if, at the time of my rape, I had ovulated. I had, and the choice the doctor gave me was between being submerged under an avalanche of sand or an avalanche of mud. Choose your hell.

Since abortion was illegal at that time (under all circumstances in that state), I could go into the hospital immediately and have what would be called a D and C. Since no pregnancy test had been conducted, the doctor felt comfortable that he would not be breaking the law. Alternatively, I could wait two weeks until a pregnancy test could be done. If the test turned out positive, I would have to plead for an abortion with every scream, moan and threat of self-annihilation that I could muster before the Board of Directors of the hospital. I would have to literally threaten suicide, and this august group of doctors would have to decide that my threat was real before handing down their fateful, illegal, never-to-be-mentioned-outside-of-that-room verdict.

I didn't endlessly bathe after my rape, as I have heard other rape victims often do. My bruises, tears and cuts wouldn't have allowed it anyway. What needed washing for me was not my outside, but my inside. Any possibility of a THING growing inside me filled me with revulsion. That THING had to be extracted and no one could get me to the hospital fast enough. To wait two weeks or not? There was simply no choice at all. It wasn't at all the fear of THE BOARD—as I came to think of them. Handling a room full of bespectacled doctors, beseeching with all my might for the return of my life as it had been before that night was a piece of cake compared to living one moment longer with that THING possibly growing inside of me.

We went to the hospital—all three of us, Steve, my mother, and me. Steve's presence was a strong shoulder for me; my mother's was a soft one. They flanked me, and, for a moment, the first moment since the rape, I felt cared for and protected.

Five steps before the entrance my mother turned to Steve and said that he would have to say goodbye to me. He started to protest, and she explained with absolute dry calm, now firmly and finally in control, that this procedure would be done only if it was not perceived as an abortion. She reminded me of the strict instructions I had received about how to lie to the admissions office, lie to doctors making their rounds, lie to any casual passer-by who might be interested. I was here having a D and C because of trouble with my menstruation.

Steve wanted to be with me. My mother wanted him gone—her reasoning being that Steve's presence (a man next to a woman having a D and C) would instantly alert the entire hospital staff—red flag: sirens ringing: emergency alert: **AN ABORTION IS ABOUT TO TAKE PLACE**. Now their flanking felt like my arms were being pulled in opposite directions, and that I would split down the middle. I began hoping for a nearby Solomon.

I was a child and yet a woman. I was a bruised, battered child who wanted nothing more than to forever bury my head in my mother's breast that had once been the safest place on earth. And I also wanted to be with the man I loved, and feel the sweet manly embrace that I was used to. My voice lost its womanly confidence and became more like a childish whimper. Fear dominated the whole of my being. There was no anger, no outrage; only fear.

A lesson in the unconscious

I woke from the anaesthetic screaming: "You killed my baby!" That was pretty silly of me. No one had killed that baby except me. There couldn't have been more than one cell in my body that wanted that baby. Yet, there it was—erupting from my unconscious—that one cell, screaming that it wanted that baby. A lesson about the power of the unconscious if ever there was one.

26

An Unmentionable Skeleton in the Closet

In fairy tales, and in real life, the child remains unaware of inner processes. Emotional growth can happen only through the development of an inner life, and this happens only when the child has escaped from the dominion of the parents. This period of growth is typically symbolised in fairy tales by years devoid of overt events; rather, the activity is internal, psychic, and silent, and this represents a period of recovery, and of deep concentration that results in the gaining of maturity.

Rapunzel and the prince both acted immaturely. Rather than openly approaching the sorceress with his love for Rapunzel, the prince spies on her and sneaks up the tower behind her back. And Rapunzel, too, betrays her mother by not telling the sorceress what she did, except, of course, through the "accident" of her revealing slip. Their deceit cannot let the fairy tale end here, as no moral dilemma has been solved, no challenge mastered.

No reason to be anywhere

Two months after my assault, at the end of my last semester at college, five hollowed out people—me, my brother and sister, and my parents—a family that had just a moment before been entirely functional, now creeping its way onto a fast track toward becoming altogether dysfunctional—joined together for the auspicious event of my college graduation. Nobody in my family was talking. The attack had seemed to propel us all into a catatonic stupor with one another. There was only one topic—and its gradients: aggression, assault, and near-murder—on our minds. No one felt comfortable asking me about what had happened that night, what I was feeling, and so, it seemed to me, that it was one of those unmentionables that later become skeletons in the family closet. In fact, I'm not sure that that wasn't how I felt—like an unmentionable, an eventual skeleton in the closet.

After graduation, I insisted on trying to continue with my pre-assault life's plans. I walked through the motions. After a short trip back home, I returned to St. Louis with plans to enter graduate school. Steve and I weren't doing too well with one another. I was enrolled in the Ph.D. counselling programme, but couldn't get myself to class. Not even a single class. I lasted a week. In defeat, head hanging down, I returned home to New Orleans. Unable to think about the future because the past/present was too haunted, I returned to the safety of my parents' home.

And so, rather than my being launched into the world as a college-educated woman about to vanquish the challenges of the world, I retreated, small and scared, back to the bedroom of my childhood, back to the home of my parents/my mother. Back to my four-poster bed and my stained glass window, my own handpicked possessions that I had selected during my mother's house-renovation when I was in high school (the Emery phase). I hoped that in my bedroom and my bed, there would still be a memory of a world where fears were assuaged and safety could exist. Four rousing years of fiery independence of college away from home had ended with a hard swallow down of freedom.

I made a valiant effort to be normal, to be as though I had not been beaten by unkind fists, nor nearly sliced to death with a razor, and had not been raped. I lived like Rapunzel after she was banished by the sorceress. I hadn't yet learned a lesson from my rape, and its effect on all of us, other than to never live on a ground floor apartment again. And no growth from the experience seemed imminent. I was wandering around in psychic space, feeling lost and miserable, feeling a sense of near-continuous/constant fear. For most of that next year, my fears would come in the dark of night. I would wake up at 3.00 a.m., and imagine men's faces peering through my window. I roused my father out of his fitful slumber, and made him circle the house to make sure that there was no one out there. He reassured me—I was safe, no one was there—but I could never quite believe him. By day, I pretended to resume a normal life, looking for things to do, hanging out with friends, searching for meaning.

The most severe pain, however, was not my fear, nor my inability to find a life. The most painful pain was what the assault did to my relationship with my mother. Whatever small seeds of conflict there had been in the past between my mother and me about my need for separation, my desire for freedom from our relationship, now became towering trees. Our relationship became defined by her attempts to ensure my safety, which she (like Rapunzel's sorceress trapping her in the tower) felt depended upon having all the house doors shut tightly and locked, with me on the inside. Every trip I made outside the house became, for her, fraught with dangerous possibilities. She asked, incessantly, where was I going, how long it would take to get there, was I making any stops along the way, when would I be home. She would give me just the proximate time to get to my destination, and then call to make sure I had arrived. She insisted that I call her before I left to come back home. If she didn't know where I was for more than ten minutes, she would start tracking me down. This would happen at high noon, as well as at midnight. One morning, I spent half an hour in the backyard, wishing to be alone, watching the ants walk on the grass. Not knowing where I had gone, she was frantic, ready to call the police. She protected the two of us with a covering whose overhang dropped so low neither of us could see where we were walking.

And there was the silence. My mother never asked what had happened that night. She never asked me to talk about it. I didn't want to talk about it. I placed my memories of that night into a dark and silent place. I became a little like a sleepwalker, uncommunicative, without the feelings that I needed to have, devoid of anger.

A temporary reprieve from an intolerable closeness

I started spending a lot of time away from the house. My mother was getting ever more frantic about not knowing where I was. I would never have been so bold as to actually stay away for a night. But I was increasingly spending stretches of time—an afternoon might stretch into an evening—away from home. With my mother's vigilance, she became my watchdog and bodyguard. My life was no longer my own. I became mute and our silent battles over my exercising freedom of my body were unending. Rather than feeling angry, rather than pushing for confrontation, I found myself sneaking around a lot, lying, saying I was going out with girlfriends when I was really going out with a man. It was no longer a question of hiding the fact that I was a sexually active woman; it was, too, hiding the fact that I was aware that men walked the face of the earth.

But she knew. She always knew. She and I were too connected, our minds almost one. I would say I was going to Cynthia's (who, like me, had returned to New Orleans after college), and she would call Cynthia to confirm that I was there. I was forced to bring my dates to Cynthia's so that I was there for the inevitable frantic phone call.

The secret of my interest in men, my sexuality that I had so carefully hidden from her for so many years, became all too visible, and all too painful to her. She feared that every trip I made out of the house might lead to a sexual encounter. What was conscious for her was her fear that what had happened to me before might happen to me again. I believe that what was unconscious for her was her inability to tolerate the fact that I had grown into a sexual woman. Not that I would be *forced*, once again, to have sex. Rather, that I *wanted* to have sex.

The silence between us grew boundless and we never really knew that what was separating us was all about the question of who was going to own my body, who was in charge of the decisions I was making about whether and with whom to share my body. Had we lived in another century, had we been another religion, I am sure that my mother would have been happy enough to send me off to a nunnery.

Fleeing from my mother

Having almost been killed propelled me to seek help. My mother's belief in psychoanalysis became the legacy she gave to me for what to do with my own pain. I found an analyst and tried. "I was raped." No details, no feelings. Just "I was raped."

And then, for the rest of the session, I let my insides spill out to this man simply because my insides could no longer be contained within my body boundaries. It was all about my mother—my feeling suffocated by her, my empathy for her pain, and my discomfort at my not being able to get away from her. I couldn't understand how my mother and I had devolved into such disharmony, how our wonderful togetherness had turned into such tension. I ended my litany of traumas by telling this analyst that I was thinking about moving to New York. I talked about wanting to move away from home, and my desire to continue my studies in the psychology of religion. The analyst made his first communication to me. He said moving to New York would be running away from my mother. (Of course, he said it as a declaration of opinion that it was a terrible idea.) Hearing it from him in the stark way he declared its unsuitability as a solution convinced me: running away from my mother seemed like the smartest thing I could do. We needed that much separation, that much distance between us. I moved to New York to flee from my mother.

27

Wandering around in Psychic Space

Steve and I, like Rapunzel and the prince, couldn't figure out how to make our relationship work. After she left her mother's home, Rapunzel found herself living in the desert alone, having forsaken her ties to her mother. The prince, too, had lost his ties to his parents. Both had to learn to care for themselves rather than be cared for by their parents. The prince, we are told, "wandered blindly through the forest, ate nothing but roots and berries, and did nothing but moan and cry because he had lost his beloved." Rapunzel, too, "lived in misery and moaned and decried her fate."

And, as master fairy-tale interpreter Bettelheim explains, because the two had not yet learned to care for themselves, they were not able to search each other out with any real determination. During their period of tribulations, they lived without hope. Yet, at the end of the tale, Rapunzel and her prince have grown into maturity, and are ready "not only to rescue each other, but to make a good life, one for the other."

The change in cellular structure

Ultimately, I suppose that the analyst who I saw for that one session after my rape/near-death experience was right in his implication that running away from my mother was not going to solve anything. Separation is never acquired from flight. It gives distance—a temporary reprieve from an intolerable closeness—but it does not bring resolution. Resolution comes only when choice is possible. Flight (half of the fight-flight impulse that all mammals have in their genes) is not a choice; it is either a compulsion or a necessity and is, at that time of the fleeing, the only possible exit perceived.

I spent many years in New York living, like Rapunzel and the prince, in misery, living as though I were a refugee who had fled from my homeland, and had left behind all my most precious possessions. In trying to prove my independence from my mother, I lived frugally, as though I were poverty-stricken. I would walk thirty blocks to save the twenty cent subway fare. I entered graduate school, and paid for it by taking a position as a teaching assistant. I shared a house in Queens with other students, and took the third-floor attic because it was the cheapest room in the house (forty dollars a month as opposed to the more princely sum of sixty dollars for the second-floor rooms).

It was during this time that I began my period of recovery that is necessary for growth, my inner search into maturation. Having left the home of my mother, having even, in some sense, "forsaken my tie" to her, I spent time wandering around in psychic space without much hope, not really trusting myself. Without my mother as my "beacon of orientation," I searched to replace her (and her love) with a man (and his love). This replacement of mother to lover succeeds, however, only when mother has been released sufficiently for a true, new bond to develop. Because I had not resolved my separation issues with my mother, I remained unable to create a true bond with another. I moved from man to man without any real determination to find a man with whom I "could make a good life together, one for the other."

It was as though the rape had changed the cellular structure of my body. Whereas before the rape I had ended all my relationships with my boyfriends, now, after the rape, they were all fleeing from me. I had lost all semblance of confidence in myself in relation to a man.

An enduring mark of transformation

From my rape, I have acquired multiple scars, both visible and invisible, both bodily and psychically. In important ways, my scars have come to define me.

This is not so odd. Throughout history, deliberate scarification has been used not only as a means of identification, but also as a proud statement of identification. According to ancient Egyptian writing, deliberate scarification dates back to 1700 BCE. Different cultures have used scarring as a depiction of one's affiliation with a particular group, the person or culture's exploits, or individual stature. In ancient Greece, people were often identified by their scars for the signing of legal documents: the name of the individual plus any identifying scar (*oulê*) was the legal description of the person. If there was no scar, the individual was labeled *ásemos*: "not marked." In ancient times, it was as though the absence of scarring meant the absence of personhood. Scars tell us who we are.

Outward scars serve the function of reminding us of our inward scars. A scar is the body's/psyche's/soul's permanent memory of its breaching, a mark of violation and yet also an endurable mark of transformation. The etymology of the word "scar" comes from the Greek word *escharõtikos* meaning hearth. In ancient Greece, the *eschara* was a portable hearth that stood on graves and allowed burnt offerings to the earth gods and to the underworld deities. In associating scar with *eschara*, a wound becomes an offering to the underworld, a sacrificial act to placate and purify demons, ghosts, and chthonic forces. The scar becomes the mark of that offering, a never-disappearing symbol of one's sacrifice.

None of us escapes trauma, and thus none of us escapes scarring. We all suffer from the original birth trauma and we all carry the initial scar of separation from Mother—the belly button—the visible manifestation of our initial breach from our mothers. This serves as a reminder of our first initiation into independent life. Also, most of us carry scars that are reminders of later wounds, both physical as well as psychic. Scars represent our initiation not just into life itself, but, as well, into the painful and injurious realities of life. Our scars, indeed, tell us who we are; but they also are reminders of who we were.

Accidental scars are often acquired in childhood from the process of attempting to master separation from Mother. Children fall off swings, jungle gyms and bicycles, all in the service of wanting/needing to be away from Mother, exploring the world away from Mother. Mothers wince, but good mothers know that bruises, and sometimes the scars that accompany injuries, are inevitable consequences of learning to negotiate the world. Good mothers don't try to unduly restrain, inhibit, or limit their children in normal childhood explorations. Rather, the nourishing mother only tries to reduce the factor of danger.

Most of the scars we carry are invisible. I attended a seminar on trauma, and the men and women attending were given strips of red cloth and asked to pin the ribbons around the areas of their bodies that had been wounded. The room soon became a sea of red. Ribbons on the heart were the most plentiful.

The human animal develops bigger, thicker scars on its body than any other animals. Theorists have offered intriguing explanations of the fact that humans scar more severely than other animals. One theory suggests that scarring evolved alongside human intelligence. As we started relying on our brains instead of our instincts to get us out of risky situations, scars developed to act as constant reminders of our previous mistakes. Another hypothesis suggests that scars serve as sexual attractors; when a cavewoman was courted by a heavily scarred caveman, she understood that he was brave and bold.

In analysis and other methods of self-growth, individuals learn to recognise the relationship between their unconscious, their wounds, the scarred evidence of their wounds, and their history. In effect, the unconscious of an individual is the history of the individual and, most particularly, of the wounds of the individual. Every emotional wound is, above all, a historical scar. Emotional scar tissue brings about emotional rigidity, and it is in these unhealed areas that we lose choice in the moment. In these situations, how we think, feel, and act are more predetermined by our childhood experiences than by an accurate processing of the momentary situation.

Pretending to ignore the information

I decide it is time to pay attention to my most visible scar, the scar that has defined so much of my life since I acquired it. I want to develop a different relationship to my scar: to be ennobled and strengthened by it, to give it the honour it deserves.

I was in the student lounge, working on my graduate degree in psychology. I happened to overhear a conversation between two students describing an article in *Time* magazine about a serial rapist who had just been caught in St. Louis.

I pretended to ignore that information for a year. I committed to my studies, and kept myself otherwise busy.

Then the day came when I decided to take a look at his picture. As I made my way up to the New York Public Library, I wondered: would his violence reach out to me from the page? Would my fear transform itself into a rage that I had yet to feel? Would there even be any sense of recognition of a face that I had never actually seen?

I stared at his picture for an hour. I waited for something to happen—some horror, some anguish, some feeling, even a sense of bonding for the shared experience. Yet, his face remained as lifeless as the page it was on.

But the story was enlightening. It said that he had attacked a dozen women in my old St. Louis neighbourhood. It had taken so long to catch him because he always had an excuse for being in the neighbourhood: he was the neighbourhood cop. He was the first hero/policeman to show up at each scene. He was the guy who soothed all the distraught/almost-dead women who had just experienced the major trauma of their lives. He was the guy who was calling me with disembodied voices of presumed suspects repeating the words I had heard that night: "I'm going to kill you if you make a sound," in order to see if I could recognise any of the voices, making sure, obviously, that it was never his voice that uttered those words to me—again.

It seemed like a good idea to try therapy again.

I tried group therapy. The group developed the idea that re-enacting my rape would free me, at last, from its lingering effects. So there I was in group therapy with a bearded man, whom I had met only a few weeks earlier, on top of me, pinning me down, pretending that pretend was real. And I didn't scream.

All the people in the group commented that I didn't scream. Actually their comments were more like accusations. Screaming would have helped, they were suggesting. Screaming would have stopped that guy dead in his tracks, they claimed. In fact, nothing appealed to me more, at that moment of re-enactment, than the idea of a good scream. But that fateful night, one year earlier, was the last night my voice had been free enough to release a scream. Now my scream was stuck too far down in my throat to even think about coming up for expression.

After experimenting with all kinds of these touchy-feely therapies, most of them asking me to do things which I felt either I couldn't do, or didn't want to do, feeling they were too irrelevant to my pain to do, I finally wound my way back to analysis—to my mother's tried-and-true method of addressing her pain. My analyst helped me through my years of wandering and became a surrogate mother to me. Unlike the sorceress in Rapunzel, who didn't want to share her, and, unlike my own mother, who, post-rape, wanted to keep me close-by out of fear for my safety, my analyst has never wanted to imprison me, only free me. She became my guide during my years of wandering in the desert, living still at times in misery, "decrying my fate," not really trusting either my future or myself.

I was moaning in one of my sessions with my analyst when I was in heartbroken anguish once again from a relationship with a lover not working out. I told her that I felt I would die without this man in my life, without his love. My analyst said, in a complete matter-of-fact tone: "Then you'll have to learn to live without love." This sentence was like a foreign language to me. The thought of living without a man loving me was incomprehensible and intolerable. Loveless living felt as dangerous to my health and well-being as the scenario of a mother abandoning her newborn. From her analytic position, my analyst didn't care whether I had love in my life or not (though from a personal perspective, I am sure she wished me happiness with a man). Her point was not whether I should have love, whether I did have love; rather, she was giving me an invitation to examine my incapacity, the limitations I was imposing on myself by requiring love. Her point was that I was not free. My analyst committed to the task of helping me to release the child-brain I was operating from, and to grow into my woman-brain.

A long-awaited cry

My group therapy did not change my relationship to my scar. I suppose my individual analysis—finally having a willing and interested listener to the story of my rape, and to the long ordeal I had with my mother consequent to my rape—helped me to process some of the trauma of the event. But, in the end, as with so many of my emotional scars, it is Molly who has had the strongest effect on me.

Molly has discovered my scar. We are still doing full-body hugs, and during one of them, her hand accidentally brushes lightly over the protrusion in my neck from my scar. She takes her hand, and lovingly caresses the long strand of the skin-eruption. I think there must be something about the unevenness of my skin that appeals to her tactile sense. The touch is so gentle, so loving: it's more of a caress really than a brush. It stimulates memories that I had long ago relished to the trash-bin of my conscious mind. I start thinking once again about how and when my scar was acquired. I think about the aftermath, and the disruption that the event caused to my relationship with my mother. Then—and all this is in one of those time instants that the mind is capable of—I start projecting into a possible future where the victim of such an event is not myself but my daughter. I know that I was angry at my mother for how she became a suffocatingly irritating watchdog to me after my assault; but now that I am an imagined-future-mother dealing with the same issues related to my own daughter, I know that, had such a thing happened to her, I would have managed it all far worse than my own mother did. I think many of us know what our unique dropping off into the deep end would look like if we ever came to that. We might become controlling and worried, as my mother did. We might get hysterical and not be able to stop sobbing, or screaming, or both simultaneously. We might become rabid with the need for revenge. I think I know what I would become: I imagine I would become what psychiatry calls catatonic: speechless, wordless, vacant, utterly uncommunicative—locked inside myself. And, all in all, I think that my mother didn't do so badly when she saw me, her precious and adored child, bodily wounded, fighting for a restoration of psychic equilibrium, with streaks of blood matting my hair and an angry stitched scar protruding from my neck.

Tears start streaming from my eyes. I am filled with the most intense sadness that I have ever felt. For hours afterwards, for the whole of the rest of the day, I am left with the feeling that I am grieving—an inconsolable grief—but I know not for whom or what—until, in that nanosecond of faster-than-the-speed-of-light-time-warp that I am occupying, I do come to know (to "learn" and "hear" what I "know")—and this is that my grief is for my long-dead mother. And my tears are watermarks of joy as well. They are for the blessing of my having this child who has touched my scar in the most loving way possible, and in her caress, healed the internal scarification of my psyche that the external scar represents.

28

Giving in to Complete Abandon

M olly is having a terrible time because we are switching nannies. She is furious, and is taking out her rage—a typical four-year-old child's murderous rage—on the new nanny, who she says she doesn't like, by hitting her. I want to help Molly to modify her behaviour, but leave her feelings intact. I want to help her to understand that hitting is not an acceptable means of expression of her feelings, but that words are.

The unreliability of feelings

The acceptance of feelings is, of course, the emotional posture that analysts aspire to take. As calibrators of our emotional states, feelings can't be wrong. Feelings define who we are in crucially important ways. The early work of most systems for emotional growth is to identify the feelings and to re-find whatever feelings have been dismissed. Therapists assist the patient in retracing the initial path that was taken as an attempt to eliminate unwanted feelings.

But this scavenger work is only the beginning. It can't be the whole of the work of psychic integration because the human brain has two separate hemispheres, and, actually, three separate brain-portions housed in the one cerebrum—each part-brain having developed at a different time in the evolution of man. Within the brain, feelings are situated in the old brain—the subcortical, reptilian brain—the part of the brain that we share with many animals. Feelings don't represent attitudes or emotional postures. Rather, they are transient motivational states, messengers of our nervous system. And although feelings give us a rich definition of part of our identity, the most misunderstood aspect of feelings is the assumption that they serve as calibrators of reality. In truth, as assessors of reality, feelings can be utterly unreliable. They tell us as little about the psychological nature of events as when my dog barks at my friendly neighbor, mistakenly assuming that her walking past the house is a threat. And when feelings are most intense, they are often the least reliable. Their very intensity is a signifier that they may have their origin in past, unresolved issues, rather than being accurate reflections and understandings of the present.

While it is true that we should take our own feelings seriously, it is also true that we can come, finally, to the point of nonchalantly dismissing our feelings with a shrug, as if to say, "Well, they're only feelings after all." The neo-cortex, the new brain, can reason and think logically, and can counterpoint the old brain that sways us to and fro with our feelings and impulses. Reason tempers the need to discharge the drives into action. We need to know that reason and logic can be brought to bear on all our murderous inclinations, real or imagined murder—that reason and logic are what, in the end, should (and can) prevail. And, it is words that are the medium of the progression from irrationality to rationality, from behaviour to wishes, intentions and inclinations. Either internal words, or spoken words, but words.

The route to accepting feelings is circuitous

Sometimes the route to the acceptance of feelings while simultaneously short-circuiting unacceptable behaviour is circuitous. Sometimes the way to encourage the acceptance of feelings is to accept unacceptable behaviour. And so I praise Molly for her angry feelings, and I encourage her to tell me about them in microscopically minute detail.

Molly, indeed, has developed an impressive ability to articulate her aggression. There are moments when the ferocity of her rage takes my breath away and I have to remind myself (which is easier to do as an analyst than as a mother) that these are the things, as hateful as they sound, that Molly should be feeling and should be saying to me, her mother, harbourer of secrets and container of rage. Molly is learning in these experiences an important but painful lesson about separation. It doesn't happen without concomitant rage and anger, hurt and pain, feelings of disappointment and betrayal.

Molly's words of rage seem a better option for what she could do with her aggression than so many other possibilities. Better than hitting, better than calling me names or criticising me, better than clinching a knot in her stomach.

Yet this freedom I have afforded Molly in her use of language has got her into trouble. Not all mothers share my belief in raising their children with the same level of freedom of speech. One of my patients tells me that when she was growing up, her mother forbade her to verbalise any negative feelings. Whenever she said the word "hate," her mother told her to stop saying that unacceptable four-letter word. My patient learned to never say she hated anyone, or anything, or even eggs, which she decidedly did hate.

So it is, I suppose, my fault that Molly is in trouble with the mother of Annie, her best friend. Molly is angry that Annie is sitting on Molly's babysitter's lap. Molly tells Annie how angry she is at her, and, furthermore, insists that she doesn't want to be friends with her anymore.

These girls have known each other from birth. They have happily told anyone who is willing to listen that they are best friends. Molly has pretended that everyone's name is Annie, or sometimes that she herself is Annie (signifying fusion as an expression of love, as when my mother left behind her born identity of Madeleine to become Madelyn). Molly has talked about Annie when they are not together, anxiously awaiting the next time she will be able to be with her. But now they are going through this rough patch. Annie is in tears at Molly's meanness, and her mother has decided that they can't see each other again, that Molly is a bad influence on her daughter.

I think the mother is being unfair and irrational. I have seen her daughter be just as mean to Molly as Molly has been to her daughter. I understand that Annie's tears are because of her trouble conceptualising that Molly's sentiment was only going to be a momentary one—that, given a chance, two minutes later they would be hugging each other with amorous fervour again, that they would resolve their difficulties as they had done a thousand times already. I expect that shortsightedness from a four-year-old. But I don't expect it from a mother.

I am terrified of the effect this separation from her best friend will have on Molly. I feel the pain I imagine my child will have to confront as though it were my own. I would rather it were my own.

I try to talk the mother out of her decision, but she is steadfast. She says that she can't stand seeing her child cry in response to Molly's meanness—that dealing with her daughter's pain is exhausting to her. I plead my case with every ounce of brilliant debating skill that I have, using my thirty years of analytic knowledge of relationships, and cruelty and hurt. I argue; I don't argue; I communicate understanding; I communicate disbelief. Yet, no matter what I say, I cannot influence this woman, and I feel anguish in anticipating the aftermath of her decision.

As we prepare for the loss of Annie in our lives, I think about the other losses in my young daughter's life. Already at four, she has lost her live-in nanny of three years who moved onto another job; her aunt (Gregg's sister, with whom we lived for a year) has moved to North Carolina; Molly's weekend babysitter moved to South Jersey; her friends Anya, Nell, and Emma moved to Pennsylvania, Belgium, and London. She is about to lose her other aunt, my dying sister, who is moving to a world vastly different to the various places on earth that all the others have moved to—and, in addition to all these losses, now her beloved Annie.

Molly develops elaborate revenge fantasies about Annie's mother. She hopes that she dies. She wants Annie to come and live with us upon her mother's death so that they can be true sisters. And if the mother doesn't die, then maybe Annie will run away from home and come and live with us anyway. Molly prepares mentally for the imminent arrival of Annie. She explains to me how she will divide her bedroom, where the extra bed will go, which drawers she will relinquish for Annie's clothes, which stuffed animals she is willing to share with Annie. It is precisely because of these fantasies, in spite of how horrifying they seem (the wish for the death of someone), that I know with certainty that my child is uninjured (if not unaffected) by Annie's departure from her life. I know that above all, this immunity to psychic damage is the gift I have given her—the ability to use words to articulate her internal experience and thus protect her from the damage of unfelt feelings. In fact, her murder-as-metaphor fantasies are not unlike my own—about the disappearance of those I love the most—even my most-beloved Molly herself, and Gregg too—when I feel angry, exhausted, or just plain overloaded. And I know that this foundation that Molly and I have laid will prepare her for much of what comes for the rest of her life.

Opening the floodgates

This is not a marriage made in heaven, this thing between Gregg and me. But it is not hell either. We have caring, sweet moments with each other. He is loyal, and he commits to improving my life every day in a thousand ways. His intelligence and the breadth of his knowledge stun me, and I actually look to him to know how I should think on core, contemporary issues (like how to think about complex global and environmental concerns). Most importantly, he is everything I would have looked for in a loving father in his direct interactions with Molly. He is playful and imaginative, receptive, and interested.

My chief complaint about Gregg does not have to do with his being Molly's father, but with his being my partner. With me, he can become impatient and critical. After Gregg demonstrates his anger at me by some snide remark, or alternatively by screaming, it usually takes us a few hours for me to settle down emotionally. Over the years, I have tried all varieties of dealing with his criticalness and his ferocious temper: I have walked away; I have defended myself; I've tried logic and reason. Generally, withdrawal works best. It is this technique that I have settled upon for most of the difficulties in our relationship, and it is this that Molly sees when she observes us at our worst: her Daddy being angry, and her Mommy quiet and withdrawn.

I ask Gregg to watch Molly for a few hours so I can visit a girlfriend:

Me: *I'm going to be leaving now.*

Gregg: *What? Where are you going?*

Me: *Remember, yesterday you agreed to take Molly.*

Gregg: *Oh—but that was before I was able to get a tennis game.*

Me: *So, what are you saying?*

Gregg: *Well, I certainly don't want to not play tennis.*

Me: *So, you won't take her then?*

Gregg: *Well, like I said, I don't want to give up playing tennis.*

Me: *I guess I'll call Lois and see if she can babysit then.*

Ten minutes later:

Gregg: *Did you get Lois?*

Me: *Yeah.*

Gregg: *Is it okay?*

Me: *I guess it's okay.*

Gregg: *Oh good, she can do it then?*

At this point, I call my battleground:

Me: *Yes, she can do it. But when you ask is it okay, I still don't know what you mean. Do you mean is she taking Molly or do you mean do I feel okay about it?*

Gregg: *What do you mean?*

Me: *What I mean is that I'm angry about this.*

This is the point where the whole conversation falls apart. Gregg is angry that I have assured him that it was okay for

Lois to take Molly; I am angry that while it is okay, he is going against his promise of the day before, and I have had to scrounge around to get Molly taken care of.

My anger at Gregg only inflames his anger at me. He accuses me of lying, telling him it was okay when it wasn't.

My reply is altogether rational, and its very calmness drives him into an even more frenzied state. He says:

> You lied. I was asking how you felt and you led me to believe you felt okay about it. You're just arguing the spirit of what I said. You know goddamn well what I meant. I meant, were you angry about it?

At this point, the floodgates open for me. I cannot stand being called a liar when I have not lied, and I particularly cannot stand being told that I am arguing the spirit of what he said when the spirit of what he said was all he wanted to know in the first place. But what I can't stand most of all is his being angry at me because I have confessed to him that I *felt* angry at him. I can't stand his anger in the face of my placating restraint.

There is one technique in my battles with Gregg that I have not yet tried. I have never, deliberately and with absolute decisiveness, given in to complete screaming abandon.

I start yelling at him. Not because I decide to start yelling. Not because I decide that he deserves to be yelled at. I start yelling because after twenty-five years of not releasing a scream of rage, my throat is stirred and an angry scream wants to emerge.

My scream is a very specific kind of scream. There are so many different kinds of screams that are expressions of feeling—yet all, confusedly, have the same name. Philosopher Emmanuel Kant described the first scream of the infant, the birth-scream, to be one "not of lamentation but of aroused wrath." Later, there is the screech of playful pleasure—the scream that baby Molly and I shared when we were together for the first few months. There are, too, screams of fear as well as screams of orgasmic ecstasy (and perhaps these are not as far apart as one might initially think). I have a patient who is a graphic artist, and her calling card is a photograph of her head, her mouth mobilised, stretched into fierce openness, releasing what can be nothing other than a full-bodied scream. When you look at the picture closely, you indeed see the mouth stretched wide, but you see, as well, unadulterated joy around her eyes, the joy of release. And, finally, there is the scream of the horrified—a scream that is almost more intense than we can tolerate. This is the scream in Edvard Munch's painting *The Scream*. I know that most people find the vision of that woman, whose mouth seems frozen wide open into perpetuity, unpleasant, disturbing. I always found the image to be exhilarating: the throat release of that long, unending scream, the expression of feeling that would be too much to bear without that scream. Or, the uplifting scream of blues and gospel singers who shout it out from their souls. I have long aspired to such fully-felt throat releases.

And then, in this angry encounter I am having with Gregg, I actually start having some fun. I bring myself to the point where I cease caring about any possible destructiveness or aftermath that is being wrought by my scream, the point of release—no doubt, the point of release that Munch's lady found herself in. I let loose and there is, finally, no throat constriction at all.

I think about the night I lost my scream, the time when my rage and outrage began its descent into the underground of my unconscious. And I think about my first analytic dream, my dog-pouncing dream, when my scream allowed itself to be resurrected in my dream-life, a glimpse from my unconscious, yet yearning to be heard. And now that I have Molly, and I understand that I have become that mother-dog that I dreamed about so long ago—willing (even needing) to fiercely protect her young. And, too, I am still the "me" who I was in the dream, the terrified-me. But now, my throat is released again at last; my scream is no longer stuck inside me, no longer unheard from that last fateful night I screamed, and no longer inhabiting only the realm of my dreams.

Gregg and I have had our first good fight that was a long time in coming. Yet, we both stay alive, and we even keep each other as Molly's parents, raising her together, loving her together, and maybe even, sometimes, loving each other too. And with a scream in my heart, I become a different kind of mother. I am no longer filled with anxieties; I am sure-footed and decisive in how I want to handle Molly's and my ongoing procession into our separate selves.

It turns out that Lois isn't available for babysitting that day after all. I take Molly with me on my lunch-date, and we have a fine time eating grilled eggplant sandwiches with goat's cheese in an outdoor café with my friend Heidi.

The protagonist is no longer governed by fear

Many of my patients come into analysis because they have become so angry with their partner that they feel their only recourse is divorce. Yet I see these rageful feelings not as the end of the relationship, but the beginning. The point where two people can experience their negative feelings about each other, communicate them effectively and non-destructively to each other, and then be released from the weight of their feelings—this is the beginning of a relationship. This is murder-as-metaphor at work. Once this skill is acquired, the main work of the relationship has been accomplished, and there can be clear sailing from then on. This is true for partners in romance (Gregg and me), for mothers and daughters (Molly and me), and for patient and analyst (Marnie and me).

Marnie and I know that we are nearing the end of her analysis, the process of telling the story of her emotional life. We have looked at the beginning of the story, and have made sense of what it was, how it formed her. We have looked at the choices she has made, and we have come to an understanding of how some of those choices represented her strengths, while others represented her fears. We have had many powerful feelings about our relationship, and we have explored and given voice to them all—positive and negative, love and rage, Eros and Thanatos. We have moved through that dreaded territory of Marnie's being consciously and verbally angry with me, and we have come out the other side still intact as individuals, still intact as a togetherness. In the course of this analysis, we have constructed a book, an autobiographical book. And now, at the end of the book, the protagonist is no longer governed by fear.

Marnie's experience of change happened because mental life has a natural affinity for narrative construction. Lawyers know that legal arguments are more convincing when built into narrative tales rather than legal precedent. Teachers know that their students remember facts more accurately if they encounter them in a story rather than in a list. And, of course, psychoanalysts know that the strongest emotional experiences in the patient's life are going to determine the kind of life story the patient has constructed.

Delicious, delectable, desirable

Psychological change comes about when the storyline of one's life is able to be altered. Life stories are neither rigid nor wildly variable. They change gradually over time, and in close tandem with meaningful life events. Psychotherapy merely speeds up and hones a process that is natural to us anyway.

In medicine, physicians talk about the notion of "cure" as though there is a fixed state that the body can reach that represents health. Because psychoanalysis was brought to this country by medical physicians, analysts co-opted the term, and talk too about "cure." But the body and the psyche are both systems of fluidity and movement; they are organic in nature, continuously expanding, contracting, renewing, dying. Used in this sense, the term is a misnomer for what happens in the process of getting healthy in body or psyche. Rather, I like the analogy of what happens to ham when it is cooked: it is, indeed, cured; but cured in the sense of well-seasoned; it's been through a process that makes it more delicious, delectable, desirable. If we, as patients and as analysts and as humans, can reach the point where we consider ourselves to be like a cured ham—delicious, delectable and desirable—then I think we will have reached a tenable and worthwhile goal.

In developing the theory and technique of psychoanalysis, Freud often referred back to the Greeks. The Greeks saw the close relationship of the gods of love (Eros), sleep (Hypnos), and death (Thanatos). It was because of the Greeks' belief in the soul that these gods were so paramount in their mythology. These three gods shared the quality of limb-relaxation. In life, the soul remains encased in the body; but when we are supine, as we are in dream-states and in analysis—when the muscles of our body are relaxed enough—the soul is set free temporarily. In telling his patients to lie on the couch, Freud evoked the limb-relaxing quality of Hypnos. The analytic patient is relaxed; but in spite of this bodily rest, the mind remains awake and alert and able to do the work of remembering, processing, articulating, integrating.

Freud discovered that when his patients were in this limb-relaxed state, they would say unordinary things, things that had formerly been unsayable. The edict the analyst gives to the patient after he has taken the couch is "to talk" (in hope that the patient will come to feel free enough in the session to say the unsayable). Talking—placing all thoughts and feelings into words—was Freud's method of cure for the disease of our being perched precariously between life and death, the never-ending conflict between our contradictory drives. Through the act of talking, the destructive aspects of the power of Thanatos are tamed, the constructive energy behind Eros is liberated, and the two drives can coexist without undue pain or disharmony.

The analyst instructs the patient to take the couch and say what comes to his mind, to talk about whatever he wants the analyst to know about him, to tell his life story, beginning wherever he wants and ending wherever he wants. The patient is both biographer and protagonist of the story he chooses to tell. In giving the instruction to talk, the analyst is challenging the patient to remain free and childlike in thought and feeling, yet mature in his ability to utilise language as his vehicle of self-exploration.

This emphasis on pure talking with no other addendums (no eye contact, no bodily gestures), is what uniquely defines psychoanalysis, and its conceptualisation of the meaning of cure, separating it from all other therapeutic methods. All methods of psychotherapy aid the patient in coming to know the world of thoughts and feelings, but psychoanalysis uniquely makes the articulation of thoughts and feelings the very definition of cure. And, ironically, the supreme emphasis on words means that they can also come to have very little meaning. I think of the language of psychoanalysis as "throwaway words." Once the words have been said, the mission has succeeded.

Once the thought or feeling has been spoken, it is released, and, like baby-Molly's cries used to do, disappears into the stratosphere. Those words that seem particularly precious, and worthy of further future consideration, can be recaptured at any time. The others can remain as throwaways.

Words have become freedom

Marnie has come to this point of verbal freedom. She no longer struggles with a strangulated voice. She is able to tell me what she thinks and feels at the moment she thinks and feels, and there is no shame. The words come and go like the wind. Or maybe even like a butterfly, constantly in motion, flitting from flower to flower, unstuck. Words have become her freedom.

She and I prepare ourselves for our goodbye, the termination of her analysis. We do a lot of remembering and reminiscing—and re-telling the old life story and comparing it to the new one. She tells about the first time she felt that I might actually care about her:

> It was one of those slushy Manhattan days. I was wearing sneakers and I walked into your office soaking wet and you asked why I was wearing the sneakers—shouldn't I have worn better shoes? You told me, with concern, that I could get sick walking around with wet feet.

That tiny bit of concern, even nurturing, meant everything to her. She had had so little regard for herself, and it had been so long since anyone had said anything remotely motherly to her—she cries even now just thinking about those times.

Marnie brings up the period in her life when she first decided to come to me. Even after twenty-five years, there is still more information to be had, more stories to be told.

This is the first time I have heard this particular explanation of her beginning therapy. She explains that a girl in her high school had just committed suicide. Marnie was considering following in this girl's footsteps. She tells me that recently a student in her husband's class (he has retired from being a detective, and is now teaching school) has jumped off a bridge. She remembers her suicidal days; she knows, with unsinkable certainty, that she is finished with them.

Marnie's pain from being rejected by her biological mother is still an ache but she is able, at last, to rejoice in the strong love that she and I have for each other. We need not be separate any longer. She says:

> *I can now accept that you care for me and it is okay if*
> *I feel the same way.*

And then we close the last page of this book that we have read together, even constructed together, with lots of intense and conflicting feelings.

29

The End of Longing

Fairy tales tell us that a good life is possible. But we must first learn to accept adverse circumstances and use them as growing experiences. Fairy tales, like the psychoanalytic experience, don't provide us with set solutions. Rather, they are suggestive, allowing us to discover ourselves, our conflicts, and our solutions within them.

The disappearance of existential aloneness

After my mother's death, I was determined to get pregnant. I succeeded after three years of trying. I remember the absolute contentment I felt during those months of pregnancy. Because I was spot bleeding, my doctor had me on bed-rest. Staying put in one place was completely antithetical to everything in me. This was the only time in my life when I have not felt an urgency to keep moving my body, whether through swimming, running, yoga, or Tai Kwon Do. Yet during those months, despite my motionlessness, I felt utterly complete. I had no longings. I had spent so much time, throughout my life, suffering over my men, tortured by the various rejections—them of me, me of them. During the time of this pregnancy, none of that mattered to me any more. This was the first time in my life when I didn't struggle with the feelings of being desperate for love and terrified of being alone. I wasn't alone. I felt a profound sense of togetherness. When I woke up in the morning, I would think about whether or not I wanted to get out of bed, or just spend the whole day in bed experiencing the completeness of my relationship with my unborn child. I had no desire to do anything. In fact, I had no desires at all. I felt full and complete.

I miscarried this baby in my fourth month of pregnancy. I wailed at the loss of my daughter; I was sure it was a girl. I felt betrayed by my body that had failed me.

For ten years, I tried to get pregnant again. During this time, I developed my relationship with Gregg. I became a successful analyst. I wrote a few books. Then I searched for Molly until I found her.

And although I don't believe in fairy tales any more, and I don't believe in true life princes, Gregg and I have reached a point of maturity where we are no longer wandering alone in psychic space, no longer living in misery, "moaning and decrying" our fate. We have undergone a sufficient period of inner growth, and we are ready "to make a good life, one for the other"—and now with Molly, the three of us together in our good life.

Mothers know instinctively that the strongest tie they have with their children is the child's longing to return to the bliss of symbiosis. It is difficult for both to move beyond the fantasy that the mother exists to meet the needs of the child. Both mother and child resist this progression. Neither wants to give up the illusion of the omnipotent mother and the helpless child—the mother who is utterly capable of taking care, the child who is utterly in need of care.

But becoming a mother oneself often results in an unconscious and automatic shifting of these dynamics of the original mother/daughter relationship. As the child moves toward the role of becoming a mother herself, she is able to let go of the fantasy that she needs her mother. Her own motherhood "fills" her psychically as a pregnancy fills her body. The sense of existential aloneness, which the attachment to the mother has helped her to withstand, disappears.

Longing ends because the girl-child/woman has found a way to actually return to the symbiotic bliss that she once knew with her mother. She is able to re-experience that sense of oneness that she herself had when she was an infant and which had been only a memory. Surely, this drive to return to oneness with mother is the origin of what we call the maternal instinct.

There are still moments when Molly and I hug, and allow our bodies to take the shape of each other, and we return, momentarily to that state of exquisite oneness that we lived in when she was an infant. This is my mother alive in me. This is the mother of symbiosis that my mother gave me, and, because of her giving me the experience of having such a mother, I am now able to impart it to my daughter.

The good-enough mother

It is primarily the mother who defines her world for the infant. The mother gives the infant a sense of reality, narrow though it is at that early time in her child's life.

The infant is born into a world of shadowy impressions. The infant's loving mother aids the infant in clarifying these flickering sense experiences, assisting the conversion into actual thoughts and feelings. The loving mother gives her infant the belief that the world will provide sure footing, as it contains and supports the child, as Mother herself does. She gives her child the sense that the insatiability of appetites can be mastered, that excitations can be formed into meaning.

The good mother gives her child the sense that aloneness will never be intolerable. Rather, it will be merely a way-station, a temporary condition until holding and comfort is re-established once again.

And when the mother is good enough, these impressions need never be entirely shattered. A self is formed that has constancy and solidity based on the security with which the mother has provided her infant. Later, as children and as adolescents, we become aware that there is no perfect mother. We come to know that those we love and cherish will disappoint us. We understand that safety is not always within our mother's or our own control. Yet we confront our letdowns; we navigate through stormy, even dangerous waters. We live through feelings of being momentarily cast adrift; and then we allow ourselves to get excited all over again by renewed expectations and hope. When the mother has been good enough, there develops enough of a sense of self-worth, enough of a sense of constancy both about ourselves and about others that we allow our experience to hold and sustain us. Our belief in others, originating in our belief in our mother, and then our own selves, lights our way toward hope and wholeness.

A call to reason

It is in motherhood that our culture, until recently, has thought of women as reaching their epitome of womanness—and all of what womanness stands for: intuition, the ability to bond and love, feelingfulness. We have most often seen women as masters of matters of the heart (as opposed to the head).

But the part of the brain that houses the neo-cortex—the new brain, the thinking brain—represents our true self as much as our fight or flight emotions, impulses, and reflexes. And surely wisdom resides in this portion of the brain as much as in the older regions.

Freud saw the good life as one that is filled with meaning by the enduring, mutually helpful relations that we have with the people we love, and through knowing that we are working in ways that help others live better lives—"*lieben und arbeiten*" (to love and to work). Life is inevitably filled with conflict and painful difficulties. Living a good life does not deny either of these, but we do not let our troubles grind us into despair, nor do we allow ourselves to give in to the dark impulses that sometimes surface in each of us. By recognising the nature of our unconscious, and becoming aware of as much as possible of it, we are less at the whim of its forces. By giving as much energy as we can to Eros, our impulse toward life and love, we can resist giving behavioural expression to our chaotic, aggressive, and destructive impulses, Thanatos. We can learn to live in a way that is both more rational and more feelingful. Bettelheim writes that, in the end, "Thanatos wins, but as long as there is life in us we can keep Eros victorious over Thanatos."

Freud understood that maternal love is essential to both life and mental health, and to the power of Eros over Thanatos. With that appreciation, in 1908, he proposed to the mental health community that an *Academy of Love* be created to scientifically study the phenomenon of love. He felt that if we, as a culture, understood more about love, we would be able to take steps to alleviate some of the human misery and suffering that comes from an absence of love.

In spite of Freud's having to flee from Vienna from the Nazis, and in spite of witnessing the global hate that had been expressed in the massive destruction of our second world war, Freud retained hope for mankind. It took almost forty years for world leaders to finally come to see Freud's wisdom in his idea of studying love. In 1945, the charter of the United Nations was signed. It was an organisation whose express purpose was based on the same underlying principle as psychoanalysis: the idea that talking is a more constructive channel for the communication of differences and hostilities than is action.

My hope for the future

Marnie's analysis has led me to think deeply about the meaning of my being an adoptive mother. I know that in observing Marnie's travails, I have been looking through a window into Molly's future. It is likely that one day Molly, too, will begin her search for the woman who birthed her. This woman, Molly's other mother, whose picture is safely tucked away in my files (awaiting Molly's interest years down the road), is forever etched in my memory, is never far from my mind. In a profound sense, this young woman, whose name I don't even know, has mothered me and honoured me by allowing me to have the privilege of raising her daughter.

I know there will come the day when my daughter will know the real meaning of the fact that she and I did not share the symbiosis of biological fusion, and she will begin to wonder about the woman who carried her in her womb. The end of Molly's journey of interest about her biological mother may be as deeply disturbing as was Marnie's. Or, Molly may find her and meet her, and feel, as many adopted children do, that she has finally come home to a part of herself from which she had been separated for all of her growing up years. I, as the mother who raised her, can only hope that I will have given her the nurturance that will confer emotional resiliency for whatever comes her way. And, perhaps with even more difficulty, I hope that I myself will have the generosity of spirit to be able to share with this unknown woman the child whom I have raised and have come to feel as just mine alone. And, I hope that Molly's other mother will give to Molly the same feeling that my mother gave to me—the feeling that *all news was good news*, and that her presence on earth was a gift to her, and that their time together was woefully too short.

Swimming in the realm of eternity

Although Molly will never know her grandmother except through me, she has been able to be with my sister, and came to know her, for several years before my sister's death.

It is the last week of my sister's life; we are all at the hospital with her. She is in a coma, but we never quite give up hope that she will awaken.

I watch my nieces and my brother-in-law this week. I observe the greatest outpouring of love possible. They never leave her side, sleeping at the hospital, crawling into bed with her, lying next to her near-lifeless body, ceaselessly stroking her, soothing her, telling her of their love, thanking her.

I am privileged to be able to participate in a religious ritual upon her death—the traditional *tahara*. It is the cleansing of the body, the preparation of the body for burial, as the soul has readied itself to take flight from that body which can no longer house it. We comb my sister's hair. We wash her body. We clean her fingernails. It is a sensitive procedure, caringly purposeful, rather like a mother removing dirt from her child's face. It is both simple and dignified. And throughout the cleansing we are performing, we say prayers, encouraging her soul to return to its original home, its God.

And, following Jewish law, my sister is buried in a plain, modest casket (as was my mother). The casket is made from wood, a material that will disintegrate in the ground, enabling her body to return to the bosom of earth as quickly as possible. There is no metal in its construction, not even nails, as metal is the material of war, and no Jew should go to the place of eternal peace aided by elements of war.

I go to synagogue with my family. It is the Saturday, Shabbos, after my sister's death. It is also the weekend of Father's Day, and the rabbi is giving a sermon on the meaning of family. He explains the five responsibilities that the Torah assigns to the parents of a Jewish child. The first four are predictable: give your child an education (or in olden days, teach him a trade); give your child a sense of being a Jew in a community of Jews; help your child to get married; help your child to honour you. And then the rabbi tells us the last: Jewish parents have the responsibility to teach their children to swim. To swim?

This fifth edict that was given from rabbis to their people five thousand years ago is particularly puzzling to me. Perhaps it was a nod to the pagan origins of Judaism—the honouring of one of the elements that are the constituents of life, the water element, from whence we all come, ontologically, as a species. Perhaps, too, it was a recognition of our individual origins, our first watery home within our mothers.

And then I think about swimming as a passion—my mother's, my sister's, and my own: I muse on the sense of freedom and carefreeness that I feel in the water, the gracefulness I feel when I am supported into buoyancy, unburdened by the weight of my own body. Floating and flying seem oddly linked to one another, and I know that my time in the water is the closest that I can come to experiencing the airborne quality of my soul, the quality of eternity. (And, thus, why I have oriented my life-style around my passion for swimming, living near natural bodies of water: my farm in Puerto Rico, my house on a lake in northern New Jersey.)

And then I think about swimming as a metaphor for emotional and cognitive growth. Having taught adult swimming lessons when I was a teenager, I saw how difficult it is to overcome the anxiety that an adult feels underwater without having had the experience of swimming as a child. From birth on, our respiratory systems can only process air, and when we deliberately cut off our access to air, as we do when we put our heads under water, we either feel assured that we will be able to find air again—and swimming is a pleasurable experience—or we feel anxious that we won't—and swimming is approached with apprehension, or even terror.

Developmental psychologists emphasise the importance of learning during what is called the "critical period." Perhaps swimming, too, can be a metaphor for learning a new skill, as we are not born knowing how to swim. With all new tasks, but especially for psychological undertakings, if the imprint for an ability is not laid down in early childhood, the neurological pathway that represents that skill doesn't yet exist. The areas of the brain that are allocated for the learning of that skill fall into disuse; they eventually adapt to perform other functions, and are then no longer available for the original purpose. The imprint for learning, then, cannot be re-awakened because it is not there to begin with. This stunted capacity is seen in the development of many of the biological systems, including auditory, visual and vestibular structures, but it has been most thoroughly researched for attachment. It is thought that the first twenty-four to thirty-six months of life are the critical period—a window of time that can never be reclaimed for sustained attachment to develop. Cooing, eye contact, loving touch, consistent feeding and dependable soothing are all fundamental to create nerve connections in the brain for attachment, from which derives empathy, sensitivity to others, and a sense of community.

In my work with patients, it is easy to discern which patients have dormant psychic and neurological pathways, and which have non-existent ones. Carrie, for instance, had a severely critical father, and a mother who stood by and watched as her father squashed her into the ground with every criticism he could think of. Carrie is an extremely smart and capable person. She doesn't know it, and it doesn't matter how many compliments she receives; they all bounce off her because her "truth" is that she is stupid and incompetent. Her therapy has consisted of a long and arduous process of implanting new neurological pathways into her brain, and thus her psyche. I am, in effect, teaching her to "swim" for the first time as an adult.

And finally, I think about the meaning of swimming in terms of separation, the psychic theme that has captured me all through these early years of Molly's life, and before that, throughout my life with my mother. In order to teach a child to swim, there must be a perfect balance between closeness and distance, between separation and independence. Hover too close and the child never meets the challenge of the task, never learns independence. Move too far away and the child experiences fear, even the possibility of death. The notion of teaching a child to swim seems to be a perfect metaphor for this primary challenge of parenting: the challenge of separation, and the task of guiding one's child through this process safely.

I have a patient, Stacey, who came to me after the loss of her child. Stacey was in her home making lunch in the kitchen while the nanny was watching her child play in the swimming pool. The nanny fell asleep and the child tragically drowned. Swimming as flying for the soul, or swimming as the end of one's physical incarnation? Stacey was unfortunate enough to have the life-endangering aspect of swimming in her life. She began therapy after she had contracted cancer, quite convinced that the cancer was her brutal—deliberately brutal—self-inflicted punishment for having been a neglectful mother, a mother who allowed herself to be too separate, too distracted from her child. Any compassionate person would be inclined to try to talk this mother out of her guilt, out of her need to inflict damage upon herself as her retribution against herself. But I knew that such an endeavour would be fruitless, that this mother *had* to make herself suffer.

We mothers are often neither compassionate nor even reasonable with ourselves when it comes to the well-being of our children. We hold ourselves accountable for their fate, whether that accountability is legitimate, rational, practical, or even realistically possible. We "know"—that is, we "feel"—that our true responsibility for our children is through our power of omnipotence. We know this and feel this to be true even though it is a patently impossible responsibility.

The world of stories

Molly understands that she will never see her Aunt Lee again. She asks me about death, or heaven, and other cosmic questions that I feel I don't really know how to answer. I have a moment of paralysis when she asks me these questions, feeling inadequate about not having a strong enough conviction of belief about these important questions to pass on to her. Then I remind myself of how it is with my psychoanalytic patients, how I am in a place with them for long periods of time where I similarly don't have answers to their questions. In this place of not knowing, I have learned, as a psychoanalyst, to retreat to inquiry.

And so, as I find myself with Molly in this place of not knowing, I resort to my analytic training. I do with Molly the same kind of inquiry that I do with my patients. I meet her questions with a question. "Molly, what do you think death or heaven is?" And she will say what she thinks. She will tell me a story that gives me a peek into the interior of her young, actively developing mind. And then I will understand her real concern. Her worry, her terror actually, is that these things will mean that she and I will not be together. Death will mean that she will not be able to find me. Heaven means that we will be apart, one on earth, the other in heaven. And, in understanding that her real apprehension, the theme of the story that most preoccupies her mind, is about our separation, I am able to reassure her about our togetherness. I say something that I believe and hope is true, though I can't honestly say I *know* it to be true. I say it because, at that moment, she needs to hear it. I tell her that we will be together for eternity. I tell her that there is no force on earth that is strong enough to pull us apart—that we will be together through life as well as through death. I even tell her that after death, we will come back in another life. We will find each other then, as we did now in this life. In hearing this, Molly develops the idea that she and I will do it all over again—in the same house, with the same dog, same cat, same bunk-bed—maybe only our names will change. Recently, she has even embellished the notion that in the next life she may be the mother and I will be the daughter, and she tells me this with a smirk in her mouth, and twinkling eyes, as though this thought of role and power reversal seems to give her a kind of childlike pleasure of grandiosity.

And then I tell her the story of her beginnings with me. I tell her of my search for her and how I came to find her. "Out of all the children in the world," I tell her, "it was you who I knew was meant to be mine, you who I looked for, searched for, waited for, even dreamed about, and I didn't rest until I found you." I tell her the story of crying when I first saw the picture of her tummy-mommy. I tell her about my sense of recognition of this woman who I have never met but with whom, at that moment, I felt an instant, overwhelming kinship. I tell Molly of my sense of knowing that my search for my daughter was over, and then I tell her that I brought her, my Molly, home with me to be my daughter.

What I want to tell my mother

We are all storytellers. The brain/mind is programmed to create and want to tell stories. It can make fiction up out of whole cloth (delusions and hallucinations), out of partial plots that are stitched together seemingly randomly (dreams), out of misinterpretations of communications (fantasies based on partially understood experience). The mind seeks to create patterns of thought even when the data it is processing represent meaningless data. It does this structuring of data to create an evolutionary advantage, making efficient neural programmes in the neural circuitry.

Psychotherapy patients are amongst the most original storytellers there are. Although they may come into therapy without a coherent storyline to their lives, the therapy emboldens them to create a personal narrative that they come to embrace as authentic. Creating this life-narrative is one of the great benefits of therapy.

The process between patient and analyst is, if nothing else, a conversation. Patient and analyst engage in the exchange of words. This is all they do: talk. It doesn't matter whether you want to call this method of talk science (as some psychoanalysts claim), art (as most psychoanalysts claim), or hogwash (as critics of psychoanalysis claim). The one thing that is indisputable is that the patient comes to tell a story about himself. In fact, the patient has decided to be in this process of self-examination largely because, as psychoanalyst Adam Phillips says, the story that he has been telling himself has either stopped or become too painful. The analyst listens to the story and talks back, and they continue doing this specific kind of dialoguing as long as the conversation is either useful, interesting, pleasurable, or even painful, but ultimately gratifying in some way. The dialogue continues in a successful analysis until the story begins to move again. One might even develop a clear beginning and end of the storyline, a cogent story that comes to have rational meaning. For a while it doesn't even matter whether the story has the authenticity of truth. The analyst suspends disbelief (as Freud originally did when his patients told him that they were being sexually abused by fathers, uncles, friends of the family) in order to enter the emotional reality of the patient. It is only later that the analyst must take on the difficult job of aiding the patient to move toward reality, into an accurate rendering of his life story. The maturing adult, then, is a storyteller who is, as Louise Kaplan describes, continually in the process of reliving and revising her memories, continually re-finding her identity, continually re-forging the shape of her very selfhood.

Molly and Marnie are at the opposite ends of their storytelling ability. While Marnie has come to an end of her storytelling with me, Molly is just now entering this phase of her development. At the age of four, Molly has herself become a storyteller. Molly tells me many stories, some wondrous and uplifting. Molly's stories drift into her dream-life (as did mine when she first came to me), and become narratives of her dreams. But every story/dream she tells me that has thematic elements of fear or aggression is, ultimately, a story of separation from me or occasionally from her father: either she can't find me, or she is taken from me against her will; she is perpetually searching for me, seeking me out, often desperately—in her dreams, as in her life. As she first begins to tell me her stories, her endings reveal that she is helpless to mend the injury from the separation. She is eager when she wakes up each morning to tell me all that has transpired in her world between the time we have said "good night" and the time we say "good morning." Her dreams are convoluted and detailed. It takes a long time for her to tell them to me. Sometimes I wonder if she is telling me dreams at all or just making it up on the spot—imagination run amok. It doesn't really matter, but I do marvel at the elaborateness of her mental creations.

Then Molly begins to have nightmares that seemingly have nothing to do with me. She dreams about the dark side of the cosmic elements. The lake (water) we live on is overcoming its limiting boundaries (earth), flooding the land. Or, our house is burning (fire), and she needs an escape route. And she dreams of falling, the other side of flying (air). She has lost her belief in the magical quality of aeroplanes floating effortlessly in the sky, and asks how they can possibly stay in the sky. Also, she no longer believes that she can skywalk. I am reminded of something Nietzsche's Zarathustra said: *"When I saw my devil I found him serious, thorough, profound, and solemn: He was the spirit of gravity—through him all things fall."*

Molly comes to dread going to sleep for fear of yet another nightmare. She asks me, *"Aren't you dead when you're asleep?"* For Molly, sleep is falling. Falling is death. She falls asleep to fall to death.

I know that the meaning of Molly's nightmares is that she has left her baby-soul altogether. And I suspect that this movement from one self to another self may be more traumatic for Molly than for her non-adopted friends—it may conjure up fears of loss and abandonment, particularly so because of her early history of leaving one mother to be with another mother. It is through my continued reassurance of our togetherness that I help Molly to resolve her fears of the savage force of the elements, of our separations, and of death itself: Thanatos. We talk about the splendor of dream-time and the lightness of feelings. We talk about using the dream-world as a time and place in which she can allow her soul and her psyche to roam, to fly about freely, unrestrained, unimpeded. We talk about the "hairy cat" (the etymological root of the word "caterpillar") who must crawl on the ground before it becomes the exquisite soaring butterfly. I tell Molly that the hairy cat has several homes during the course of its lifetime, and that it must leave one in order to inhabit the other.

When Molly regains confidence in her placement in relation to me, she begins to handle the art of separation, and, as well, the skill of transforming fears into mastery. Her images of dreadful falling are replaced with fantasies of ecstatic flying once again. Molly becomes eager for sleep in order to have this experience of soul-flight in which all feelings are possible and are lighter than air.

Molly knows now that when she dreams of flying she is leaving one home, and returning to another home—the true home of her psyche and her internal self. Home is everywhere when one is comfortable with oneself.

Then, we have an experience in waking life. It feels like an awake-dream, a surrealistic story. We are walking down the street. We spy a little girl, Molly's age, Molly's size, who is walking ahead of us with her mother. Molly decides she wants to catch up with them. We walk a little faster; Molly pushes me to walk a lot faster. Then she starts running, and I do too. We catch up with them and are standing side by side: two mothers, two girls. The girl looks at Molly. There is a moment—call it a moment of dramatic tension. And then Molly and this unnamed character simultaneously throw their arms around each other, like long-lost friends having finally found each other after years of searching. Molly has decided that this little girl, whom she has never met before (and will never see again), is worthy of her ardour for that moment.

Molly the storyteller has created a narrative within her imagination. She has imbued her story with a plot, a protagonist, with desire and intent, suspense, and even a satisfying climax.

My act as observer, witness to her story, makes it *our* story, and now that this little story that she has concocted has been written, it can become reabsorbed by her in the future. She will understand that her mom writes books, sometimes even about her, and she will read this story one day, and it will become *her* story again.

And then I realise the meaning behind this narrative of my own story that I have told. I have talked to my analyst, telling her my life-story, such as I have remembered it and given meaning to it. I have talked to my daughter, telling her aspects of her life-story, short as it is thus far, as well as parts of the life-story of the ancestors of the family she has found herself in. The person who I have stopped talking to is my mother. The meaning of constructing this narrative is so that I may continue to talk to my mother. This narrative that I have created about my mother's life, about my life, about my daughter's life, and about the lives of some of my patients is what I want to be telling my mother, what I would be telling my mother were she still alive.

All of Molly's mothers

Because my mother had a substitute mother in her analyst, and I, too, have had my own substitute mother in my analyst, Molly is now on the receiving end of two generations of analytic mothers—four mothers, in a sense. She is quite a different child than either my mother or I was. Molly is infinitely more confident, more outgoing and outspoken, more enthusiastic about life at an earlier age. She is more forceful in her anger and more despairing in her sadness. Her feelings are total in a way that neither my mother's nor mine were at the same age.

As Molly grows into becoming her own person, she will have characteristics that move her in specific directions: she may develop into being either a blamer or a forgiver, vindictive or compassionate, listless and dull or full of sparkling life energy. She could be someone who responds either with courage and eagerness to adversity, or someone who is defeated by it. Her past will be fused with her present, and will determine her psychological future. How I help her to manage her separation from me, how I myself manage my own separation from her, will be crucial to this process of maintaining harmony within the multiplicity of her various selves, the numerous possibilities for the direction in which her growth will take her.

And suddenly and unexpectedly, Molly's fifth mother enters our lives. After four years of my having Molly, her very first mother, Shawn, and I have found each other.

Shawn has called the adoption agency to request that I send her a picture of Molly. I use that opportunity to write to her through the agency, thanking her for loaning me Molly. (I see all children as on loan, if not from another mother, then from the universe.) I spend three months composing my letter. I want her to know how miraculous being a mother to this child has been for me. I want her to have a sense of who this child is that she gave birth to four years earlier. And through our writing back and forth, Shawn and I have become friends and I have learned the story of Molly's origins.

Shawn had her first child when she was fifteen. In that first marriage, she had two children; Molly was her third. At twenty-one, her marriage had failed, and she had just entered into a new relationship. She found herself unexpectedly pregnant, felt unable to take on a third child as a single mother, and was unprepared for any sort of commitment with the man who became Molly's father. Shawn grew to feel extremely attached to Molly during the pregnancy. She dreaded the birth, knowing that birth would mean final and absolute separation from her child. As the birth time got closer, Shawn wanted to hold on ever more tightly to her daughter.

I remember this time. I remember waiting for Molly's birth. I remember fearing that Molly was never going to be born. I remember the agency telling me that if Molly couldn't (or wouldn't) be born on her own, the doctors were going to have to induce labour. I understand now the reason for Molly's delay. She and Shawn were mother and daughter, and they wanted to honour that relationship just a little bit longer—to grab every extra minute they could get with each other before their final goodbye.

Shawn has written a letter to Molly and I read it to Molly. It is sensitive and respectful. It is devoid of platitudes.

Molly is very excited about having another mother, her first mother. I tell her that Shawn would be happy to meet her whenever she wants, and that Shawn lives close to New Orleans. We have gone to New Orleans several times since I read Molly the letter, and though Molly talks about Shawn on occasion, she has never asked to meet Shawn. I think she will want to one day. I know she will ask when she is ready. I will analyse her request, as her mother, and as the inquiring analyst I am. I will ask all sorts of questions about what she expects, what she hopes for, what will happen if she is disappointed. I will be emotionally with Molly as I was with Marnie, helping her to understand the full meaning of the step she wishes to take. And if it seems that it is the right thing to do to have Molly and Shawn meet, then we will have a happy reunion, mothers and daughter.

Waiting to see if anything else falls out of the sky

First my mother; then my sister. And now, my other mother through most of my adult years: my analyst. All have died. Thus has ended my thirty-year relationship with this woman whom I knew for almost as long as I knew my own mother. Her death has been entirely unanticipated. I had imbued her with powers of omnipotence and immortality throughout our relationship. I imbued myself, too, with a sense of omnipotence, sure that if she only followed my instructions about how to cure her cancer (as my mother did) that she would be able to stay alive. Even today, I remain convinced (unrealistic/grandiose as I know it sounds) that I could have saved her, should have saved her.

I am left with Molly. She is the one female remaining in my life who holds my whole heart. I know that I have such a short time to enjoy as well as to learn from Molly the Buddha, the teacher of feelings in flight, before she becomes Molly the human, Molly, the individualised, whole self.

I have another dream:

> *I am standing on our dock with Molly. We are watching the sky because there is a lot of activity in it. There is a bunch of helicopters. We see that one of them starts spinning and then sputtering. We watch it closely and I tell Molly that I think it's going to crash. We see lots of men bailing out; they look like small little objects falling from the sky. But they land in the water so they seem all right. One of them is in charge and he comes close enough so that we can see him. I want to invite him in and help them all. But he proves that he is entirely self-sufficient, and instead of coming over, he pulls out a huge cardboard piece that he uses as a boat. I am relieved that they don't have to stay in the water, don't have to keep swimming because I know the water is deep and cold. He and his men get on this boat that he has invented, and somehow he gets it to move. They go off in one direction. I realise that they are going back to their base that is actually not that far off. It's just on the other side of the lake. I realise*

that they will be okay, but I feel rudderless, useless—not having been able to help—and I feel homeless, too. I have a terrible feeling of aloneness—and it feels like this is how it has always been for me—that I have always been alone and felt this lonely. Then I look down and see Molly standing next to me and I am filled with joy from remembering the experience that we have just shared of looking up at the sky and seeing things falling out of it. I feel together with her and we stand there, looking at the sky again, waiting expectantly to see if anything else will fall out of it.

I wake up. I find Molly. And then we grab onto each other, falling into each other's arms, falling into life.

THE END

Bibliography

Crescent City Jewish News Source, 2013-14 / 5774, p. 4
(http://www.crescentcityjewishnews.com/blog/wp-content/
uploads/2013/08/CCJN_SOURCE.pdf).

Lucille Hoerr Charles. "Drama in First-naming Ceremonies", *Journal of American Folklore* 64 (1951) pp 11-35.

A.K. Nongrynrih. *Khasi Society of Meghalaya, A Sociological Understanding* (New Delhi, India: M.L.Gidiwani Indus Publishing Company, 2002) p. 144.

Gurmukh Kaur Khalsa. *Bountiful, Beautiful, Blissful* (New York, NY: St Martin's, 2003).

Rabbi Goldie Milgram. *Living Jewish Life Cycle: How to Create Meaningful Jewish Rites of Passage at Every Stage of Life* (Woodstock, VT: Jewish Lights Publishing, 2009) p. 79.

Walt Whitman. *Passage to India* (Amsterdam, Netherlands: Fredonia Books, 2004).

Priscilla Dunstan. *Child Sense* (New York, NY: Bantam Books, 2009) p. 8.

Dylan Evans. *An Introductory Dictionary of Lacanian Psychoanalysis* (New York, NY: Routledge, 1996).

Valeria Gazzola, Lisa Aziz-Zadeh, and Christian Keysers. "Empathy and the Somatotopic Auditory Mirror System in Humans", *Current Biology 16, 1824–1829,* (September 19, 2006 Elsevier Ltd.) p. 3.

Tze-ki Hon. *The Yijing and Chinese Politics: Classic Commentary and Literati Activism in the Northern Song Period 960-1127* (New York, NY: State University of New York Press). p. 92.

Graham Faiella. *Mesoamerican Mythology* (New York, NY: The Rosen Publishing Group). p. 19.

William P. Fifer and Chris M. Moon. "The effects of fetal experience with sound", in Jean-Pierre Lecannuet et al, eds., *Fetal Development: A Psychological Perspective;* (Mahwah, NJ, Lawrence Erlbaum Associates, 1995).

Anthony James DeCasper, Ph.D. and William P. Fifer. "Of Human Bonding: Newborns Prefer Their Mothers' Voices", *Science*, (New Series, Vol 208, Issue 4448, June 6, 1980) pp. 1174-1176.

Anne Karpf. *The Human Voice* (New York, NY: Bloomsbury, 2006) p. 62.

Marius Wernig. *Proceedings of the National Academy of Sciences* (January 30, 2012).

Alice Miller. *The Drama of the Gifted Child* (Translated by Ruth Ward, New York, NY: Basic Books, 1994) p. 52.

Ellen Junn, Chris Boyatzis. *Child Growth and Development* (New York, NY: McGraw-Hill Higher Education, 1999) p. 28.

Finer L. B. and Zolna M. R. "Shifts in intended and unintended pregnancies in the United States, 2001–2008", *American Journal of Public Health*, 2014, 104(S1): S44-S48.

Paul D. MacLean, *The Triune Brain in Evolution: Role in Paleocerebral Functions* (New York, NY & London, UK: Plenum Press, 1990).

Otto Rank. *The Trauma of Birth* (Mineola, NY: Courier Corporation, 1929).

Margaret S. Mahler, Fred Pine, and Anni Bergman. *The Psychological Birth of the Human Infant: Symbiosis and Individuation* (New York, NY: Basic Books, 2000).

Alessandra Piontelli. "Pre-Natal Life and Birth as Reflected in the Analysis of a 2-Year-Old Psychotic Girl", *International Review of Psycho-Analysis* 15 (1988): 7 3-81.

Stephanie S. Swales. *Perversion: A Lacanian Psychoanalytical Approach to the Subject* (New York, NY: Routledge, 2012) p. 24.

Daniel Stern. *The Interpersonal World of the Infant* (New York, NY: Basic Books, 1985).

"Parkinsonsism and Music's Ability to Heal: Oliver Sachs interview", *Music and the Brain,* http://www.pbs.org/wnet/musicinstinct/video/music-and-the-brain/parkinsonsism-and-musics-ability-to-heal/51/ (May 21, 2009).

John Shelby Spong. *The Living Commandments* (New York, NY: Seabury Press, 1977).

Louise Kaplan. *Oneness and Separateness: From Infant to Individual* (New York, NY: Simon & Schuster, 1978) p. 19.

Plato. "What is Love?" *Euthypbus, Crito, Apology and Symposium* (South Bend, IN: Regency/Gateway, 1953).

Robert L. Burgess, Robert G. Burgess, and Kevin MacDonald. *Evolutionary Perspectives on Human Development* (Thousand Oaks, CA: Sage, 2005) p. 176.

Maoshing Ni. *Second Spring: Dr. Mao's Hundreds of Natural Secrets to Revitalize and Regenerate at Any Age* (New York, NY: Free Press) p. 140.

Anne Karpf. *The Human Voice: The Story of a Remarkable Talent* (New York, NY: Bloomsbury, 2006).

Mark Twain. "Letter to George Bainton, 15 October 1888, solicited for and printed in George Bainton", *The Art of Authorship: Literary Reminiscences, Methods of Work, and Advice to Young Beginners* (1890) p. 87-88.

Joseph Jaffe and Stanley Feldstein. *Rhythms of Dialogue* (New York, NY: Academic Press, 1970).

Bob Doman. "Brain Injury: 'Daniel'", *The NACD Foundation, Volume 10 No. 9*, 1996.

Theodor Reik. *Listening With the Third Ear* (New York, NY: Farrar Straus & Giroux, 1983).

Michael Davis. *William Blake: A New Kind of Man* (Berkeley, CA: University of California Press) p. 103.

David Eagleman. *Incognito* (New York, NY: Vintage Books, 2012) p. 7.

Beatles. *Anthology* (San Francisco, CA: Chronicle Books, 2000).

Trudy Fox. *Afflatus: A Collection of Dreams and Their Gnostic Influence on Human Evolution* (Bloomington, IN: Balboa Press).

David Bakan. *Sigmund Freud and the Jewish Mystical Tradition* (Mineola, NY: Dover Publications, 2004).

Bruno Bettelheim. *Freud and Man's Soul* (London, UK: Pimlico, 2001).

D.W. Winnicott. *The Family and Individual Development* (London, UK: Tavistock, 1969).

Newsweek. "It's a Wise Father Who Knows…" (Vol. 129, New York, NY: Newsweek Inc., 1997) p. 73.

Carl Jung. "Psychology and Religion", *Psychology and Religion: West and East* (CW 11: 1938).

Marion Woodman. *Addiction to Perfection: The Still Unravished Bride: A Psychological Study* (Toronto, ON: Inner City Books, 1982) p. 82.

Loren Eiseley. *The Immense Journey: An Imaginative Naturalist Explores the Mysteries of Man and Nature* (New York, NY: Random House, 1946).

Deborah Anna Luepnitz. *Schopenhauer's Porcupines* (New York, NY: Basic Books, 2003).

C.L. Meyer, and M. Oberman. *Mothers Who Kill Their Children: Understanding the Acts of Moms from Susan Smith to the "Prom Mom"* (New York, NY: New York University Press, 2001).

J. Weston. "The Pathology of Child Abuse", *The Battered Child* (Eds. R. Helfer & C. Kempe, Chicago, IL: University of Chicago Press, 1968).

J. B. Watson. *Psychological Care of Infant and Child* (New York, NY: W.W. Norton & Co., 1928).

Anna Freud and Dorothy T. Burlingham. *War and Children* (New York, NY: Medical War Books, 1943).

H. W. Loeward. "The Waning of the Oedipus Complex", *J Psychother Pract. Res.* (1978) p. 757.

Joshua S. Goldstein. *War and Gender: How Gender Shapes the War System and Vice Versa* (New York, NY: Cambridge University Press) p. 44.

Sigmund Freud. *Civilization and its Discontents* (London, UK: Hogarth Press, 1946).

Sigmund Freud. *The Interpretation of Dreams* (London, UK: Macmillan, 1913).

Deborah Anna Luepnitz. Edited by Lewis A. Kirshner. *Between Winnicott and Lacan: A Clinical Engagement* (New York, NY: Routledge, 2011) p. 10.

Bruno Bettelheim. *Truants from Life: The Rehabilitation of Emotionally Disturbed Children* (New York, NY: Free Press, 1964) p. 324.

Barry G. Gale. *Love in Vienna: The Sigmund Freud–Minna Bernays Affair* (Santa Barbara, CA: Praeger) p. 145.

Adam Phillips. *Missing Out: In Praise of the Unlived Life* (London, UK: Picador, 2013).

Louise Kaplan. *Adolescence: The Farewell to Childhood* (New York, NY: Touchstone Books, 1995).

Jean Graybeal. *Language and the Feminine in Nietzsche and Heidegger* (Bloomington, IN: Indiana University Press, 1990) p. 44.

Christian Gottlob Heyne. "Odysseus and Eurycleia" https://www.coursera.org/learn/mythology/lecture/jWzcM/4-4-the-scar .